Dilemmas of Italian Socialism

THE UNIVERSITY OF MASSACHUSETTS PRESS   AMHERST, 1980

SPENCER DISCALA *Dilemmas of Italian Socialism: The Politics of Filippo Turati*

For my mother and the memory of my father

ACKNOWLEDGMENTS

I AM VERY grateful for the support I have received from a number of persons while working on this book. Among those in Italy, I wish to thank especially Dr. Cipriana Scelba, Director of the Fulbright program, and Professors Renzo De Felice, Arturo Colombo, Brunello Vigezzi, Mario Stoppino, and Franco Della Peruta, who either read the manuscript or were otherwise helpful. The late Senator Lelio Basso allowed me to use his library, and the late Giuseppe Faravelli shared with me his experiences of Turati. The staff of the Società umanitaria, and especially Elio Sellino of the Istituto Giangiacomo Feltrinelli in Milan, were particularly generous with their time. The Einaudi publishers kindly allowed me to consult the unpublished portions of the Turati-Kuliscioff correspondence. My discussions with William Salomone, Eric Robinson, Robert D'Attilio, and the members of the Columbia University Seminar on Modern Italy especially stimulated me. I thank Carlo Golino, formerly Chancellor of the University of Massachusetts at Boston, for his encouragement, and I owe a special debt to Professor Max Bluestone, who read the manuscript and made invaluable suggestions for improvement. I am also grateful for grants from the Fulbright program, the Kentucky Research Foundation, and the University of Massachusetts at Boston, which helped make my research possible.

CONTENTS

Filippo turati, the father of Italian reformism, founded the Italian Socialist party, created a working-class political tradition in Italy, and raised important questions still debated by Italian Marxists. Although they cannot write histories of Italian socialism without discussing his policies and influence, few historians have focused on Turati's activities. Scholars have not treated him well, and Marxists, especially, have attacked his political understandings with liberals. Thus, Palmiro Togliatti vilified Turati after his death in 1932 because his alliance with Giovanni Giolitti supposedly betrayed the working class, but when, eighteen years later, Togliatti praised Giolitti's policies, he ignored Turati, who helped make those policies possible.

Turati followed a flexible policy of alliances, especially when they were necessary to defend democracy and to obtain reforms. He believed in the nonviolent, gradual achievement of socialism.

The Socialist party's left wing and the Communist party denounced these ideas as simplistic but years later accepted and followed them. After a review of Turati's policies, for example, Pietro Nenni acknowledged in 1977 that the Socialist left wing did not understand how consistent Turati's policies were or how skillfully Turati avoided many of the pitfalls inherent in political compromises. In 1960 Nenni himself had been forced into an alliance resembling the one Turati made in 1901. Without admitting it, the Italian Communists have also adopted policies similar to Turati's. An editorial by Luigi Longo in the 12 July 1966 issue of *L'unità* could have been lifted from one of Turati's articles in *Critica sociale*: Longo protests that his party "aims at the gradual socialist transformation of Italian society by means of cooperation with all political and social forces aspiring to renovate Italian society, which must then be managed democratically, not by a single party, but by many parties and economic and social organizations." This statement and the Communist repudiation of the dictatorship of the proletariat, foretold by Turati, exemplify the influence of reformism even after ninety years. The "historic compromise" is a new edition of the reformist policy of political alliances to guarantee liberty and reforms.

Perhaps the lack of serious Marxist discussion of Turati's methods derives from the disturbing nature of the analogies between the problems confronting Turati before World War I and those confronting Italian Communist leaders since World War II. Marxism is an ideology for revolution, but both the Socialists and the Communists had to subordinate revolutionary objectives to reformist tactics. Both realized that they could not take power immediately, both became parliamentary, and, to increase their support among the electorate, both demanded reforms. These policies produced debates and splits among the leaders and friction between leaders and the rank-and-file members of the parties. In the early years of the twentieth century, the conflicts often led to bloody strikes, and some leaders propounded a theory of urban violence; in recent years the friction has taken the form of strikes and terrorism.

Because a historical study of Marxist politics before World War I may provide insights into the Italian situation after World War II, this book will focus on Turati's political action and the ideological debates within the Socialist party, the nature of the Giolittian system, and Turati's efforts to prevent reaction and to establish the strongest possible base for Italian democracy. Because Turati was primarily a political leader and not a thinker, this book does not discuss the intricacies of Marxist ideology. Moreover, the book ends with an account of events in 1912, the year in which Turati's influence in the Party ceased to be dominant. I have concluded with a brief sketch of events after that date, showing how Turati remained a major protagonist in Italian history in the years between 1912 and 1932, which deserve two further volumes in themselves. That undertaking would also provide many insights and lessons.

Dilemmas of Italian Socialism

CHAPTER I

The Ideology of Filippo Turati

Filippo turati's career as a writer and politician lasted for fifty years and crucially influenced the history of modern Italy. He propagated Marxism in Italy, founded the Italian Socialist party, set the tone for its policies, and played a central role in the post–World War I crisis that ended in the rise of fascism. He died in exile in Paris in 1932, at the age of seventy-five.[1]

This essay is not a biography of Turati, nor does it examine all aspects of his enormously productive career. Rather, it discusses Turati's politics during a key period of Italian history, from the foundation of the Socialist party by Turatian reformists to the left-wing takeover of the organization, which profoundly changed the nature of Socialist politics.

During these years, the Italian lower and lower middle classes entered the political system of the country and, at least in the North, forged a political tradition of their own. Although the desire to bring the system down remained strong among extremists, reformist Socialists were able to contain it within limited bounds before World War I by mitigating the harsh realities of Italian life.

It is essential to analyze the Italian Socialist party's responses to the problems of Italy in order to understand the vicissitudes of modern Italian history. The Socialist party had wide support, even if the representative institutions of the country and government policies generally reflected this support very imperfectly. The frustration this caused and the numerous splits that prevented the Party from becoming a dominant political force contributed heavily to antiparliamentary criticism in Italian politics and helped to stimulate the later rise of fascism.

Filippo Turati gave Italian reformism its moral tone and ideology.

His prestige as the pioneer of Italian Marxism and as a founder of the Socialist party allowed him to influence—at crucial junctures, to dominate—the Party for most of the period between 1892 and 1912. Many rivals challenged and some occasionally unseated him as leader, but he still determined the Party's course through his maneuverings in Parliament and his influence with powerful unions or with the Milanese working class—the most organized and vocal in Italy. Because Turati's politics and aims were both tortuous and complex, their significance has oftentimes been misinterpreted or lost to the view of historians. Analyzing Turati's philosophy is the key to understanding his practical political action, that of the Socialist party, and, indeed, that of his rivals in the Socialist movement.

The Young Turati

Turati was born in Canzo, a small town north of Milan, on 26 November 1857. His father, Pietro, was a career civil servant who had attained the rank of prefect before the Left retired him in 1876. An amateur poet, Pietro Turati translated French, German, and Slavic verse. His translations drew praise from the Nobel Prize winner Giosuè Carducci.[2] Filippo was also a poet in his youth, contributing to avant-garde reviews and eventually publishing a volume of his collected poems.[3] His mother, Adele, was an intelligent and strong-minded woman to whom Turati remained attached all his life; his first youthful poem bore a dedication to her.[4]

Turati's family was not rich, but they were relatively well off. He could afford to buy books and to take numerous trips around Italy and abroad. His parents sent him to the best doctors to treat his nerves and his extremely melancholy bent.[5]

Turati's intellectual growth seems to have been steady rather than spectacular. The year 1873 apparently marked the beginning of an important phase in his intellectual development. In that year his father was transferred to Cremona, a bustling, northern industrial city, where Turati met Leonida Bissolati, who was successively to become his teacher, follower, and opponent.[6] Bissolati, the son of a defrocked priest, was a serious boy,[7] and he and Filippo quickly became good friends. They attended the same *liceo* and upon graduation entered the University of Pavia, from which Pietro Turati had received his law degree in 1839. In 1875, however, the two friends decided that Pavia was not stimulating enough and transferred to the University of Bologna, where a more heady atmosphere prevailed.[8] Situated at the crossroads of northern and central Italy in the radical Emilia-Romagna section of the country, Bologna provided the students congenial surroundings in which to discuss the new and radical ideas that entered Italy from the rest of Europe via the city.[9]

When he obtained his law degree in 1877, Turati went to Milan, where he became part of the Milanese *scapigliatura*, a group of "angry young men," mostly artists and writers, such as Felice Cavallotti, the poet-politician, and Giovanni Verga. Turati contributed articles and poetry to cultural reviews published by members of the group,[10] *Il preludio* and *La farfalla* being the most well known of these journals.

The *scapigliatura* signaled the intellectual vitality of Milan during the late 1870s. Milan, the most advanced industrial and commercial city in Italy, would soon become the center of Italian Marxism and Turati's political stronghold, as it was the crucible of all of modern Italy's political movements.

The Milanese *scapigliatura* had profound effects on young Turati's intellectual development. He once admitted that until the age of twenty he was still a monarchist whose only goal was to teach. His friend, Arcangelo Ghisleri, atheist, republican, and prolific founder of reviews, attacked Turati for his lack of a "mature" ideology or sense of criticism.[11]

Of the three friends who made up the so-called *sodalizio lombardo*—Turati, Bissolati, and Ghisleri—Turati seemed intellectually least settled during this period. His neurasthenia tormented him, and he came close to committing suicide.[12] Bissolati attributed Turati's deep pessimism to his lack of a goal. Once Turati found an aim to which he could dedicate himself, the crisis would be over, Bissolati thought, and he was right.[13] Turati, "half poet, half sociologist, half lawyer, and half journalist," found his ideal in socialism.[14]

Turati's closest friend and most impatient critic during this time was Arcangelo Ghisleri, who might be dubbed the editor of the *scapigliatura*. In 1875, at the age of twenty, Ghisleri founded *Il preludio*, the first of several successful periodicals. Turati wrote for *Il preludio*,[15] and both edited the *Rivista repubblicana*, the journal of the Lombard Republicans.[16] Ghisleri, who later became a famous geographer, flirted with socialism for a short time but eventually opposed it.[17]

Turati's debates with Ghisleri and the other intellectuals of the *scapigliatura* helped him to sort out his intellectual life.[18] Ghisleri considered Turati undisciplined, not well read, and more susceptible to a well-turned phrase than to a logical argument.[19] Ghisleri stimulated his friend to undertake serious study and once publicly ridiculed him in the pages of *Il preludio* for what Ghisleri considered Turati's vague thinking about God. Turati replied, but Ghisleri's counterattack was so effective that it changed Turati's moral orientation.[20] Within two years, Turati had adopted materialism.[21]

In the late 1870s Turati seemed to be moving toward a vague socialism.[22] His personal situation paralleled the confused nature of the Italian left at this time; Italian intellectuals were turning away from Mikhail Bakunin's revolutionary anarchism but had not yet replaced it with a consistent Marxist system. Turati dissociated himself both from anarchism and from the confused mélange of "integral" socialism advocated by the followers of the French Socialist, Benoît Malon.[23] Although Turati had not yet worked out his own ideas, one basic feature of his ideology had emerged: his belief in gradualism rather than violent revolution.[24] But Turati was not well acquainted with Marx, and his ideology was not fully formed until after 1885, when he met Anna Kuliscioff, the woman who was to be his companion for forty years.[25]

Nevertheless, much of Turati's later ideology can be discerned in his writings of the late 1870s and early 1880s.[26] A good illustration is his most important early work, *Il delitto e la questione sociale*, which appeared as a series of articles in the Socialist newspaper, *La plebe*. *Il delitto* refuted the theories of the criminologist Cesare Lombroso, who maintained that criminals were born, not made. Not so, answered Turati. The bourgeois economic structure caused crime. The capitalist state robbed the poor, forced them to commit crimes to survive, and then punished them. The law could not be equal for all until social conditions became equal. Turati wrote that "The penal question is above all one of social reform"; crime, he said, would disappear after society had been reformed. Thus, crime was not an isolated phenomenon to be cured by laws directed against criminals, and "natural" factors considered important by Lombroso's school—race, physical type, climate—were only incidental. The criminal state had no right to punish anyone.[27]

Il delitto emphasizes social reform, the organic nature of society, the inevitability of evolution, and the need for gradual change. These elements, erected into a system, were the fundamentals of Turati's reformist socialism.

"Socialism is light, it is life, it is the future"

Like most Italian Socialists of the period, Turati arrived at socialism through humanitarianism and philosophical positivism, rather than Hegelianism. "Heaven falls," he wrote in a letter of 10 July 1878, "Christianity is transported to Earth, comes alive . . . and takes the name of socialism."[28] By the 1890s, when he helped found the Italian Socialist party, Turati's ideology had become "scientific" and

Marxist, but his deep feeling and passion for humanity explain his conversion to socialism.

His humanity also explains his lifelong aversion to violence. Turati emphasized that socialism could only come about as the result of a slow, peaceful, transformation of capitalism. As early as 1878, he saw revolution as a "bogey" that might serve to accelerate the evolution toward socialism, but he believed in education as the best means to achieve this end.[29] He denied that violence was an integral part of Marxian ideology. "A revolution is not such *because* of violence," Turati wrote in 1893, "but *despite* violence." Force degraded the human spirit, killed freedom, and made socialism impossible. Violence caused mental paralysis, servility, and terror. Revolutionary violence indicated that society was not ready for socialism:

> The revolution, when it erupts into violence, denies itself wholly or in part and confesses its own weakness because it must fight and crush [others] . . . at the risk of shattering itself and deviating from its goal. The revolution may fulfill itself and generate effects in the same way a piece of fruit torn with violence from a tree may be ripe enough to serve as seed, not *because* it has been pulled off, but *despite* it.[30]

According to Turati, Socialist ideas must be spread peacefully until they so permeated society that men would have no will to resist them. Such a spiritual revolution would involve intensive preparation, and this groundwork would spur the evolution which, for Turati, was synonymous with revolution. Those who preached violence and the "dictatorship of the proletariat" deluded themselves. The revolution would come only when it had evolved from bourgeois society, and its hallmark would be either the absence or the absolute minimum of force.

Turati's concept of social evolution underlay all his thought. He believed that the internal contradictions of capitalism would eventually cause it to collapse, as did all Marxists, but his aversion to violence and his stress on gradual evolution colored his interpretation of Marx. For Turati, the idea that capitalism would fall of its own weight was an abstraction. He never imagined that capitalism would end in a relatively short period of time, and socialists could wait. Socialists must speed up, by means of reforms, the "natural" tendency of capitalism to collapse. Thus, when Turati spoke of the "class struggle," he meant the proletariat's struggle for reforms, a process that depended on the human will and excluded violence. Thus, evolution and revolution were the same thing.[31]

Turati's concept of evolution played a crucial part in his analysis of the Italian proletariat's role. Because it would be unable to improvise a Socialist society, it was not desirable for the Italian working class to achieve power immediately.[32] Through the years, the proletariat itself had absorbed bourgeois culture and had adopted "bourgeois principles and tendencies. The proletariat has the enemy which it confronts externally also within itself. The proletarian must strip himself and jettison the man who now exists. This does not come about in a day."[33] Hence, the political and moral preparation of the proletariat for socialism would take a long time.

For socialists to promise the workers immediate and total satisfaction through violence, Turati argued, showed either fraud or ignorance. The Italian proletariat could not be unconscious and backward, as the socialists claimed, and at the same time demand the establishment of a dictatorship in order to lead civilization to new heights. The concept of a dictatorship of the proletariat led straight to an oligarchic principle within socialism: leaders imposing their own ideas on the masses. This principle would bring about a dictatorship not *of* the proletariat but, eventually, *against* the proletariat.

For Turati, "socialism is a force that becomes," not the violent imposition of a plan by socialist leaders. Socialism would come about through the daily action of the proletariat in its economic organizations, even if the workers did not belong to the Socialist party. The Party's function was to assure political conditions guaranteeing the proletariat's freedom of action and to translate its achievements into law, not to act as a revolutionary elite or advance guard. Indeed, Turati so greatly feared the Party's Jacobin tendency that in 1902 he attempted to dissolve its executive organ, the Directorate. He narrowly missed this objective, but his steady weakening of that body led, finally, to a violent reaction against him in 1911. Preventing what a scholar would later call "totalitarian democracy" and still maintaining a modern, efficient, centralized organization presented insuperable difficulties.[34]

The Party also had to make the workers understand those irresistible forces operating in bourgeois society that made socialism inevitable. It had to help "elevate" the proletariat. Elevation meant the gradual conquest of existing political institutions. "Elevation," Turati wrote in 1892, "is not so much economic as it is intellectual and moral—and, therefore, necessarily political."[35]

According to Turati, an ever-increasing crescendo of reforms would slowly train the proletariat for its future role as administrator of the socialist society. Reforms would have a cumulative effect. The proletariat could attain "these most beautiful reforms," which would slowly sap the vitality of the capitalist system, only by working positively within bourgeois political institutions. Working within the capitalist system did not imply its acceptance. Ultimately, the socialists aimed to overthrow capitalism, but emphasis on violence reduced this aim to trivial violations of the Civil Code. Reforms, on the other hand, stimulated the inexorable evolutionary process already taking place within capitalism. Leftist arguments that the bourgeoisie consented to reforms only to preserve itself failed to convince Turati. Of course, capitalists aimed at self-preservation, but if the bourgeoisie became stronger by granting reforms, those reforms would strengthen the proletariat even more. Thus, the bourgeoisie followed its own interests in the short run but committed suicide and made socialism inevitable in the long run. Turati branded as anarchists those socialists who rejected these conclusions, not only in 1892 but throughout his career.[36]

More important than the reforms themselves was the process by which the proletariat became galvanized to obtain them. Turati considered this process the kernel of the concept of "elevation" and the real socialist contribution to the proletariat's cause. The struggle for reforms "exercised" the workers and prepared them to govern and to manage the emerging socialist society. Reforms also fulfilled an educational purpose. Turati's formula was "organization, study, propaganda." By organizing itself, the proletariat would develop into an important bloc wielding great power within bourgeois society. Study involved intensive investigation of the workings of society and produced guidelines for political action. Propaganda meant the diffusion of socialist ideas in all possible ways—press, lecture, club, correspondence, and, above all, example.[37]

Reforms required democracy, the essential political precondition for the spread of socialist ideas. This requirement accounted for Turati's willingness to enter into political alliances with radical middle-class parties. Because he considered Italian society too prone to reaction, Turati supported progressive "bourgeois" ministries. Ironically, the Socialist party would defend the Constitution from its supposed friends who, according to the Party, would destroy it in panic-stricken attempts to save themselves from socialism.

The preservation of democracy was so critical to Turati's thinking that he believed the Italian Socialist party might have to act as a substitute democratic party in order to establish or maintain conditions favoring the evolution of socialism. A radical democratic phase was essential for the establishment of socialism. If no democratic party capable of bringing about this development existed in Italy, then the Socialist party would have to perform the task itself.

Revolutionaries condemned this "bourgeois" concept of the Socialist party. As the Party toned down its demands when it collaborated with radical bourgeois groups, the revolutionaries objected that it had been co-opted by the capitalist system. In the resulting struggles between Turati on the right and different kinds of revolutionaries on the left, nobody won. Although Turati was the Socialist party's most prominent leader, he could not exercise complete control over the organization, nor could his opponents. Disunity deprived the Party of a solid political base. Many of the "socialist" and "petty-bourgeois" reforms coincided, making collaboration possible, but in the process Socialist party deputies often found it necessary to modify even their most modest proposals, thus alienating the Party's left wing, which opposed collaboration on principle. Moreover, the "revolutionaries" could exploit the frustrations of the masses simply by belittling any results of parliamentary action.

Turati's willingness to cooperate with certain factions of the establishment, under certain conditions, did not mean that he minimized Italy's problems. Parliament, he wrote, was a den of thieves, the judiciary was servile, the police corrupt, the schools squalid, the bourgeoisie cynical, but these problems could be overcome with hard work and dedication.[38] Social reforms would slowly destroy the bourgeoisie's political monopoly and ultimately render economic monopoly meaningless.[39] Marxism provided the guidelines, but they must be used with caution and adapted to special conditions in different countries. Socialists could not apply Marxist theories in Italy automatically or dogmatically.[40] As long as the Socialists kept alive the ideal of a just society, they could modify Marxist dogma.[41] "The class struggle," Turati wrote, "is humanity's struggle."[42] As Turati conceived of socialism, it became a moral imperative, not the mechanical application of dogma.

Turati's ideology resembled that of the other major leaders of European social democratic parties before World War I—for example, Emile Vandervelde in Belgium, Wilhelm Liebknecht in Germany, Jean Jaurès in France, Viktor Adler in Austria, and Keir Hardie in England. There are also interesting parallels between Eduard Bernstein and Turati: the emphasis on the ethical desirability of socialism, the condemnation of violence, the rejection of the dictatorship of the proletariat, the importance of political alliances with middle-class groups.[43] The similarity stems from common situations and dilemmas, rather than from reciprocal influence. All of the prewar parties were parliamentary organizations attempting to win reforms for their followers, who then became less instead of more revolutionary. None of the parties gained a majority, and all found it necessary to fight repression or gain influence through political alliances with democratic bourgeois groups or governments.

As a result, they provoked attacks from militant left wingers within their ranks and further weakened the potential force of the organizations.

Anna Kuliscioff and Filippo Turati

Turati's ideology resulted from the interaction and exchange of ideas with Anna Kuliscioff.[44] Anna Kuliscioff (née Rosenstein) came from a small Crimean town near the city of Simferopol. Three years older than Turati, she came from a relatively wealthy family able to give her a good education. Because Russian institutions of higher learning were closed to women at the time, Kuliscioff studied medicine in Zurich, where she joined a group of conspiratorial Russian revolutionaries. She returned to Russia, but few details are known about her political life there; she fled in April 1877.[45]

By this time Anna Kuliscioff had joined the anarchist movement. She went to France, where she met the Italian anarchist Andrea Costa, by whom she had a daughter. Arrested for her anarchist activities by the French police, she was liberated through the intercession of the Russian novelist Ivan Turgenev.[46]

Kuliscioff was expelled from France and went to Italy, where she actively participated in anarchist intrigues. Charged with plotting insurrection, she was tried and acquitted in 1879. By then, however, she had become disillusioned with the anarchists.[47]

Her change of heart apparently influenced Andrea Costa to abandon anarchism, a crucial event in the decline of that movement. She influenced Italian socialism to an even greater extent and was instrumental in turning it toward social democracy.[48]

Her relationship with Costa had already cooled off when she met Turati in Naples in 1885. She moved to Milan where, in the offices of their review *Critica sociale*, in the Galleria Vittorio Emanuele, Kuliscioff and Turati established a salon, which all the important personalities of the Extreme Left attended:

Dalle undici alle otto,
Nel bel mezzo del salotto,
Splende il sol dell'avvenir.[49]

The salon was the center for the diffusion of socialist ideas in Italy, the credit for which goes to Turati and Kuliscioff.[50]

Anna Kuliscioff introduced Turati to the serious study of Marxism. She had converted to Marxism before she met him,[51] and, under her influence, Turati's ideology acquired the "scientific" basis that was the boast of Marxist socialism at the end of the nineteenth century; she convinced him that to comprehend the political and social changes in society one must understand "the transformations of the means of production and exchange, that is, the economy of an age rather than its ethics or abstract philosophy."[52]

Although Anna Kuliscioff not only influenced Turati decisively at a crucial point in his life but inspired him until her death, it is difficult to separate the pair's actions.[53] Their correspondence demonstrates that she was a keen political observer and that many of Turati's political actions had their origins in her suggestions or complaints. Furthermore, she often provided Turati with the basic ideas for his editorials in the *Critica*.

The two did not always agree. Kuliscioff maintained the political perspective of an outsider and often warned Turati not to isolate himself in Parliament. Turati displayed the frustrations and doubts of a person who had very little room to maneuver in a political world where the odds were overwhelmingly against him. The convergence of ideas and the working out of positions on the major problems of the period make their twenty-five-year correspondence important for modern Italian history. Anna Kuliscioff summarized their dialogue in these words: "Our letters are a long-distance conversation. Our ideas, sentiments, and projects meet as if the space that divides us were suppressed, as if we only had one brain and one soul. What union will ever be able to boast such a complete and perfect identification?"[54] Despite their differences, Filippo Turati and Anna Kuliscioff shared the same ideology and the same goals.

Although Turati assimilated the "scientific" aspects of socialism under Kuliscioff's influence, the true basis of his political philosophy was not science. Some authors have remarked that Turati lacked speculative insight.[55] The positivist vogue in fashion in Italy during his youth left a lasting mark on him, and he always billed himself as a "positivist" whose theories were rooted in "facts" and who took changing conditions into account to modify his political ideology. This realism made him more susceptible to "revisionist" ideas.[56]

Despite his emphasis on "positivism," and the "science" he believed was part of it, Turati's real strength derived from his humanitarianism and his emphasis on the ethical and moral justification for socialism.[57] These feelings underpinned the reformism he had fully developed by the time he founded the Italian Socialist party.

CHAPTER II

The Foundation of the Italian Socialist Party

THE FEATURE that stands out in the foundation of the Italian Socialist party is the opposition to its establishment by groups of leftists, especially anarchists and *operaisti*. The latter advocated a labor party exclusively composed of and led by workers and concentrating upon improving working conditions. For ideological reasons, the anarchists opposed the founding of any political party on the extreme left. Both groups believed that systematic participation of a proletarian organization in politics meant the "absorption" of proletarian energies by the capitalist system.

In addition to anarchists and *operaisti*, Antonio Labriola, then the nation's most renowned Marxist philosopher, also opposed a mass political party at that stage of Italy's political and economic development. He argued that such a party could not survive or that it would have to accept a program that would be meaningless from a Marxist point of view.

These opponents, however, were no match for Turati's political and organizational abilities.

Preludes

Although Italian socialism has roots going back before 1848, its modern history begins with Mikhail Bakunin's efforts to disseminate socialist ideas in Italy on behalf of the Workers' International. Bakunin destroyed the influence of Mazzinianism among Italian workers and gained the allegiance of many Italian intellectuals against Marx during the struggle between them in the 1860s and 1870s.[1]

Bakunin advocated the immediate overthrow of the state by violence. In the 1870s anarchist bands attempted to spark a nationwide revolution, but the police had little trouble suppressing their activities because of the lack of popular support.[2] After 1877 the failure of anarchist methods became clear, and prominent leaders began to desert the movement. In August 1879, Andrea Costa pronounced anarchism a failure in a famous letter to his colleagues.[3] He advised the socialists to enter Parliament and to gain control of local government. He was the first socialist elected to the Chamber of Deputies, the young Turati being among those urging him to take the oath. Costa, however, was not a reformist in the sense Turati was. Costa wished to infiltrate, undermine, and destroy existing political institutions, rather than transform them into tools that would lead to a proletarian victory. He proposed the union of all socialist factions in Italy, and the broadening of the movement's base by establishment of a political party.[4] He founded the Partito socialista rivoluzionario di Romagna in 1881, intending it as the nucleus of a nationwide political organization; this, however, was not to be.[5]

A more immediate forerunner of the Italian Socialist party was the Partito operaio italiano (POI). Founded in Milan in 1882 and composed of salaried workers, its members were "the sons of the working class . . . which is always derided, insulted, oppressed, and kept in ignorance."[6] Party leaders vowed to improve working conditions and denounced the quibblings of intellectuals.[7] The workers, distrusting the socialists' middle-class origins, founded their own party in order to take advantage of the right to vote, which most of them received in 1881.[8]

The stimulus for a party had come directly from Engels, who, in a letter of 1877, had urged the Italian workers to try the legal road to power. Engels communicated with a group, organized around the newspaper *La plebe*, which rejected violence and favored more conventional forms of political activity.[9] Originally inspired by a French "evolutionary" socialist, the group's confused ideology sometimes resembled that of middle-class radical reformers but was an important strand within Italian socialism.[10] The group's leaders helped found the POI in Milan and had an indirect role in the Socialist party's formation ten years later.[11]

Both the POI and Costa's Romagnol organization suffered from unclear or confused programs and unsettled tactics, and both had little success.[12] The POI failed to elect any candidates in the elections of 1882 and 1886.

Immediately afterward, Felice Cavallotti's Radical Democrats launched a violent campaign against the POI, which they blamed for some of their own losses in the election. Cavallotti strongly intimated that the POI had the support of the police during the elections and that the government subsidized the party's newspaper.[13] The government took advantage of the dispute in June 1886, dissolved the POI, and jailed its leaders.[14] The POI had probably reached a membership of 40,000.[15]

Turati, the defense attorney for the POI leaders, argued that the POI did not advocate violence but worked to improve social and working conditions causing unrest among the workers.[16] He accused the government of attacking the entire Italian proletariat through the POI.[17] The defendants received light sentences.[18]

Although the POI reorganized after the government's attack, it failed to remain viable, despite attempts by the *operaisti* to revitalize it.[19] By excluding socialist intellectuals a priori, the POI deprived itself of highly educated, professional personnel who might have become its leaders. For Turati the POI's failure proved the futility of the exclusionist principle and of an "apolitical" policy. On the other hand, the POI showed that a proletarian political organization could count upon substantial support in Milan and northern Italy.

The POI did not declare itself Marxist, although Marx's ideas influenced its leaders. The POI's anthem, the "Canto dei lavoratori," illustrates this influence. The "Canto," with words by Turati, diffused Marxism among the masses. It explained Marxist dogma in simple terms that uneducated people could understand: capitalist exploitation, labor theory of value, surplus value, self-emancipation of the workers. It stressed:

Il riscatto del lavoro
de' suoi figli opra sarà;
o vivremo del lavoro
o pugnando si morrà![20]

Turati's main vehicle for the propagation of his ideas was not the "Canto," however, but his journal *Critica sociale*, which grew out of *Cuore e critica*, a monthly founded by Arcangelo Ghisleri in 1887. Turati became de facto editor of the review in 1889, two years before he took control and changed its name and format.[21] Turati promised that the journal would be open to all opinions and would not have a rigidly ideological tone.[22]

The *Critica*'s success depended upon his close collaboration with Anna Kuliscioff, who frequently provided the ideas. Turati's lively, scathing style ensured its appeal. He wrote the articles signed with his name, his initials, "La critica sociale," and "Noi." The imprint of his eloquent ironic style permeated the publication. As Roberto Michels wrote, Turati's writing could "boil the blood, caress, slap, become tender." His metaphors have been described as "grandiose and unforgettable," his sentences as "being able to pull the skin off." His style was lively, impatient, nervous, energetic, his criticism penetrating. Benedetto Croce maintained that Turati's review was livelier than its German counterpart, Neue Zeit.[23] Antonio Graziadei was drawn to Marxism by Critica sociale, as were Arturo Labriola, the future theoretician of Italian revolutionary syndicalism, and a host of other intellectuals.[24] Labriola pronounced Critica sociale's Marxist ideas superior to those of any other radical journal. "And," adds Michels, "for a while it seemed to be true."[25] Critica sociale thus helped prepare the way for the Italian Socialist party.

An institution with a similarly important role was the Lega socialista milanese (Milanese Socialist League), which Turati and Anna Kuliscioff founded. A "cell" for the future Socialist party, this organization enunciated the principles that later inspired it.[26] The league's platform was influenced by the German Socialists and concisely expressed Turati's reformist socialism.[27] The program advocated gradualist methods, stating that the revolution would require an "epoch," the culmination of a great *evolutionary* movement making use even of the "most hostile elements, which become, in their turn, its helpers." The revolution had to graft itself upon "and penetrate all the most vital organs and strata of the old society." Therefore, "scientific socialism does not believe in miraculous renovation . . . by decrees from above or revolts from below." The document stressed the Marxist theme of self-redemption of the working classes. Because they would teach the workers to help themselves, the socialists had to organize the proletariat as an autonomous party.[28]

In order to implement this program, it was essential to enter Parliament and work for reforms. Italian socialist tradition, however, had been overwhelmingly antiparliamentarian, and Turati set out to attenuate the workers' distrust by throwing the league's support to the POI in 1887, convincing the Fascio dei lavoratori to participate in local elections, planning demonstrations for 1 May, and giving numerous lectures. A secret report by the prefect of Milan, written in July 1900, details Turati's activity during this period—preparation for a final drive designed to culminate in the foundation of a party.[29]

Turati and the Drive for the Socialist Party

There was still so much opposition on the left to the idea of establishing a Marxist Socialist party that Turati had to deal with this point first. He emphasized the need for immediate political action to help the proletariat.[30] The workers, the "revolution in the making, socialism which *becomes*," had to organize in order to achieve their aims.[31] Above all, socialist action had to be "realistic," had to root itself in concrete events.[32] Socialists must work to attain the reforms that spur social evolution.[33] It was this need for action that made a political party with a practical, realizable program imperative.[34] Marxist precepts had no value without immediate objectives.[35] Socialism in Italy had to become parliamentary, as it was in more advanced countries.[36] Turati then denounced the *operaisti*, who either foolishly threw away the vote or believed that only workers should belong to a proletarian party.[37]

The *operaisti*, however, had widespread support among the Italian workers, and Turati proved unable to defeat them at an important National Workers' Congress convened in Milan by the Milanese socialists on 2 and 3 August 1891. The meeting, however, was far from a total defeat for Turati. The congress began well, accepting Turati's proposal for recognizing the validity of social legislation as a means of curbing the excesses of capitalism and rejecting a motion advocating electoral intransigence.[38] Debate then occurred on a motion clearing the way for easy entrance of nonproletarians in the future Socialist party, but it soon became clear that the motion would fail if put to the vote. When he became aware of this, Turati presented a compromise motion, which the assembly accepted by a near-unanimous vote. Turati's motion gave way to the *operaisti* on the membership issue but achieved some practical results. The delegates declared that all the organizations present at the congress constituted a party and nominated a commission to draft a tentative program within a month. The commission would remain as a provisional central committee until a national congress could establish the new organization on a permanent basis, not later than the summer of 1892.[39]

Turati's concessions were aimed at winning over the *operaisti*, who still suspected socialist intentions. Turati later claimed that he had made a mistake; the *operaisti* proved not less suspicious when the Genoa congress convened, and in the meantime they allied with anarchist groups, a development Turati had long feared.[40]

Probably, however, the gains outweighed the losses.[41] The Milan congress had done more than give the go-ahead for a party, it had in some measure determined its policies. The delegates had endorsed social legislation and active participation in politics to transform the existing political apparatus into "a ponderous force for evolution."[42] These policies coincided with Turati's reformism.

Turati intensified his campaign for a Socialist party after the Milan congress. He and Kuliscioff tripled *Critica sociale*'s circulation and helped found *Lotta di classe*, its "popular complement," designed to reach the workers who were untouched by the more intellectual journal. He and his friends had agreed to found this newspaper on 26 June 1892 at a restaurant in Piazza Fontana in Milan. In order to meet growing resentment against Milanese domination of the Italian socialist movement, Turati pressured Camillo Prampolini, a popular Reggio Emilian leader whose ideas coincided with Turati's, to accept editorship of the new publication. Prampolini was unwilling, however, to leave his own newspaper, *La giustizia*, and, although his name appeared as editor of *Lotta di classe* until shortly after the Congress of Genoa, he never managed the newspaper.[43] During the crucial period leading to the foundation of the Socialist party, Turati himself edited *Lotta di classe* along with Costantino Lazzari.[44]

The Italian Socialist movement was, if not exclusively, overwhelmingly Milanese. Milan, the most highly industrialized city in Italy, remained the center of Italian socialism until World War I. In addition to being the headquarters of Turati's Socialist League and of the POI, Milan established the first successful *camera del lavoro*. The *camere* quickly spread all over Italy and provided centralized leadership and welfare services to the workers.[45]

It was also in Milan that an embryonic Socialist party had experimented with electoral politics before the Congress of Genoa. On 18 June 1892, a *numero unico* of *Lotta di classe* was printed to support the socialist campaign for the local elections that month.[46] This pilot issue introduced *Lotta di classe* as the voice of "the democratic socialist workers' associations of Milan for the local elections of 1892." The articles were unsigned, but the most important one, "The Modern Class Struggle," is in Turati's style, and his ideas clearly permeate the issue. The article denounced violence, for example, because it could never profoundly alter the economic structure of society or achieve the proletariat's aim, collective ownership of capital. This goal could be attained only gradually by capturing the institutions that defended the bourgeoisie's economic privileges—state, commune, court, school. The vote, a bourgeois instrument of power, could more potently arm the workers because of its value as a means of recruitment and training, and the most powerful means of gaining ascendancy in public life. Violence could succeed only in bringing about "simple" political change. The workers had decided to organize themselves to achieve political power by means of the franchise.[47]

Lotta di classe then urged a wide range of people to vote with the socialists, even asking the aid of groups generally considered middle class, a clearly Turatian policy. The newspaper invited white collar workers, former aristocrats, and bourgeois into the socialist ranks[48] and explained how landlords and government exploited small businessmen.[49] The newspaper turned socialism into a moral crusade and urged all exploited groups to join in it.[50]

Lotta di classe's campaign had implications beyond the local elections. Turati and the Milanese socialists were clearly implementing their own policies in the name of the "party" before a congress had determined them. Furthermore, the approximately 1,300 votes received by the socialist candidates allowed the Turati group to claim widespread support, which it could use against the *operaisti*.[51] The Turatians demonstrated that socialism could appeal to other groups exploited by Italian society, not only the workers.

It was essential to counteract the influence of the *operaisti* because they were on the verge of having their way. The "provisional" Central Committee charged by the Milan Workers' Congress to draft a party program reported in March 1892. The seven-member committee reflected the many factions represented at Milan and was dominated by Antonio Maffi, an ambitious radical democratic deputy anxious to ingratiate himself with the *operaisti*. The draft program, therefore, was practically a carbon copy of the POI program of 1887.[52] This draft went out to interested groups along with invitations to a congress that would ratify it.[53]

Turati attacked the draft program at once, charging that it consisted of vague or meaningless words and slogans. "Popular sovereignty," "All men being born equal," and like phrases were nebulous and overexploited; "emancipation," "union," "common end," were words conservatives would have no trouble with. The new program should eliminate all equivocation and be specific. Socialists should say "collectivization" if that is what they mean. The new party should not exclude anyone who accepted its program, but neither would it be an old-fashioned political organization open to everyone; the prerequisite for membership was an ideological commitment to socialism.[54]

Next, Turati criticized the draft constitution for the opposite reason—it was too specific. Because the proposed constitution included an article limiting admission to proletarian workers, Turati had finally to confront the compromise he had accepted at the Milan Workers' Congress. He now objected that he had proposed the compromise only because the congress had been in a hurry. For the socialists to refuse admission to white-collar workers, professionals, or anyone else who accepted the party program would provoke "the intellectual, moral, and political suicide of the party."[55]

Turati's objections to the program were similar to those Marx had made to the German Socialist party's Gotha Program.[56] In fact, he was heavily influenced by Antonio Labriola's application of Marx's principles in his critique of the Central Committee's draft.[57]

Labriola criticized Turati's attempts to establish a Socialist party in Italy. He remained unconvinced that conditions for the foundation of a Socialist party existed and castigated Turati for being too accommodating and too ready to compromise ideological principles. Labriola favored a small, close-knit party of vigorous ideologues, capable of rapid expansion under favorable conditions. He refused to attend the Congress of Genoa.[58] Nevertheless, it was Labriola's criticism of the draft program that spurred Turati to publish his articles.[59] The two men complemented one another.[60]

While Turati went on the offensive, the *operaisti* organized their own campaign against him. On 23 July 1892, the associated workers' organizations met in Milan to determine their policy for the upcoming Congress of Genoa. The representatives agreed with the *operaista* leader, Alfredo Casati, that the new party should be composed exclusively of workers' associations, that it should consider all problems from an *operaista* viewpoint, and that it should turn over control of the party newspaper to the workers. Turati's representative, the glovemaker Giuseppe Croce, proved unable to block these decisions.[61]

That was just the beginning of the *operaista* onslaught. On the eve of the Genoa congress, the Fascio dei lavoratori (the workers' union to which many of the *operaisti* belonged) published a statement expressing its grave concern with the "turn several bourgeois and ideological socialists, who have recently infiltrated the ranks of the Italian workers' movement, wanted the workers' party to take." The Fascio wished the "bourgeois socialists" to remain separate from the workers and authorized Casati, its representative to the Genoa congress, to oppose the admission of political associations composed jointly of workers and bourgeoisie. Moreover, the Fascio announced its opposition to any description of the new organization as "socialist" because "even if the Partito operaio is inspired by economic concepts suggested by socialism, it still cannot call itself socialist since its program does not consider the complex philosophical problems that modern socialism seeks to resolve."[62] In other words, the Fascio demanded a new version of the POI.[63]

The *operaista* position threatened Turati. It not only challenged his conception of a modern Socialist party but also exposed the divisions in the worker-socialist camp on the eve of the Congress of Genoa. If he failed to work out an understanding between socialists and workers, all hope of establishing a Socialist party in Italy would disappear.

Turati was therefore obliged to respond immediately to the Fascio's statement. He argued that the Fascio's principles meant reversing the direction the Italian workers had already chosen and nullifying the decisions of their congresses. Such a position would make them the laughingstock of the workers of the world. Furthermore, Turati maintained, the Fascio represented only Casati's ideas and those of a few of his "acolytes," not those of the Partito operaio, or of the Milanese labor movement.[64] Casati, who was no match for Turati, replied weakly that the socialist leader was attempting to bury the Partito operaio while it was still alive.[65]

Clearly, the possibility of founding a modern Socialist party in Italy now depended upon Turati's political acumen, as it was generally believed that the new party would be a reincarnation of the POI.[66]

Moreover, a coalition between anarchists and *operaisti* had jelled by August 1892. The anarchists were anxious, for ideological reasons, to prevent the establishment of a party under socialist auspices, fearing that they would lose influence among the workers.[67] Turati and the socialists made plans to resist the anarchist threat. Anna Kuliscioff presided at a meeting on the night of 13 August to plan socialist reaction to predictable anarchist harassment during the congress. The socialists rejected suggestions to exclude the anarchists and to call the carabinieri but agreed upon measures to prevent anarchist sabotage of the congress.[68]

The Congresses of Genoa: Birth of the Italian Socialist Party

The Congress of Genoa opened on the morning of 14 August 1892. Delegates representing more than 300 labor associations attended, but the persons packed into the meeting hall, the Sala Sivori, numbered many more, according to *Lotta di classe*. The anarchist-*operaista* coalition materialized immediately to combat Anna Kuliscioff's motion nominating four men to chair the scheduled sessions of the congress. After a loud, disorderly debate, Kuliscioff's proposal passed by a 106-to-46 roll-call vote. Anarchist attempts to disrupt the meeting continued, however, even after Turati proposed, in an attempt to resolve the dispute, that the anarchist Eugenio Pellaco be one of the chairmen. The assembly finally came to another vote over the issue, but the delegates could not proceed as new incidents and disturbances broke out. Cries of "shame" were heard as the delegates took still another vote and agreed to continue their business. At this point, Casati proposed expelling all "political" associations, but a new vote defeated the anarchist-*operaista* coalition.

After a brief lull punctuated by outbursts from the floor, anarchist obstruction began anew. When the provisional Central Committee reported, Pellaco asked the anxious assembly to postpone discussion until the next day. This time the angry delegates rose to their feet shouting and accusing the anarchists of sabotage. They came close to fistfighting as Turati shouted, "Out with the despots!" Finally, Prampolini proposed meeting in different places on the next day. The anarchist leader Pietro Gori threatened to follow the socialists wherever they went, but Turati answered: "We do not wish to discuss further problems that we resolved long ago. . . . Tomorrow we will meet someplace else without you. You have your own meeting wherever you like."[69]

That evening the Milanese socialists called a meeting of delegates favoring a Socialist party. Delegates from about 150 organizations attended. The Central Committee "dissolved" the congress, convened a new one for the next day, and specifically excluded the anarchists.[70] The socialists' speedy decision and their ease in securing a meeting place suggest that they had planned for such an eventuality. A number of delegates, including Costa, were unhappy with these developments, but there was little they could do. In the end, representatives of 197 organizations, the great majority of the delegates, adhered to the "socialist" congress,[71] while anarchists and *operaisti* continued to meet at the Sala Sivori.[72]

Filippo Turati, now in control, attempted to rectify the defects of the draft program according to the analysis he had published in *Lotta di classe* the previous month. Under the circumstances, he could do so only by amending the program to make it more precise. For example, where the draft had asserted that all men were "born equal and have the same right to live," Turati's modification read, "That all men have an equal right to enjoy the benefits of society . . . provided that they contribute to maintain those benefits to the best of their ability." Instead of advocating organization in order to "oppose existing institutions," the final draft emphasized that "the workers cannot emancipate themselves except by the socialization of the means of work (land, mines, factories, transportation, etc.) and the socialized management of production."[73]

There was some opposition to Turati's proposals. Antonio Maffi favored a flexible program that would allow as many schools of opinion as possible to adhere to the party. Costantino Lazzari worried that a program as scientifically sound as the one proposed by Turati was premature.

Turati opposed Maffi's and Lazzari's suggestions, which would produce an old-fashioned political organization, composed of loosely organized and widely diverse factions. Only a strong commitment to socialism could engender a new political party. Turati believed that clear statements of principle would aid, not hinder, the party's growth. He wanted the new organization to welcome everyone who accepted the program, but he demanded a clear program to ensure that only persons with strong socialist convictions would join. A smaller party was better than a large, amorphous organization. According to Anna Kuliscioff, it was better "to have one cell capable of development than a great, inert, dead mass."[74]

Turati won his case. The congress endorsed his suggested changes in the program and bylaws, and the new organization now became open to all who accepted its program. In addition, the delegates recognized participation in electoral contests as a duty and agreed that the Socialist party should be a compact, disciplined organization capable of rapid growth.[75]

The program that emerged from the "socialist" Congress of Genoa, therefore, combined the POI platform of 1887, carried over by the Central Committee named to write a draft in 1891, and Turati's reformism, as expressed in his amendments. Socialist policy was to have a "double aspect," economic and political:

1. *The struggle of the occupations* for the immediate improvement of working-class conditions (hours, salaries, factory rules, etc.), a struggle which is to devolve upon the chambers of labor and other labor associations

2. *A wider struggle having as its goal the conquest of the organs of public power* (state, commune, public administrations, etc.) in order to transform them from the tools of oppression and exploitation they are today into instruments of economic and political expropriation of the dominating class.[76]

Although Turati's dream of establishing the Italian Socialist party had finally come true,[77] his success was marred because he had to accept the main outlines of the draft program and to make concessions to the feelings of worker representatives. The program resembled the platforms of the Milanese Socialist League and the German Erfurt Program only where Turati modified it.[78] However, it excluded "revolutionary" means—violence—as a method of achieving power, and the Party was formally committed to gradualism.[79]

But there remained in the Socialist party groups still advocating violence against the capitalist system. As the Party attempted to define its policies, these groups clashed with Turati and his followers, and the struggle weakened the Party.

The Socialist party, as created at Genoa, was the first modern Italian political party and as such served as a model for later organizations. The Party was highly centralized, at least on paper: Party policy derived from the rank and file; an executive committee enforced Party decisions in all its collateral organizations in order to maximize the effectiveness of Socialist political action.[80] "The Party is a disciplined one," stated the stenographic report of the Congress of Genoa.

The Party's bylaws spelled out its organization. National congresses representing all member organizations (each with one vote) determined Party policy. Individual organizations were guaranteed "administrative" autonomy.[81] The Central Committee, an executive group of five persons elected at the national congress, was charged with carrying out the congress's policies.[82] The Central Committee corresponded with and advised the member associations and was obliged to submit a complete report of its actions at the next congress.[83] In addition, the Party fixed norms for the payment of dues, the violation of which could lead to exclusion from the national congress.[84]

There was a fundamental structural defect in the Party's organization: workers' organizations or political clubs joined the Socialist party, not persons.[85] Because these groups elected to associate themselves by majority vote, a person could find himself in the Socialist party against his will or, more likely, apathetic members could artificially swell the Party's rolls. The enormous gains made during the Party's first year, therefore, were misleading.[86] Furthermore, associational organization proved a liability, as became obvious when the government banned the Party in 1894. In attacking the Party, the authorities also dissolved its affiliated labor organizations and in one blow undid many of the organizational accomplishments painfully achieved by the workers themselves over the years. Another weakness of this structure was that some Italian regions, notably the South, lacked organizations that could join the Party, and thus individuals from those areas were effectively excluded from Party membership. These liabilities outweighed any ideological reasons for associational membership—for example, Turati's desire to prevent the Party from turning into a centralized machine, which would impose on the workers the will of articulate intellectuals.[87] As a result, the Party was restructured in 1895.

Conditions at the Congress of Genoa prevented the Socialists from discussing concrete policies, but the next congress completed the work of unification.

The Congress of Reggio Emilia

The Socialists met again at the Congress of Reggio Emilia in September 1893 to determine the Party's position on two major issues, electoral alliances and the relationship between Socialist deputies and the Party.

Surprising agreement occurred on the question of electoral alliances, a continuing problem in later years. The congress agreed to absolute political intransigence—no cooperation of any kind with other parties. The vote was 106 to 62. In the minority on this question, Turati favored a minimum of cooperation with other parties under certain conditions, provided a regional congress approved and the Central Committee was informed.[88] He thus foreshadowed his role as champion of a more flexible electoral policy and of radical decentralization of the Party structure.

Turati opposed cooperation with "bourgeois" parties for tactical, not ideological, reasons. Because the Party had not become sufficiently independent, Turati supported intransigence during this period. Once it had done so, political alliances could even become desirable, as he had explained in a speech to the International Socialist Congress in Zurich in 1893. Turati contradicted Emile Vandervelde, the Belgian Socialist leader, who had endorsed electoral alliances for weak and recently founded socialist parties, such as the Italian. Turati argued that intransigent separation from radical democratic parties in less advanced countries was a condition of socialist affirmation. Firmly entrenched parties, on the other hand, could ally without fear, because, already sufficiently distinct, they would not confuse the workers. Turati explained how the Italian Socialist party had elected several deputies within a month of its foundation by using intransigent tactics, but, he stated, once the Party became strong it would ally itself with other political groups to achieve its major goals.[89]

This position was perfectly consistent with the point he made in 1890, that alliances "should not be rejected a priori and in all cases, but can be discussed and accepted, providing it can be done in a manner that does not create any confusion of men, of ideas, or of programs."[90] This was his position at both Zurich and Reggio Emilia. It is probably true that government reaction in 1894 convinced him to accept alliances in self-defense sooner than he otherwise would have done, but the view of Turati as a committed intransigent suddenly shifting gears under government repression is erroneous.[91] Nevertheless, when the Socialists faced the question of an alliance with "bourgeois" political groups against government repression, the easy accord reached at Reggio simply dissolved.

Significant friction occurred at Reggio Emilia over the issue of de facto cooperation. A Socialist deputy had voted for the government, justifying his action with the argument that non-Socialists as well as workers had cast their votes for him.[92] Angered by his reasoning, the leftist Costantino Lazzari presented a motion that completely subordinated the deputies to Party discipline and simply forbade them from participating in parliamentary votes. Kuliscioff objected that a party with long-range goals could not condemn itself to parliamentary sterility but must struggle for social legislation in addition to exercising its ideological function. Otherwise, the

Socialists might as well keep out of the Chamber of Deputies. Turati demanded that Lazzari strike from his motion the clause forbidding participation in votes, but Lazzari flatly refused. Another delegate broke the stalemate by offering Lazzari's motion minus the offending article.[93]

According to the successful motion, the deputies became Socialist party delegates who were obliged to coordinate their actions under the command of the Central Committee. The committee would convey its orders through a secretary, with whom the deputies were required to be in continuous communication. The deputies could support only measures the Party had deemed to be "socialist," and their actions would be evaluated by regional and general congresses. The deputies also had to participate in strikes, to ignore "adulterated" reforms, and to absolutely refrain from voting confidence in the government.[94]

The Party proved incapable of enforcing these requirements, especially since the Gruppo parlamentare socialista became the center of Party resistance to government reaction between 1894 and 1900, a role to which parliamentary status—which conferred power, privileges, visibility, and immunity from arrest—was particularly suited. The Socialist parliamentarians lost no time making a case for relief from the requirements for reasons of expediency. It was impossible, they argued, to consult the Central Committee when surprise votes came up in the Chamber, nor was it possible to lay down general policy because circumstances in Parliament could not be foreseen. With one exception, the Party secretary had little importance in Italy. In the end the deputies created their own policies, their only concession to the Party being a report summarizing their actions before the national congresses. This caused increasing conflict, which from time to time erupted into a violent reaction against the deputies.[95]

The delegates at Reggio Emilia, therefore, resolved the questions before them only on paper. The congress did not consolidate Party unity but opened a rift that plagued the Socialist party throughout its history.

CHAPTER III

Government Repression and
Socialist Response

THE LAST YEARS of the nineteenth cen-
tury were troubled ones for Italy. Economic crisis, financial chaos,
corruption, international difficulties, rapid industrialization, revolt,
government repression, and colonial conflicts all contributed to the
country's woes. The troubles affected the fledgling Socialist party,
which stormed onto the political scene vowing to end class domination of Italian society and threatening the hegemony of the ruling
groups. The government, especially fearing Socialist organization,
reacted by initiating repressive measures. Given the Party's imper-
fect and fragile structure, the measures might have proved fatal,
had not the Socialists closed ranks, changed their organization, and
modified their intransigent policies. Turati's prestige imposed a coherent and consistent line of action on the Party until Italy's an-
guished fin-de-siècle came to a close.

Repression and Self-Defense

The Italian political situation at the time of the Party's foundation
seemed propitious for the Socialists. In May of 1892, Giovanni
Giolitti took office. Giolitti had greater respect than his predeces-
sors for the rights of dissidents and recognized the workers' right
to organize themselves into resistance leagues, *camere del lavoro,*
and finally into a political party.[1]
    Giolitti's permissive attitude caused him trouble with the Right
and the dominant political figure, Francesco Crispi,[2] and in 1892
and 1893 a number of incidents combined to topple Giolitti's cabinet: the bank scandals, and the resulting charges of corruption
against Giolitti;[3] the disturbances in the country after French work-

ers at Aigues-Mortes killed several Italian emigrants;[4] and, finally, the Sicilian revolts. Giolitti had allowed the constitution of workers' organizations in Sicily, the *fasci*, many of them under Socialist influence. He had resisted demands for their dissolution[5] and, indeed, had announced a more liberal program in late 1893.[6] At the same time, however, Sicilian peasants protesting poor conditions began storming government offices, and in December widespread rioting took the lives of ninety-two persons.[7] Giolitti resigned, and Parliament called upon Crispi to reverse Giolitti's "soft" policies. Crispi proclaimed martial law, dissolved the *fasci*, dispatched 50,000 troops to the island, and established military tribunals.[8]

These events had repercussions in the Socialist party. According to Marxist theory, the Sicilian agricultural troubles could not herald the start of the revolution, which could begin only in the industrialized North, although Sicilian socialists had been instrumental in founding the Party and in establishing the *fasci*.[9] The Party newspaper, *Lotta di classe*, condemned the disorders because they smacked of anarchism.[10]

Turati, however, objected that the Sicilians were reacting to intolerable repression and exploitation. He considered the revolts as the first rumblings of the future socialist revolution.[11] This stand opened Turati to unjustified charges of inconsistency. Although Turati opposed violence, he was unwilling to abandon the Sicilians merely because violence had erupted on the island—especially since the Socialists had not provoked it. On the other hand, he opposed striking in the North to protest the Sicilian events and channeled Socialist action into meliorative activities such as collecting funds for the victims.[12]

In short, Turati interpreted the disorders as an incident in the class struggle, an opinion that received fast confirmation. Because the violence had spread, Crispi extended restrictive measures to include Socialists all over Italy. The police confiscated *Critica sociale* and initiated similar action against the rest of the Socialist press. In March 1894, Parliament voted Crispi full powers, provoking complaints from the Socialists that he had become a dictator.[13] In June came the so-called exceptional laws, passed ostensibly against the anarchists but really intended to curb the Socialists. These laws severely limited freedom of expression, provided severe penalties for infractions, and put *domicilio coatto*—exile to remote parts of the country—under police jurisdiction.[14] Turati, for example, was sentenced to three months' "exile" in Udine for his defense of the Sicilians.[15] Ultimately, Crispi aimed at abolishing the significance of the vote, Turati believed,[16] and he soon compared Crispi's regime with the reactionary czarist government.[17]

Crispi's policies set off an important debate within the Socialist party. Should the Party modify its political intransigence and ally itself with Crispi's bourgeois opponents to present a united front? We have already seen that Turati did not oppose alliances with other parties on ideological grounds. His tactical prerequisite was a clear identity for the Party. By the beginning of 1894 the Socialist party had affirmed itself sufficiently that there would be no confusion in the minds of its members if it contracted alliances with other parties.

In light of the Party's injunction against alliances, Turati had to act cautiously. He undertook a carefully planned campaign to obtain ideological approval for his policy of alliances from none other than Friedrich Engels.[18]

On 19 January 1894, Anna Kuliscioff wrote to Engels and asked for his advice. She summarized conditions in Italy and concluded that no socialist revolution could occur in a country still "two-thirds medieval," because a political revolution leading to a democratization of the country might break out. What should be the attitude of the Italian Socialists? The "doctrinaire" Socialists, who Kuliscioff said were in the majority, advocated a hands-off attitude, but she believed that "a political revolution in Italy would be such a boon to the future development of the Socialist party that, even if only a republic were attained, for us that would be enough."[19]

Anna Kuliscioff's assessment of the Italian situation turned out to be too optimistic. Marxist ideology prescribed a "democratic revolution," such as had taken place in France after 1789, after which radical bourgeois elements would seize power. During that phase Italy would become a capitalistic, industrial state, and conditions would mature for the revolution of the proletariat. Anna Kuliscioff and Filippo Turati believed that Italy had reached the stage for such a "democratic revolution."

In his reply, addressed to Turati, Engels endorsed the Turati-Kuliscioff thesis of a "democratic revolution" or a more radical government in Italy. Engels wrote that the Italian bourgeoisie "did not know how, nor did it want" to complete its victory after unification. As a result, the working classes were "crushed" by a combination of ancient, feudal, and capitalistic abuses. This situation led to revolts among the lower classes, but obviously conditions were not ready for a socialist revolution because of the lack of modern industry and of a well-developed proletarian class in Italy. If the revolts succeeded, they would lead either to a radical government, which would institute important reforms, or to a republic.

Engels emphasized that Marx, in the *Communist Manifesto*, had indicated the role of the Socialists in such cases. Socialists should help further the cause of all radical movements. Every advance for the progressive forces of the country was also a gain for the proletariat. But the primary role in any bourgeois revolution must belong to the Radical Democrats, not the Socialists. The Party could ally itself with the radicals and aid them, but it must take precautions to remain independent from them. Socialists must keep their own goals clear in their own minds and remember that even if the radical bourgeoisie achieved its aims, these would become means to further the march of socialism. Alliances must therefore be limited. Socialists could cooperate with bourgeois radicals today, as long as they remembered to oppose them tomorrow.[20]

Turati and Anna Kuliscioff interpreted this letter as a confirmation of their theories, but consulting Engels was only part of a cautious strategy to induce the Party to accept the principle of political alliances.[21] On 16 February 1894, two weeks after receiving Engels's letter, Turati wrote that he did not favor electoral alliances, given present conditions, but he left the door open for a change in tactics.[22]

In July 1894, Turati came out boldly in favor of alliances. On 22 October, Crispi dissolved the Socialist party and all its affiliated organizations. The government also prohibited the imminent Socialist congress scheduled for Imola. Under these hammer blows, Turati brought about the first practical changes in the Socialist policy of intransigence. The Milanese Socialists allied themselves with radicals in preparation for the local elections scheduled for February 1895.[23] More important, they also joined the Lega per la difesa della libertà, composed of Milanese radicals opposed to Crispi. The Party newspaper, which had escaped dissolution, argued that the league's goal was to restore the basic political liberties. The Milanese Socialists would henceforth form electoral alliances with any group fighting for the same cause. This was a reversal of the complete intransigence voted at Reggio Emilia in 1893 and still official policy. Indeed, the Party newspaper went so far as to state that if "moderates and clericals . . . also demanded this same liberty, we would join in a common front even with them."[24] *Lotta di classe* theorized that Crispi had welcomed the violence in Sicily and other parts of Italy in order to crush the Party while it was still relatively weak and that alliances were a justified response to the challenge.[25]

After much urging by the Socialists, Turati commented that true bourgeois liberals had finally awakened to the threat the government posed to Italian liberty. Radicals such as Cavallotti had emerged as Crispi's most bitter critics. A Socialist alliance with the rest of the Extreme Left remained the only means of struggling "for the conquest of liberty."[26] The Socialists could not react with violence, even in the face of force.[27] In Socialist theory, the task of defeating reaction devolved upon the democrats, but until the end of 1894 Turati had doubted whether Italian social conditions had produced a viable progressive bourgeoisie. The establishment of the Lega showed that it did exist, thus confirming that the conditions for alliances, spelled out in the *Communist Manifesto*, also existed.[28] The determination of bourgeois democrats to organize against Crispi removed Turati's last doubts about alliances.

The Milanese Socialists took concrete steps to implement their new alliance policy soon after they joined the Lega in November. On 12 December they decided to present only a restricted number of candidates in the local elections of February 1895 and to give no other Socialist candidate their endorsement. The goal was to elect as many democrats as possible while still affirming the Socialists as an independent party.[29] In November, a letter from Engels endorsed the Italian Socialists' struggle for political power,[30] and *Lotta di classe* initiated a campaign in favor of parliamentary institutions. According to the newspaper, the Socialists defended Parliament against Crispi because "the representative system is the only means by which the political power necessary to transform the economic structure and to construct the foundations of the Socialist society can be achieved."[31]

The Milanese decision on alliances caused growing discord in the Party, as Antonio Labriola reported to Engels.[32] The young Arturo Labriola complained because Turati was too accommodating.[33] Turati's closest friend, Leonida Bissolati, also objected to the new policy.[34] Costantino Lazzari, formerly a close ally of Turati, wrote an article against alliances for *Critica sociale*, which Turati refused; Lazzari went to see him and they "had a short, sharp dispute and, irritated, [Lazzari] left, violently slamming the door. From then on it was a continual polemic on the question of tactics."[35]

Turati maintained that Italian political and social conditions required the Party to be more flexible. With the Party on the defensive, complete intransigence was unjustified. Furthermore, he stated, it was untrue that all bourgeois parties belonged to a common anti-Socialist front, a view he had already argued against. The Socialist party could mitigate unfavorable political situations only if its tactics were skillful. The time had come for the Socialist party to abandon outmoded tactics and to become mature.[36]

Turati's position foreshadowed his later policies. His endorsement of political alliances in 1894 signified that he did not conceive of them as temporary expedients, although he could not say so. During the local elections of February 1895, *Lotta di classe* continually stressed the transient nature of the alliances, reiterating the antagonistic goals of democrats and Socialists.[37] Turati, however, made a special appeal to the lower middle classes to continue co-operating with the Socialists even after the elections. He emphasized their common objectives—universal suffrage, tax reform, tariff reductions, a decreased military budget.[38]

Turati also initiated a campaign to change the official Socialist policy of intransigence. He justified the abandonment of that policy by citing local issues, developments, and disparities that could force Socialists in a particular region to adopt attitudes unforeseen by general congresses.[39] Milan, for example, was economically and politically the most progressive city in Italy,[40] and Claudio Treves argued that local conditions had imposed the adoption of political alliances there. The Milanese proletariat, the most advanced in Italy because it was the product of modern industry, understood that in the elections it had an excellent opportunity to alter the city's political situation. He did not advocate a similar policy in backward parts of the country, Treves wrote, but it was unreasonable to expect the Milanese Socialists to follow tactics suited to rural towns completely dominated by reactionary interests.[41]

Thorough discussion of the issue took place at the next Party congress, held secretly in Parma on 13 January 1895. The Tuscan Party representatives charged that the Milanese had harmed the Socialist cause, while the Emilian Socialists, led by Prampolini, defended Turati. Turati insisted that a realistic political line had to be adopted to meet Crispi's challenge. Once again, he denied the accepted view of the bourgeoisie as a single reactionary mass. In Milan, cooperation with liberal bourgeois factions was not only useful but a political fact of life.

The debate ended in a modification of the Reggio Emilia policy. By a 34-to-20 vote, with two abstentions, the delegates allowed Party members to vote for democratic candidates on the second ballot, although they obliged the sections to present an independent list of candidates on the first ballot in both national and local elections. Although this motion failed to endorse Turati's principles, it did permit the Socialist party greater cooperation with the democrats. Furthermore, the assembly made an exception for Milan and agreed to allow the more advanced Milanese alliance policy to remain in effect. A limited success for Turati, it nonetheless "was destined to have an enduring effect on Italian history."[42]

The Parma congress also made a crucial structural change, instituting personal membership for all those who accepted the Party program. Government repression had clearly demonstrated associational membership to be a liability. It was imperative to separate the political and economic strands of the movement and to protect the labor organizations from any future political action against the

Party. The Socialists also hoped that personal membership would result in a more compact and dedicated organization, even if a smaller one.[43] There was general agreement on this point, although Turati feared the entrance of "dilettantes," who might join the Party for personal gain.[44]

Such a radical change necessitated a complete restructuring of the Party. Socialists in a specific area would form *gruppi* or *circoli* (clubs), the Party's basic units. The clubs in an electoral district were obliged to federate, thus constituting the "sections" of the Party. The sections federated on the provincial and regional levels. Regional federations held congresses, which established local regulations, discussed regional affairs, and nominated representatives to the National Council (Consiglio nazionale). The Parma congress also established a Central Executive Office (Ufficio esecutivo centrale, UEC), composed of five members elected by the national congress. Its duties were to register new sections, count their members, and receive dues. Each section nominated a secretary to correspond with the UEC. The Parma congress also issued rules for the payment of dues and for the convening of national congresses. In addition, a complex executive organ called the Party Directorate replaced the old Central Committee. The new body was composed of the National Council, the parliamentary deputies, and the members of the UEC.[45]

The Party Directorate had an extremely troubled existence. Despite numerous structural reforms, the Directorate had trouble enforcing its orders. If powerful enough, the sections could, and often did, defy the Directorate's rulings. Powerful labor organizations did the same. The unstable nature of the Directorate's composition, which was determined by the congresses, weakened the executive's authority and gave the edge in determining policy to the Socialist deputies, who had more prestige and constituted a practically irremovable group.

The Congress of Parma also acted to clarify the Party's immediate objectives by commissioning the Minimum Program, which listed the reforms the Socialists aimed to achieve within bourgeois society: universal suffrage, freedom of the press and association, regional and municipal autonomy, reform of agricultural contracts, tax reform, nationalization of railways. Some demands, such as abolition of the standing army and creation of the "armed nation," were more radical. Turati and his ally, the Genoese reformist Giuseppe Canepa, drew up the program, which provoked a split with the third member of the committee, Arturo Labriola. This dispute was a sign of things to come.[46]

The Congress of Parma succeeded in reorganizing and strengthening the Party. To an extent, also, the Socialists submerged their differences, as symbolized by their adoption of the name Partito socialista italiano.[47]

The Fall of Francesco Crispi

The new Socialist electoral tactics produced good results in the elections of 26 May and 2 June 1895. Despite Crispi's elimination of 700,000 voters from the electoral lists, the Socialist vote doubled, and Crispi failed to elect a more docile Chamber.[48]

At this point foreign affairs took on more importance, although Crispi's persecution of the Socialists continued. Perhaps in an attempt to divert the country's attention from its internal woes, Crispi pushed Italian expansion in East Africa.[49] Crispi had long been interested in the area and had sponsored the Treaty of Uccialli in 1889, which supposedly gave Italy a protectorate over Ethiopia.[50] In 1893 the Ethiopian King Menelik denounced the treaty, and sporadic hostilities broke out between the Ethiopians and Italians. In 1895 the Italian commander in Ethiopia asked for reinforcements, but Crispi refused because of the opposition of the northern bourgeoisie.[51] The industrial revolution had begun in the North, necessitating a period of peace and stability.[52] The emerging industrial bourgeoisie's opposition was so great that it allied itself with radicals and Socialists, thus thwarting Crispi's African ambitions and eventually bringing him down.[53]

The center of this opposition was Milan, whose evolving social, economic, and religious forces Crispi, a southerner, had never comprehended. Crispi considered the Milanese crass materialists, and they hated him for his anti-French policies and because he symbolized the despised South, which had "captured" political control of the country. This feeling persisted despite his tariff policies, which fostered Italian industrialization.[54] By the beginning of 1896, the Milanese industrialists were casting around for someone to replace Crispi as prime minister.[55]

Crispi's colonial policy was also a major issue for the Socialists, who objected to it on practical and moral grounds. Turati linked the war in Africa and repression in Italy. It followed that Italian arms had to be defeated in Africa if there was to be any further social progress in Italy. Dynastic and military ambitions spurred the government to press the conflict, while Socialists understood that Italy was too poor to make war and pay for reforms at the same time. A disastrous defeat in Ethiopia, therefore, was a prerequisite for the fall of Crispi and the initiation of reforms, Turati wrote:

Because of our concept of evolution, and because we do not
see any other way out, we frankly hope that our arms and our
flag . . . will be so solemnly defeated as to deny the thieves who
rule us the moral possibility of ever undertaking such a campaign again. . . . We hope for this . . . so that a fruitful policy of
work, which would otherwise continue to be a dream, can start
in Italy.[56]

The idea that war and military spending inhibited Italy's development became a constant theme in Turati's thinking.

Turati's vision of an Italian humiliation in Africa became an actu-
ality in March 1896. The failure of the government to send reinforcements and the blunders of the Italian commander combined
to produce the defeat at Adowa.[57] Riots and popular indignation
followed the battle.[58] The Milanese in the forefront of the demonstrations against Crispi poured into the streets and led the nationwide call for his resignation. Turati denounced him in fiery speeches.
Clamoring crowds induced the mayor of Milan to send a telegram
to Rome asking the government to resign, and the City Council
voted in favor of getting out of Africa. Disorders all over the country
and indignation in the Chamber forced Crispi to resign in disgrace.[59]

Antonio Starabba Di Rudinì, an old political enemy of Crispi's,
formed a new government. He was the leader of a liberal reform
faction and the candidate of the Milanese industrialists who had
opposed Crispi, although they were uneasy with Rudinì's projects
for social and administrative reforms and preferred a conservative
fiscal policy that would further the industrial activity then gaining
momentum in the North.[60] Rudinì seemed to have a mandate to
liquidate Crispi's heritage at home and abroad.[61] He retreated to the
borders of Eritrea and gave a partial amnesty to Crispi's victims.[62]
In the beginning the Rudinì cabinet had the support of a part of the
Extreme Left and survived only because of it.[63]

This development raised once more for the Socialists the issue of
whether or not a Socialist deputy could vote for a bourgeois government. The deputy Giuffrida De Felice voted for Rudinì, arguing that
Socialist support was necessary to prevent Crispi's return, considered a real possibility at the time.[64]

Turati defended De Felice's right to vote as he thought best. According to him, there were two fundamental points to consider:
First, did De Felice make a political mistake by voting for the government? Second, and more importantly, would any Socialist deputy who acted similarly be guilty of breaking discipline? Turati answered no to both questions.

Rudinì may have been a reactionary, Turati reasoned, but he was still an improvement over Crispi. Although it was true that the Reggio Emilia congress had prohibited Socialists from voting confidence in any government, Turati questioned the validity of this policy after all that had happened since 1893. The man who did the voting and his justification were more important than the vote itself. De Felice had voted for the lesser evil and was perfectly justified in doing so, as would any other Socialist deputy under similar circumstances.[65]

Although Turati's arguments are in line with his conception of the Party as a decentralized organization and foreshadow his role as future leader of the Socialist deputies in their defiance of Party control, they were also an extension of his policy of cooperation with the Radical Democrats. Before he issued his statement on De Felice, Turati asked the advice of Cavallotti, Rudinì's friend, and most certainly received it.[66]

The Party newspaper opposed Turati's views and criticized him for his stand in favor of De Felice,[67] and the Sicilian deputy eventually submitted to the Party's will under threat of expulsion.[68] Turati defended De Felice as part of his new drive to secure official status for the policy of alliances. The Turatians had raised the issue at the Lombard Regional Congress in Brescia in May 1896, in preparation for the national congress to be held in July. The salient feature of a long motion presented by Bissolati was to allow Socialists to support democratic candidates on the first ballot in localities where they determined that it would not be profitable to present their own candidates, provided they stressed their "fundamental opposition to all bourgeois parties." Although read by Bissolati, the motion was written by Turati.[69] When the delegates defeated the proposal by a 33-to-8 vote, an angry Turati complained that the Socialists continued to act as if time stood still.[70]

Illness prevented Turati from arguing his case at the Congress of Florence, held from 11 July to 13 July 1896. As a result, Anna Kuliscioff backed a compromise motion presented by Ivanoe Bonomi, a close friend of Turati and Kuliscioff and future exponent of theoretical revisionism in Italy.[71] Bonomi would have allowed Socialists to support candidates of the Extreme Left on the first ballot in local elections only. In her speech supporting the motion, Anna Kuliscioff said: "Personally, I would have accepted a motion that allowed for greater cooperation, which Turati would certainly have presented had he been here."[72] (Turati advocated voting for other parties on the first ballot in general elections.)

The delegates, however, rejected even Bonomi's more moderate proposal by a 147-to-71 vote. Indeed, they not only reaffirmed the Parma status quo but made alliances more difficult by requiring Socialists to support only those democratic candidates accepting the Minimum Program.[73]

In addition to the debate over electoral tactics, the old question of the relationship between Party and deputies came up again at the Congress of Florence. The intensity and the tone of the debate indicated a widening schism in the ranks of the Italian Socialist party on the issue. The De Felice case contributed to the heat of the discussion.[74]

The debate opened after a spokesman for the deputies presented a report listing the accomplishments of the Party representatives in Parliament. Several delegates angrily accused the Parliamentary Group of negligence because of their failure to appear at the scene of several important strikes and because of their insufficient zeal in the Chamber. The deputies replied that the Party made impossible demands upon them. The Party could not expect its elected officials to participate full time in parliamentary proceedings and actively take part in strikes while earning a living.

As a result of this debate, the Florence congress agreed that other Party workers should substitute for the deputies in activities outside of Parliament as often as possible. The congress also endorsed salaries for Italian deputies. As a gesture in this direction, the congress voted 350 lire per month for the Parliamentary Group, a sum the deputies were to divide among themselves.[75] These actions, however, did not heal the growing rift between deputies and Party.

The congress managed to avoid debate on another divisive issue when Anna Kuliscioff sidetracked Arturo Labriola's report on the Minimum Program. The Minimum Program embodied Turati's ideas, and Labriola intended to attack it as too moderate.[76]

In contrast to the disagreement over parliamentary tactics and the Minimum Program, the delegates quickly agreed to found an official Socialist daily newspaper.[77] Because the normal means of financing such a business enterprise were closed to the Socialists, they had to rely on individual contributions and Socialist organizations to fund the new periodical, which took the name *Avanti!* after the German *Vorwarts!*. Turati's friend Leonida Bissolati was named editor.[78]

The Socialists aimed for a newspaper that would be truly national and not Milanese, as *Lotta di classe* was, so they decided to publish *Avanti!* in Rome instead of Milan.[79] From Rome the newspaper could reach areas of the country where Socialist ideas and Party organization had not yet penetrated, especially the South. Indeed, the influence of southerners during *Avanti!*'s early years was much greater than Socialist strength in the region would indicate.[80]

Avanti! first appeared on Christmas Day 1896. Forty thousand copies were printed and sold out, and the paper eventually attained a daily circulation of 50,000. *Avanti!* was a professional newspaper. Bissolati aimed at a wide audience, including non-Socialists. He sent regular correspondents to foreign countries, published articles on the arts, sciences, literature, and sociology, and periodically asked foreign dignitaries to contribute articles.[81] *Avanti!* was a forum for the exchange of ideas and a vehicle of political and social criticism. The newspaper increased the influence of the Socialists in Italian political life and may be considered as the last act in the Party's foundation.[82]

Avanti! opened its career by denouncing Rudinì. The premier had dissolved a number of *camere del lavoro*, claiming that they instigated class hatred, and then repressed other Socialist organizations.[83] A qualitative change had indeed taken place in the Rudinì government by the beginning of 1897. Spurred by the growth of Socialist influence, including the election of Turati to the Chamber of Deputies, and the increasing power of intransigent Catholicism, the basis of a political agreement between Rudinì and Giuseppe Zanardelli, the most prominent leader of the Left, had been set. The anti-Socialist coalition was strengthened by the addition of Cavallotti and by pressure from the Right to take action against the unrest. Rudinì had to be cautious because Cavallotti was still persona non grata with the conservatives, and this collaboration in the end dashed his hopes of uniting them behind him. This anti-Socialist, anti-Catholic combination of Rudinì, Zanardelli, and Cavallotti provoked the elections of 1897 designed to stem the emerging influence of these two forces that threatened the existing order.[84]

The Socialists reacted vigorously to the attacks upon them, charging that the bourgeoisie was attempting to suppress constitutional liberties.[85] In August 1896 Turati concluded that Rudinì had become another Crispi and called upon the Socialists to unite against him.[86] Turati denounced government actions against the Socialist press and associations as being clearly unconstitutional.[87] He also joined with non-Socialist groups attacking the *domicilio coatto*, by which thousands of persons not guilty of any criminal offense were secretly condemned to forced "exile" by the police.[88]

This was the atmosphere in which new elections were held in March 1897. The Socialists campaigned on a platform of complete Italian withdrawal from Africa, reduction of military expenses, government observation of the basic constitutional freedoms, universal suffrage, tax reform, social legislation, and "popular sovereignty" over foreign affairs.[89] The elections were a qualified success for the Socialists. They increased their votes to 121,000 and sent fifteen deputies to the Chamber instead of the previous ten.[90] *Avanti!* was confident that now the Socialists could resist an expected new wave of reaction.[91] In fact, Rudinì's plan to curb their influence had failed.[92]

The electoral success of 1897 did not end the debate over electoral tactics. The debate intensified at the Fifth National Congress held in Bologna from 18 September to 20 September 1897. Indeed, the debaters struck a particularly bitter note, which foreshadowed the tone of later polemics between the left and right wings of the Party. Giacomo Ferri attacked the Socialists of Cremona because they had violated the precepts outlined at the previous congress by supporting the Radicals during the recent election. Ferri demanded the expulsion of the Cremonese. Turati defended them and presented a motion legitimating their action and allowing other Socialists to do the same. Turati's proposal allowed maximum liberty to the local Socialist organizations, freeing them to contract political alliances as the Milanese Socialists had already done. In fact, the Socialists of Cremona had merely followed the example of Turati and the Milanese.

The Cremonese dispute was finally settled in a manner that avoided the wider question. Enrico Ferri presented a compromise motion simply confirming the previous policy, and the congress adopted it over Turati's by a narrow vote of 97 to 90. Although Turati's attempt to change the Party's official policy had failed once again, the closeness of the vote implied much more sympathy for Turati's ideas than in previous years. The Party was heading toward cooperation with other political groups.[93]

The representatives at the Bologna congress also discussed a related issue, the Minimum Program. As has been mentioned, Turati and Arturo Labriola represented the opposing views. Labriola charged that the Minimum Program was not Socialist. According to Turati, the Minimum Program was a plan of action for the *attainment* of socialism, that is, for the proletariat to gain control of the fundamental institutions of political power. Turati argued that the Minimum Program is

a progressive guide, capable of continuous change, to those major reforms which, *while seemingly compatible with the fundamental economic order of a given moment*, will stimulate gradual evolution to higher forms by elevating the workers' standard of living, by allowing a more normal and conscious development of the class struggle, and by increasing the strength of the Socialist party.[94]

Turati's main concern, now as in later years, was to prevent reaction. "The real Minimum Program," Turati told the congress, "is the reconquest of the elementary liberties, without which everything else is vain."[95]

There were irreconcilable differences between Labriola and Turati. Whereas Turati believed that socialism could be achieved only by a gradual, guided evolution, during which the Socialists would exploit conventional political methods, taking care to preserve freedom, Labriola looked for more rapid means to achieve socialism. Labriola was less cautious than Turati and was willing to use methods that might provoke official violence and repression. By the end of 1897, therefore, the serious divisions that would paralyze the Party after 1901 were already present.

CHAPTER IV

Political Crisis and Party Unity

The LAST TWO years of the nineteenth century in Italy brought not only disorder, violence, and political crisis but also rapidly increasing economic wealth and growing political maturity. In 1898 the country's rulers saw themselves threatened by the rise of mass political parties, the Socialist and the Catholic. In order to hold onto their power, they resorted to violence and repressive legislation. The government repeated the tactics Crispi had used in 1894 and again failed to crush the Socialists, who fought back with great effectiveness, not in the streets but in Parliament. During the grave political crisis of 1898–1900, the Socialist party formed an alliance with the Extreme Left, the policy Turati had advocated, and eventually with the Constitutional Left. This alliance defeated the reactionary movement that began with the violent disorders of 1898.

"For eight hours the cannon has been thundering in Milan"

The reasons for the violence varied by region. Sporadic disorders had continued since the Sicilian uprising of 1893, but in the fall of 1897 more serious disturbances occurred in the Marche, the Romagna, and other regions.[1] The disorders in the South have been attributed to a rise in the price of bread, because of bad harvests and the outbreak of the Spanish-American War, which raised transportation costs for American grain.[2] Even without these exceptional circumstances, the protective duty and other taxes were enough to depress the consumption of this basic commodity.[3] The average Italian consumed 330 grams of grain compared to 533 for a Frenchman, and the price increases of 1897–98 raised the specter of famine for the poorer classes.[4] Before 1898 Rudinì did little to lower the protective tariff, despite repeated Socialist warnings that a revolt was inevitable if the government did not immediately lower drastically or eliminate the tax.[5]

Conditions within the Rudinì government, however, made tax relief politically difficult.[6] The state received most of its revenues from such indirect taxes as those on grain. One writer estimated that the total taxes represented a staggering 75 percent of the real cost of bread.[7] The Socialists' warnings implicitly called the whole tax system into question.

Other political factors contributed to the tense atmosphere. On 22 April 1897 there was an unsuccessful attempt on the life of the king.[8] The police questioned an anarchist, who later was found beaten to death in his cell, whereupon the Socialists accused the police of murdering him.[9] A great crowd attended his funeral in Rome, and the Rudinì government, fearful of alienating Cavallotti, kept the police away from the demonstration.[10] This alarmed conservatives, who considered Rudinì weak and overly influenced by Cavallotti.

Similarly, the whole nation demonstrated its grief in March of 1898 when Cavallotti himself was killed in a duel. The Chamber of Deputies suspended its business and draped itself in black in sign of mourning. Turati delivered an emotional funeral oration. "It seemed as if it was not the death of a man that was being mourned," writes a historian, "but an irreparable disaster for the Fatherland."[11] Again, Rudinì took no steps to halt the demonstrations or to prevent the transportation of Cavallotti's body to Milan from turning into a triumphal procession. These events further alarmed the conservatives.[12]

Rudinì's regime had been shaky for a while. In 1897 the increasing influence of both Socialists and Catholics provided a basis for a political agreement between Rudinì and Giuseppe Zanardelli, who found the Catholics particularly threatening. In December 1897, Zanardelli entered the cabinet, which, however, failed to win support either on the Right or among the Socialists.[13] Turati himself denounced it for its artificiality, and Rudinì received only a slight majority.[14] With the death of Cavallotti, who supported the Rudinì-Zanardelli entente, the government became more anxious to placate the Right. This meant taking energetic action against disorder.

In February 1898, when riots broke out in Sicily, the police killed at least ten people and wounded over a hundred.[15] After a calm of about two months, the disorders spread with amazing rapidity throughout the South, and then to the North. Demonstrators and police clashed in Palermo, Foggia, Aversa, Minervino Murge, Bari,

Ravenna, Pavia, Florence, and other cities. In Naples the army placed cannons at strategic points.[16]

The unrest climaxed in Milan. On 6 May workers for the Pirelli rubber company staged a demonstration protesting the arrest of several persons for distributing Socialist leaflets denouncing the government for its failure to reduce significantly the price of bread and for its refusal to cut military expenses but appealing to the people to remain calm.[17] In making the arrests the police probably acted illegally and certainly inopportunely and inflamed the passions of a crowd already incensed by the killing in Pavia of Muzio Mussi, the son of a popular Milanese deputy.[18]

At the height of the demonstration, Filippo Turati and Dino Rondani, another Socialist deputy, tried to calm the people. Turati announced a number of conciliatory measures taken by the local authorities. When this announcement failed to defuse the situation, Turati warned the demonstrators that the time for the revolution had not yet come, that the government was prepared to suppress them, and that when the day came for action he would be with them. This strong language quieted the crowd. As the crowd broke up, two or three hundred demonstrators singing the "Inno dei lavoratori" ran into some soldiers, who fired on them, killing two people. Toward evening knots of people began to gather, but a heavy rain dispersed them.

The next day, surprisingly enough, started normally, but then business establishments suddenly closed. Workers poured out of the factories and gathered in groups. As their numbers swelled, troops attacked them. Barricades appeared in the principal streets of the city but were mostly symbolic and undefended. Troops fired wildly into the windows of homes, and the military commander, Fiorenzo Bava-Beccaris, called his cannon into action against the crowds. The Republican deputy Luigi de Andreis was almost executed on the spot when he was discovered carrying a map on which *f* and *b* were marked in red: the soldiers interpreted the letters to mean "fire" and "bombs."[19] Officially, 80 civilians died and 500 were wounded, but estimates have gone as high as 400 dead and 1,000 wounded.

After the firing stopped, the arrests began. Anyone who had opposed the government was suspect—Socialists, Republicans, Radicals, Catholics. Turati, Kuliscioff, Oddino Morgari, and de Andreis were arrested. Bissolati and Costa, who had rushed to Milan in response to a rumor that Turati had been killed, found themselves in jail immediately after their train pulled into the station.[20] Don Davide Albertario, editor of the *Osservatore cattolico*, was also arrested. Numerous opposition newspapers had to suspend publication, among them Turati's *Critica sociale*, the Republican *L'Italia del popolo*, the Radical *Secolo*, the Socialist *Lotta di classe*, the Catholic *Osservatore cattolico*, even the monarchist *Il mattino*. An important exception was *Avanti!*, which continued publication despite continued harassment by government officials.[21]

Rudinì had panicked.[22] He feared that Italy might fall apart as the result of domestic violence and external attacks. There were reports that "Swiss bands" were marching toward the Italian border, groups of anarchists who aimed to seize power.[23]

Political factors, however, were more important. Eugenio Torelli Violier, the founder of the *Corriere della sera*, described the government's actions as a "coup d'état in favor of the bourgeoisie and against the people."[24] This view, which is the main theme of a recent work on the subject, substantially coincided with that of the Socialists.[25] Turati, for example, believed that there had been a conspiracy against the workers by the bourgeoisie, especially its most "advanced" industrial elements in Milan. It was not necessary that every detail be planned. "In the conduct of governments and parties," he wrote, "deeds are the results of complex motives and are to a great degree the product of tradition, instinct, and unconscious tendencies." Thus, disturbances that would have been easily controlled by the police in any other country were brutally suppressed by the army in Italy. Although Turati refused to attribute murderous motives to Rudinì, the premier's calls for severe repression were so interpreted in Milan. In Turati's talks with government authorities, he "got the impression that the idea of a massacre did not at all trouble them." Finally, the sudden closing of the factories incontrovertibly proved "the precise and explicit intention to provoke a massacre." Turati believed that the conservatives had long been looking for an excuse to crush the Socialists but failed because of the Party's peaceful methods. When violence broke out, they welcomed the opportunity to destroy the opposition.[26]

There seems, indeed, to be little doubt of the reactionary nature of the Milanese bourgeoisie and about the ill treatment of the workers.[27] Poor conditions helped Socialist labor organizers, and the Party threatened to take control of the city government in the local elections scheduled for June 1898. As a result, conservative groups in Milan and elsewhere pressured Rudinì to do something about the Socialists.[28]

This helps to explain why the government took drastic measures as soon as the tumults spread to the North. Violence in the South was explained in terms of the poor conditions there, but no one was willing to grant this for the North. When disorders broke out in the "rich" North, conservatives believed that they resulted not from poor economic conditions but from a conspiracy to destroy the state. Rudinì, whose "soft" policies the conservatives blamed for the outbreaks, came under great pressure to crack down hard.[29] He threatened to punish the prefects should they fail to keep the peace and called out the army to recoup his support on the right, to halt what he believed was a general revolution, and to block Zanardelli, whose advisors had been urging him to leave the cabinet so that he would be in a position to put together a cabinet of "national reconciliation" at a later date.[30] But the contrasting elements in Rudinì's cabinet came to the fore, and his conservative foreign minister, Emilio Visconti-Venosta, resigned. The Milanese industrialists refused to forgive Rudinì for his moderate policies, which they considered responsible for the revolts. Sidney Sonnino first asked Rudinì to resign in order to make way for a "strong government" and then unleashed a furious attack on him in the Chamber of Deputies.[31] Rudinì resigned on 18 June 1898 without waiting for a vote.[32]

The Failure of Reaction

The immediate result of the disorders was the trial of opposition leaders and demonstrators by special military courts.[33] The tribunals made no secret of their political bias, especially against Socialists.[34] Although she had done nothing, Anna Kuliscioff received a two-year sentence.[35]

The Chamber of Deputies sanctioned the trial of Turati, his fellow Socialist Oddino Morgari, and de Andreis.[36] Turati was charged with being "the soul and the mind of the Socialist party in Milan, of which he was the recognized chief and official representative during the most solemn occasions." Army lawyers tried to prove that Turati was the center of a conspiracy among all the "subversive" parties and that he had plotted to overthrow the government at least since 1896. They alleged that the plot had been conducted by means of propaganda, party organization, pamphlets, and lectures; they insisted that the Socialists had organized 4,000 exiles in Switzerland and had moved them to the Italian border despite the testimony of Swiss authorities that no such event had occurred. They tried to prove that Turati had incited the workers to revolt, despite Pirelli's testimony to the contrary. The evidence of a plot was so circumstantial and the case so ridiculous that the military court itself had to dismiss the allegations. What remained, the tribunal decided, was the "individual" guilt of the defendants. It found Turati guilty of belonging to the Socialist party, editing the *Critica sociale,* inspiring "class hatred," advocating a railway strike, and making an inflammatory remark. The court condemned him to twelve years in prison and interdiction from holding public office, and it ordered him to pay the court costs. De Andreis received the same sentence, and Morgari was acquitted.[37]

At first, events at the highest level of government appeared to contradict these developments. A liberal general, Luigi Pelloux, replaced Rudinì and immediately withdrew proposals for restrictive legislation presented by his predecessor.[38] Pelloux, however, received emergency powers on a temporary basis and then asked for permanent legislation that would have severely restricted freedom of the press, association, and assembly.[39] These bills alarmed the Constitutional Left as well as the Socialists.[40]

Having previously denounced the grant of emergency powers, and seeing themselves as the principal targets of reactionary legislation, the Socialists fought the bills in earnest on the grounds that if the bills became law they would "permit the government to rebut the 'subversive' deputies by maintaining that they are not protesting against caprice but against the application of the law."[41] *Avanti!* called upon the Socialists to defend the Constitution "repudiated by the bourgeoisie."[42]

Pelloux's unwillingness to amend the bills alienated not only the Socialists and other parties on the extreme left but also the Constitutional Left.[43] As a result, Pelloux turned to Sonnino and the Right for support.[44] Sonnino now seemed to be in a position to put into effect the conservative revisions of the Italian Constitution he had been advocating for years.[45]

These developments led to the formation of a cohesive new bloc, the Estrema sinistra. Pelloux's proposals and fear of Sonnino had convinced thĕ Socialists to coordinate their efforts with the "bourgeois" Radicals and Republicans.[46] Not endorsed by any Socialist congress, the new policy was the same one Turati had been advocating for years and which Kuliscioff was still working hard to get adopted in February 1899.[47] The previous efforts of Turati and Kuliscioff had cleared the ground for the rapid acceptance of a policy of alliances in this emergency.

In the Chamber, the Estrema could count on only about 67 deputies out of 508, but the rules and regulations of that body allowed a determined group of deputies to delay business indefinitely.[48] As a result, the government's supporters began to tire, and Sonnino moved to change the rules in order to limit debate.[49] The Estrema saw the changes as an attempt to crush the opposition and to alter the Constitution,[50] and so it continued to obstruct proceedings.[51]

The government then tried to circumvent the Chamber by embodying its bills in a royal decree issued by the king.[52] Clearly unconstitutional, this procedure contributed to the later political understanding between the constitutional and Extreme Left.[53] On the Chamber floor, fistfights broke out, and the king ended the session.[54]

The government had played its cards badly. Under ordinary circumstances the methods of the Extreme Left might have resulted in their condemnation by the Chamber and the nation. But by July 1899 almost half the deputies opposed Pelloux, and outside the Chamber Pelloux's lack of support became patent.[55] Widespread agitation for an amnesty forced the government to grant several pardons.[56] Turati was reelected to his seat while still in jail, declared ineligible, and reelected again.[57] De Andreis also won reelection twice while in jail. In 1898 and 1899, a Socialist-Radical bloc led by the reformist Luigi Majno defeated the conservatives in local elections in Milan. In 1899, 463 Socialists won election in 156 municipalities, a great increase over previous years.[58] Popular feeling against the government remained just below the boiling point during this period.[59]

All these activities testified to the renewed energy of the Socialist party.[60] In June 1899, Turati was released from prison, and Critica sociale reappeared. The review pledged continuing resistance to the government's policies.[61]

Turati outlined the future strategy of the party in an interview with Walter Mocchi, a correspondent for Avanti!. In response to a question about the new tactics, Turati pointed out that he had been a long-time advocate of cooperation. He regretted that his ideas had been adopted by the Socialists only under pressure of reaction, thus making it seem as if fear had forced them to do so. He emphasized that alliances with the other parties of the Extreme Left would be necessary for a long time. Turati believed that cooperation with the Radicals and Republicans was not a temporary expedient, destined to end once Pelloux had been defeated, but a permanent feature of Socialist party policy. It was the beginning of a new era, he said. Because the Italian ruling classes inherently inclined to reaction, the Socialists must work with the Italian democrats as well as the Extreme Left in order to protect liberty and modernize Italy. The policy of alliances, therefore, "is not transitory, it is the beginning of a new phase of the Socialist party's existence. For the policy of absolute intransigence, the Party now substitutes regulating relations with the "cognate" (affini) parties according to the varying necessities of time and place."[62] At the end of 1899 the Regional Congress of Lombard Socialists solemnly sanctioned Turati's ideas.

Now, however, Turati and Anna Kuliscioff went beyond the opinions expressed in Turati's June interview. Alliances served not only to ward off reaction, they wrote, but to attain reforms that led to socialism. They argued that collaboration with "bourgeois" parties was fully justified by Marxist thought because history was not a simplistic struggle between two classes; "these classes are numerous and most diverse, intertwine in the most complicated patterns, and conflict with and influence each other reciprocally." According to the reformist leaders, Italy was a special case in Marxist terms. The classic struggle between great landowners and industrial bourgeoisie had yet to emerge, and these classes *together* formed the real exploiting class. The opposition included not only the industrial and agricultural proletariat but also small property holders, white-collar workers, and small shopkeepers. These representatives of the lower middle class also suffered greatly from exploitation by industrialists and landowners and would support reforms along with the Socialists.[63]

As we have seen, these ideas were not new, but in 1899 the political crisis made them more palatable to the Socialists. Turati was thus free to develop all the implications of his earlier thinking, in the hope that the Party would be receptive.

There was one corollary to Turati's reasoning that many Socialists would later consider an abomination. According to Turati, the democratic bourgeoisie had to make Italy into a modern industrial state with an advanced political and social structure to prepare the country for the coming of socialism. If the democratic parties were weak, the Socialists should help them, but if it proved impossible to invigorate them, Turati was convinced that the Socialist party would have to take over the role of the democratic Left. As time went on, reformist leaders tended more and more to view the Party as a surrogate Radical-Republican organization preparing the way for the coming of socialism. Left-wing Socialists considered this view an abdication of the Socialist mission, whereas right-wing Socialists believed that it was the only realistic way for the Party to operate within the Italian context.

Although he believed it necessary, Turati did not relish this corollary, and this explains his eagerness to effect a reform of the "decrepit Constitutional Left,"[64] especially through Giolitti, whom he believed most likely to attain power and restore Italy's political liberty. Turati thus initiated a campaign to increase the prestige of the democratic leaders. The bourgeois Left had finally awakened to the threat from the Right, Turati wrote in November 1899, and he praised Giolitti and Ettore Sacchi, the Radical leader, for acting like statesmen. He hoped that the Constitutional Left would become strong enough to form a government and liberalize Italian politics, and he urged the Radicals to join it. In the Chamber, Turati said of Giolitti that "someone on the other side has understood us."[65] A broad coalition stretching from the Turatians to the Giolittians was taking shape.

The country's legal institutions now gave greater impetus to these developments. Pelloux had ended the legislative session on 30 June 1899 without having secured approval of the royal decrees, but, as he had announced, his government began enforcing them as law after 20 July. In February 1900, however, the Court of Cassation dismissed charges against an anarchist based upon the decrees. Because Parliament had not approved them, the court ruled, the decrees remained simple legislative proposals and could not be enforced as law. Because the president of the court was friendly with Giolitti, its decisions have been interpreted as reflecting the desire of a large part of the ruling classes for a liberal solution to the political crisis.[66]

After the court's rebuff, the government attempted once more to force the decrees through the Chamber, but the Constitutional Left was hostile and the Extreme Left obstructed parliamentary business.[67] Conservative deputies such as Rudinì and Luigi Luzzatti also objected.[68]

Pelloux and Sonnino, faced with the prospect of losing their majority, resorted to highly unorthodox measures in order to limit debate. The government proposed authorizing a committee to make rules changes, which would go into effect automatically, without discussion or a vote. The Extreme Left filibustered, but Pelloux announced that the proposals would be voted upon on 3 April.[69] An uproar broke out, with the government supporters shouting for an immediate vote on the motion. Suddenly, the president of the Chamber requested a stand-up vote, declared the motion passed, and quickly adjourned the meeting over the howls of the Extreme Left. The next day the opposition deputies chased the president out of the hall.[70]

The victory turned out to be a Pyrrhic one, however, because the government's actions definitively alienated the Constitutional Left.[71] After a declaration by Zanardelli, the Constitutional Left joined the Extreme Left in walking out of the Chamber, thus leaving the majority alone "to commit this crime" of changing the rules. The new rules were to apply at the 15 May sitting of the Chamber, but the Extreme Left considered them null and void and demonstrated every time the president made a decision according to the revised regulations.[72] The Extreme Left created so many distur-

48 CHAPTER IV

bances that it was impossible to carry on business, and the next
day the king ended the session. New elections were scheduled for
3 June and 10 June 1900.[73]

This strategy turned out to be a mistake because feelings were
running high against the government. Pelloux himself did not wish
new elections but agreed when he saw the impossibility of operating
the Chamber as it was then constituted.[74] The government hoped
to make a good showing by throwing all its resources into the campaign; by using the electoral lists of 1898, which had been purged
of the subversives arrested in that year; and by using to maximum
advantage the short notice on which the elections were called.[75]

Turati's strategy of cooperation reached its apogee during these
elections. There was no significant dissent to Socialist collaboration
with the Radicals and Republicans or with moderately liberal "bourgeois" political factions in order to defeat Pelloux. Avanti! claimed
that the Socialists were fighting for the survival of parliamentary
institutions in Italy. The ultimate goals of socialism were deemphasized by the Socialists and their new allies, because "they wanted
liberty, without which no party could survive."[76]

The election spelled the end of Pelloux's cabinet. Although the
government emerged with a majority of about eighty-five votes in
the Chamber, it had lost the popular vote. The Socialist delegation
doubled, claiming 32 seats instead of 16. The representation of the
Extreme Left went from 67 to 95.[77] Moreover, Pelloux recognized
that his majority was no longer solid and announced his intention
to resign.[78]

Pelloux's resignation essentially ended the political crisis of 1898–
1900 but did not end the controversy over his role among contemporary observers and later historians. Arturo Labriola argued that Pelloux was the front man in a widespread plot led by King Umberto I
to undermine Italian parliamentary institutions.[79] A recent work
takes its point of departure from Labriola and other contemporary
sources and argues that the crisis was a coup d'état of the bourgeoisie
against the proletariat.[80] This view sees as the main result of the crisis
the triumph of Turati's ideas within the Socialist party, a development that deprived that organization of its revolutionary impetus.[81]
It is true that this was an immediate result, although Turati's leadership was seriously challenged within a couple of years.

His feelings about Turati's victory also led Labriola to make the
opposite argument to the one previously cited, that is, that there
was no reactionary party in Italy and that, therefore, Turati was unjustified in emphasizing the perils of reaction.[82] This raises the question of why Pelloux failed to use force against the opposition. Clearly,
there was little support for such a course of action in the country,

even among conservatives who tended to support Pelloux in the Chamber.[83] The Socialists hinted that they would meet violence with violence, and no responsible person would willingly provoke such a conflict. Most important, however, was Pelloux's desire to achieve his aims by means of laws regularly voted by the Chamber. Pelloux took liberties with procedures, but he did have strong constitutional scruples.[84]

The Socialists, of course, saw themselves as defending Italian liberty and the Constitution against Pelloux's and Sonnino's proposals.[85] It was a dangerous precedent, they felt, to allow any group, even a parliamentary majority, to limit freedom of speech, press, and association because certain ideas seemed dangerous.[86] The Socialists were preserving these freedoms, Turati argued, for themselves and for all groups against all arbitrary governments, present and future.[87]

Perhaps this was the most important result of the political crisis of 1898–1900. Under Turati's tutelage, many Socialists became convinced of the Statuto's viability and learned that "liberty is not a bourgeois or class concept."[88] In practice, however, this meant that the reformists wished to continue using the tactics of 1898–1900 in more normal times and to extend them to other issues besides the defense of civil liberties. Future attempts to do so set off a dispute within the Party that was never resolved.

THE SOCIALISTS believed that the twentieth century would see the working classes take power everywhere. The proletariat was becoming more highly organized and had resisted all attempts to break its political power. This seemed especially true in Italy where Socialist policies during the crisis of 1898–1900 had made the Party very popular. Socialists and their sympathizers were sure that the fight against Pelloux would be a prelude to other great victories, but now the struggle against the "bourgeoisie" changed character. Turati was more than ever convinced that liberty was essential if the Socialist party was to succeed in its goals and that socialism could only be achieved gradually through reforms. Both of these objectives, given the present political situation, required greater cooperation with the liberal groups that had helped the Party during the late crisis. Systematic opposition to governments was obsolete from all points of view.

The revolutionary left wing of the Party denounced Turati's methods as dangerous and ineffective. In its view, the bourgeoisie had abandoned the use of systematic, overt violence against the workers and had substituted the more subtle method of seducing their leaders and dampening their revolutionary élan. The conflicting views of Turati and the left wing greatly weakened the Socialist party's political effectiveness.

"It is the greatest crime of the century"

After Pelloux's resignation the king asked the eighty-one-year-old president of the Senate, Giuseppe Saracco, to form a government.[1] A journalist opined that just "when Italy most desperately feels the need for a lusty male to impregnate her, she consummates a union with an old man already betrothed to Death."[2] Saracco, Umberto's intimate adviser, had known Cavour and had participated in the cabinets of several Risorgimento figures. Given the king's influence over Saracco, the new government has generally been viewed as a stopgap designed to restore the normal functioning of the Chamber.[3] The Socialists were unhappy with the solution, *Avanti!* announcing its opposition and Turati accusing the king of having ignored the significance of the recent elections.[4]

The government lost its main prop at the end of July 1900, when Umberto was assassinated in Monza. The murderer was Gaetano Bresci, an anarchist incensed by Umberto's nomination of Bava-Beccaris to the Senate.[5] Demonstrations against the Socialists took place, and the conservative press exhorted the new sovereign to crack down on the Socialists, whose propaganda it held responsible for the assassination.[6] The Socialists, however, denounced the assassination, and Turati expressed the sympathy of the Parliamentary Group in the Chamber.[7] When Bresci asked Turati to handle his defense, he refused and wrote privately, "After having fired three shots at the monarchy, he wants to fire a fourth at socialism."[8] The danger of reaction passed when Vittorio Emanuele promised to uphold Italian liberal institutions.[9]

Vittorio seemed to favor more tolerance for political opponents of the regime. In September 1900 the Socialists held their first congress in three years. They had for some time been debating the most important issues to be decided at the congress, and in January 1900 Turati and Anna Kuliscioff gave a polemical edge to the ideas they had previously expressed. They openly stated the need to revise Socialist assumptions in the face of reality. Only a democratic government could ensure the freedom necessary to allow the Party to work for socialism, and such a government could come to power in Italy only through Socialist cooperation with the Extreme and Constitutional Left. Socialists should deemphasize revolutionary rhetoric and concentrate on more concrete goals, such as improving the mental and physical environment of the proletariat. Real revolutions were not only political but social and economic as well.[10]

Despite criticism that he was being overly optimistic about the reforming zeal of the Constitutional Left,[11] Turati now tried to ensure his freedom to implement his policies in the future. He proposed that the congress leave local party organs free to determine their own tactics.[12] This policy, labeled "autonomy," had deep roots in Turati's fear of Socialist "Jacobinism," as we have seen, which was so strong as to spur him to undertake a campaign at a later congress to eliminate the Party Directorate.

Turati had little trouble in achieving his aims when the Socialists gathered in Rome, for his opponents lacked unity and coherence. The main proponent of intransigence, Enrico Ferri, was ineffective. He agreed that alliances suited Socialist needs in the most developed centers but not in the more backward sections of the country. Because there were more underdeveloped centers than modern ones in Italy, the Party should impose intransigence; and since autonomy was a smoke screen for legalizing alliances, he opposed it.[13]

Turati's friend Giuseppe Emanuele Modigliani, the main orator for autonomy, contended that autonomy encouraged debate, close investigation of problems, and decisions made by the people most directly involved. Autonomy encouraged full participation in the intimate life of the Party, whereas intransigence ultimately resolved itself into a few clichés. Ferri's fear that autonomy might cause the Party to deviate from its principles was legitimate, but the autonomist motion included a provision charging the Directorate to review the policies of individual Party sections. Marxist doctrine was the basis of Party unity, not force. Finally, Modigliani concluded, local organizations would be perfectly free to institute a policy of intransigence, if they so desired.[14] Claudio Treves reinforced Modigliani's arguments, stressing that the Party had to adapt to changing conditions.[15]

The autonomists defeated the intransigents by a vote of 106 to 69, with two abstentions,[16] in a motion proclaiming the full freedom of the local organizations to contract alliances with the Extreme Left, "except for the Directorate's obligation to oppose methods which are obviously incongruous with the aims of the Party."[17]

The congress went beyond this general approbation of Turati's methods. It encouraged Socialist infiltration of local administrative organs, sanctioned political alliances for this purpose, and suggested model reforms.[18]

Turati's viewpoint failed to win on another important issue, however, that of freedom of action for the Socialist deputies. The prestige of the deputies was at its height, and the congress voted its appreciation.[19] But when it was asked to relinquish its supremacy over the deputies, the congress refused.[20] In fact, the deputies had grown used to acting independently, and their unwillingness to change would cause major rifts within the Party.

There was also a dispute over the role of the Party newspaper. Several delegates complained that *Avanti!* had become too parliamentarian. This elicited the significant comment from Modigliani that the Socialist movement in Italy *was* parliamentarian. In the future Bissolati's removal as editor had high priority among the objectives of the left wing.[21]

Another important development at the Rome congress was the adoption of the Minimum Program embodying Turati's ideas. The program listed important reforms that could be achieved in a capitalist society, that would help prepare the way for socialism, and that included universal suffrage, tax reform, and local autonomy.[22]

This time the Minimum Program encountered criticism among recalcitrant reformists as well as revolutionaries. Gaetano Salvemini criticized it as being too long and general and suggested stressing a few crucial reforms, on which the Party would concentrate all its energies. He advocated lowering the interest on the public debt, abolition of the standing army, and a drastic reduction of taxes, all of which were prerequisites to other reforms.[23] Salvemini's proposals failed, but he continued his campaign to get them adopted.[24]

If the Minimum Program failed to become a symbol, the Rome congress did, however, adopt measures of practical importance. The deputy Angiolo Cabrini suggested the establishment of a secretariat, which would specialize in economic questions. Ettore Reina, a labor leader, asked the Party to help organize workers on the land and to take measures to foster the founding of agricultural leagues. Another reformist, Quirino Nofri, proposed that the Party pay special attention to the founding of cooperatives and mutual help societies on the land. Other delegates asked the Party to support the demands of small proprietors, also considered exploited. The congress voted all of these proposals.[25]

The measures were particularly significant because Italy would soon be enveloped in a vast strike movement, which had its epicenter on the land and which was spearheaded by agricultural leagues under the influence of reformist Socialists.

In addition to cementing the Party's ties with the labor movement on the land, the Rome congress tightened the Party's organization by strengthening the Directorate, despite Turati's attempt to deemphasize it.[26] A weak executive was a corollary of the "autonomy" voted at the same congress, but Enrico Ferri managed to secure adoption of a motion that streamlined the Directorate and made it more efficient. Henceforth, the Directorate would consist of five members elected at the national congress, five chosen by the deputies, and the editor of *Avanti!*.[27]

Despite minor disappointments, Turati and Anna Kuliscioff were happy with the results of the congress. The delegates had focused on practical issues and had avoided a doctrinal fight, which would have paralyzed the Party. There were many roads to socialism, they wrote.[28] This analysis was only partially correct. Unity was the main theme, but ideological disputes were surfacing. Hostilities between the Right and the Left would recur, and the Socialists would be obliged to make a practical decision as to exactly how far they should go in giving the country a government that would guarantee civil rights.

The decision was not far off. Giuseppe Saracco had survived the shock of Umberto's assassination, but his cabinet fell in February 1901. Saracco had given his permission to the prefect of Genoa to dissolve the local *camera del lavoro*, which had been causing trouble for the commercial interests in the city. The militant dock workers immediately struck, and the movement spread. Soon Italy's largest port city was completely paralyzed, and sympathy strikes took place in other parts of the country. Saracco gave in to the pressure and allowed reconstitution of the *camera*, but it was too late.[29] The Socialists denounced him for attacking the right of association,[30] and the conservatives turned against him for yielding to pressures from below and consenting to the reconstitution of the labor organization. In the Chamber the government fell under the combined votes of Left and Right.[31]

The "Liberal Springtide" and the Great Schism

Finding a replacement for Saracco presented unusual difficulties. Government crises in the Italian system were usually "extraparliamentary"; that is, a prime minister headed toward defeat resigned before a vote could be taken. In this way the Chamber could not indicate its choice of a successor. This gave the Italian monarch a much larger role in selecting the person who would form a government than was the case in the most advanced parliamentary systems. Because Saracco was defeated in the Chamber, that body had the opportunity to express its opinion as to a successor. Probably the Chamber would have preferred Sonnino, but political maneuvering obscured this preference, so that it was unclear exactly who had a majority. The king then appointed Zanardelli to form a cabinet.[32]

The Left praised Vittorio Emanuele for this decision but failed to consider all its implications. Presented with the opportunity to designate the president of the Council of Ministers, the Chamber relied meekly on the king to name Saracco's successor.[33] The monarch had three alternatives. He could have asked Saracco to form another government, but Saracco offered no lasting solution to the crisis. He might have followed the inclinations of the Chamber and designated Sonnino. But while Sonnino was well liked in the Chamber, he was unpopular in the country. The third choice was Zanardelli, who would come to power with Giolitti, whose ideas were popular in the country. The problem was that Giolitti advocated tax reforms, and any significant tax reform meant less money for the army. The king, like all the Savoys, was opposed to cutting the army's budget. He opted for Zanardelli and Giolitti but made impossible any cuts in military expenses, leaving Giolitti the choice either of joining the government or of fighting for tax reforms outside of it. The king accomplished this by naming the ministers for war and the navy and heavily influencing the choice of the foreign minister. These measures wrecked the chances for meaningful fiscal reform.[34] Giolitti believed that the nation needed a liberal government that would end the reaction and begin a dialogue with the Socialists, and he joined Zanardelli in putting a cabinet together.[35] The Socialists were also aware that secret military commitments undertaken by the monarchy made impossible both a reduction in military expenses and tax reform, but they went along with Zanardelli and Giolitti out of fear of Sonnino.[36] When the Radicals requested, as the price for their participation in the cabinet, a pledge not to exceed "by even a penny" the sum of 239 million lire earmarked for the army, Zanardelli and Giolitti refused.[37] Ironically, the liberal solution to the crisis of 1901 confirmed the weakness of Italian parliamentary institutions, even if it had very positive results in other areas of Italian life.

The Zanardelli-Giolitti cabinet did not have a majority in the beginning, and only the votes of the Socialists and the Extreme Left could guarantee its survival. Indeed, the Socialists began receiving overtures from Giolitti even before Saracco fell.[38] On 4 February Turati's views favoring an alliance with Giolitti carried over the objections of Ferri and the Republicans at a joint meeting of Extreme Left representatives. Ferri remained adamant on the reduction of military expenses, but Turati did not believe that the question should prevent agreement between the Extreme Left and Giolitti.[39] Eventually, Radical representatives worked out a compromise that allowed the Extreme Left to support Zanardelli. Zanardelli promised to "consolidate" military expenses at the 239-million-lire mark and to withdraw all requests for supplementary funds then before Parliament.[40] On 7 March Turati wrote to Anna Kuliscioff that the Socialist and Extreme Left deputies had accepted "our point of view" and had agreed to cast their ballots for Zanardelli-Giolitti.[41]

This decision, however, concerned only the deputies, not the rest of the Party, where the situation was extremely delicate. Kuliscioff informed Turati that the imminent Socialist vote for the government would certainly aid the "semianarchist" (revolutionary) faction. She advised the Socialist deputies to refrain from defending every action of the government and to press their own demands.

They must oppose military expenses and grain duties and should intervene to rescue the cabinet only if it demonstrated a willingness to concede democratic reforms.[42]

On 29 May the Party Directorate mobilized to prevent the deputies from voting for the cabinet. Despite all of Turati's arguments, the Directorate reaffirmed existing Party policy and told the deputies not to vote for the government, leaving them free to approve only single legislative measures they might favor. This was the *caso per caso* formula endorsed by Enrico Ferri.[43]

Turati considered *caso per caso* a superficial and pernicious policy. It meant either denying a reforming cabinet the chance to come to power or overthrowing it, even if the Socialists approved its objectives. A cabinet with a liberal program could survive only if it had Socialist votes. The Socialists could well make compromises, especially when the alternative was a rightist and probably reactionary government. The best way to achieve reforms was to support a reforming government.[44]

In the end, Turati's point of view won out. A caucus of the Socialist deputies accepted a Turati motion to vote for the Zanardelli government, the Directorate's prohibition notwithstanding. Ferri and Angiolo Cabrini both resisted Turati but were overwhelmed by a 12-to-4 vote. Ferri first pushed *caso per caso* and then suggested a vote for the government in the secret ballot and against in an open ballot. Turati refused. Cabrini was unhappy with the appointment of Giulio Prinetti, a conservative Milanese industrialist, as foreign minister. Turati countered that the overwhelmingly liberal constitution of the cabinet as a whole made Prinetti acceptable.[45] This vote, which clearly violated Party discipline, led to a state of continuous warfare between the deputies and the Party.

As far as the Socialist deputies were concerned, the presence of Giolitti as minister of the interior compensated for any deficiencies in the cabinet. Giolitti had announced the bankruptcy of reaction in Italy in a well-publicized speech in October 1899 and outlined a program that included respect for civil rights and the Constitution, the overhaul of the judicial and administrative systems, and, above all, reform of the fiscal system. He vigorously condemned fixed and indirect taxes and protective tariffs and advocated proportional taxation. He argued that the government could no longer be at the service of "restricted cabals" but must provide justice for all groups. Specifically, it must consider the requests of the lower classes and grant their most reasonable demands.[46] During the Genoese general strike, Giolitti had defended the *camere del lavoro*, had set out to unseat Saracco, and had cooperated closely with the Extreme Left to achieve this end.[47] As soon as he became minister of the interior, he ceased making use of government resources on behalf of employers in labor disputes.[48]

The government's withdrawal from strikebreaking encouraged strikes, especially on the land, where they had been rare. Newly formed agricultural leagues in which Socialists were prominent took the lead in this movement. Whereas in 1900 there had been 27 agricultural strikes involving 12,517 participants, in 1901 there were 629 strikes and 222,985 participants.[49] The Italian Socialist movement was winning a large following on the land.

At this point a conservative counterattack forced the Socialist deputies to intervene in Parliament on behalf of the government. At the end of April 1901, the Senate attacked the cabinet's liberal policies, and criticism continued in the Chamber during discussion of the Interior Ministry's budget.[50] Sonnino alleged that the government was "enslaved" to the Socialists and called for a government of conciliation and "discipline" that would not rely for support on deputies who aimed to destroy the Constitution.[51] Giolitti answered that there was no way to stop the workers from organizing and striking, except to "return to the concept of restricting constitutional freedoms." The Chamber had to choose between liberty and repression.[52] The Socialist deputies had already selected relative freedom over probable reaction, even though Sonnino said that he had given up his earlier reactionary ideas.[53]

On 22 June 1901, the Socialist deputies announced that, for the first time, they would support a cabinet.[54] The question of confidence came up later on the same day, and the Extreme Left voted as a bloc for the government, keeping it in power by a 264-to-184 margin.[55] It was, *Avanti!* commented, "the victory of liberty."[56]

Then, suddenly, as if to mock the opening of a new era, soldiers fired into a crowd of striking agricultural workers in the town of Berra (Ferrara). Three people died, and thirty were wounded.[57] This incident threatened the cordial relations between the Socialists and the government by making the reformists vulnerable to attack within their Party. The revolutionaries now had an emotional issue that reinforced their opposition to all support for bourgeois governments: the Socialist-backed government had fired on the people.[58]

The Socialist delegation's response to the "massacre" fueled the polemics. When Bissolati questioned the minister of the interior, Giolitti denounced the employers for bringing in strikebreakers and said he wished that Socialist influence in the area had been stronger; but, he said, the soldiers had done their duty because they were protecting private property.[59] Bissolati contested Giolitti's version of the incident, strongly criticizing the government for failing to keep its functionaries in check, the army for violating regulations, and the landowners for trying to break the agricultural leagues. He concluded that the minister of the interior was indirectly responsible for the shootings but that the government could not have desired such an occurrence. The incident, Bissolati believed, resulted from an "incomplete application of liberal principles" and did not alter basic political realities. There was still no acceptable alternative to the Zanardelli-Giolitti government.[60] This response infuriated the revolutionaries, who now began a massive attack on reformist policies.

The principal defender of these policies, Turati, published his ideological justification on 16 July 1901, in a *Critica sociale* article concisely stating reformist political thought in this period.[61] He began his exposition by reiterating that the basic cause of socialism was the increasing industrialization of society, a gradual development about which individuals and parties could do very little. A corresponding moral growth accompanied the slow transformation of the basis of society, to which corresponded "a transformation and elevation . . . of the thinking, the habits, and the capacities of the proletarian masses." This transformation, however, would occur not automatically or mystically but by means of reforms and the constant use of existing rights. This fact provided a guide to everyday action, which the Party had spelled out in its Minimum Program. It was thus useless for the Socialists to attempt to seize power because they could do little or nothing to speed up the transformation of the industrial base of society or the elevation of the proletariat.[62]

The Party must train the workers for political power by moving toward the conquest of bourgeois institutions now, Turati wrote. To succeed, however, the Socialists had to resist all attempts by the reactionary elements of the bourgeoisie to curb freedom of association, speech, the vote, and the press. Given the Italian political situation, this resistance could be successful only through cooperation with the more liberal bourgeois elements concerned with protecting the same rights. The Socialists should feel free to cooperate without troubling themselves about the Marxist tenet that it was dangerous to collaborate with the bourgeoisie because it constituted a "single reactionary mass." This was not only illogical but had been disproved by experience.[63]

Indeed, the realization that the bourgeoisie had conflicting interests had opened a new phase in the history of Italian socialism, Turati said, because the proletariat would exploit the differences in order to win reforms. After the periods of "affirmation" and "defense" came that of "conquest." While the first phase had been marked by violence and simplistic doctrine, and the second by a fight to survive, the third—"the present political moment"—required more subtle action. Until February 1901, the Party had adapted itself to fighting for civil rights and to deemphasizing policies exclusively Socialist. Now it could initiate action for reforms because the Zanardelli-Giolitti government had instituted a policy of respect for liberty and the law. In effect, this was a parliamentary revolution because it had ushered in a *"period of conquest* for the proletariat." The cabinet represented a modern and enlightened bourgeoisie, which had already proved its commitment to liberty and reform. Because the cabinet depended on Socialist votes in the Chamber, it was receptive to Socialist suggestions and looked with favor upon some of the workers' demands. This process would lead to an accelerating rhythm of reform and would eventually transform Italy's political, economic, and social structure. Far from overthrowing the government, Socialists should defend it from increasing pressure by conservatives. The revolutionaries who attacked the government were hangers-on from the anarchist "prehistory" of socialism, given to "infantile simplicity, . . . catastrophic solutions, and the cult of redemptive violence." They threatened to slow down the whole process of change currently taking place.[64]

In this context, according to Turati, the Berra *eccidi* acquired a crucial political importance. The government had neither desired nor provoked the killings, but its compulsion to defend the culprits proved its vulnerability to pressure from the Right, which, indeed, hoped for even more violence that would justify a new round of reaction. "For the first time . . . liberty is being tried," wrote Turati, "and it is surrounded by danger: *periculosa libertas*." Socialists who attacked the Party representatives for supporting the government were playing the reactionaries' game; the Party must purge itself of them at all costs.[65]

In 1899 Jaurès and his followers had voted for the Waldeck-Rousseau cabinet because of the clerical threat to the Third Republic. This vote provided a precedent for the Turatians. In France, a Socialist had actually broken away from the Party and entered a bourgeois cabinet, and this also had repercussions in Italy. The Italian reformists never condemned him, and the revolutionaries dared Turati to follow his example. In theory Turati had nothing against Socialist representation in a bourgeois cabinet, although in practice he had strong reservations and never joined a government.

The economic growth taking place in Italy during this period lent credence to Turati's arguments and helps explain the strength of reformism in the early years of the twentieth century. The industrial revolution reached northern Italy in the closing years of the nineteenth century, and until 1907 there was a strong boom punctuated by small crises until the more serious recession of that year. After 1908, expansion began again and continued, although at a lower rate, until 1913.[66] Workers' salaries increased significantly under reformist leadership, especially during 1901 and part of 1902. Giolitti estimated that in the first six months of 1901 alone, the strike movement increased workers' salaries by 48 million lire.[67]

The revolutionaries, however, did not consider these facts significant in the struggle for socialism. Arturo Labriola argued that the events preceding and following Pelloux's fall were the "triumph of liberty" only in Turati's imagination. He believed that Zanardelli's coming to power signified a change in tactics on the part of the ruling class. The era of force was over, and that of blandishments had begun. The bourgeoisie hoped to split the Socialists. By voting for the cabinet, the Socialist deputies had accomplished little or nothing. Salaries did rise a bit, but in return the Socialists had condoned increased military expenses, a repressive police, a reactionary administration, a regressive foreign policy, an oppressive fiscal system—in short, everything they had denounced. Labriola dismissed Turati's argument that the Socialists had compelled the government to respect the law. The government upheld the law because it defended the interests of the middle class. Labriola predicted that Turati's tactics would cause the moral, theoretical, and practical bankruptcy of socialism. The Party was being transformed into an admiring claque for the bourgeoisie, denying the existence of the class struggle, and helping bourgeois governments perform their duty of safeguarding capitalist interests.[68]

Despite his strong attack, Labriola ended by weakening his own case. He admitted that he had no theoretical objection to voting for a cabinet, or even to participating in one, when the Party was strong enough to obtain at least part of its program. He argued that he did not oppose reforms and agreed that socialism could be defined as a "becoming of successive reforms." Unlike Turati, however, he was willing to accept violence as a means of attaining them. He wished to excite the revolutionary spirit of the workers, in order to wring reforms from the ruling classes. Conservative violence had scared the Socialists into becoming "legalitarian," and he wanted to reverse the process.[69] In effect, Labriola reduced the dispute to a pragmatic question of the best way to secure reforms, and on this ground Turati got the better of him.

Labriola's weakness was immediately obvious to Anna Kuliscioff, who advised Turati on how to refute him and other critics. Labriola criticized Turati's program for obtaining reforms but suggested no viable alternative, she wrote. Labriola believed that *threatening* violence would frighten the bourgeoisie into making concessions, a belief she attributed to his southern heritage. Kuliscioff could understand that revolts were necessary in the South, but Labriola "is myopic and one-sided if he thinks he can impose those backward methods upon us."[70] Labriola mistakenly equated a vote for a government with approval for all its actions, a sophism that she recommended be attacked. As for his accusation that the deputies had contributed to the end of "revolutionary combativeness," she wrote that in modern societies, the

> revolutionary spirit of a people is demonstrated by its active participation in public life, by the conquest of legal institutions in its own defense, by its zeal in educating itself, by the conscious realization that it is part of a community with similar interests. Revolutionary spirit intended in the 1848 sense of the word has had its day.[71]

Very similar to Labriola's criticisms were those of Francesco Saverio Merlino, a former anarchist and revisionist of Marx. Merlino's assignment of the Party's revolutionary role directly to the workers organized in unions foreshadowed Labriola's revolutionary syndicalism. He also argued that revolutionary spirit meant having the will to resort to illegal means to achieve proletarian objectives, including reforms. He accused Turati of justifying the Berra killings and of planning to found a labor party under government protection.[72]

Turati objected that the Socialist vote for the cabinet did not imply "approval" for policies the Party had always condemned. It was a question of avoiding something worse. The Socialists could have provoked Zanardelli's fall, but then military appropriations would have been increased and the Chamber would have replaced Zanardelli with a reactionary. What would that have accomplished? If "reform is revolution," as even his opponents admitted, reforms could only develop the revolutionary will of the masses, not destroy it. "Revolutionary spirit" could not be reduced to a police matter, as the revolutionaries seemed to imply. To transform society by means of reforms was a long, slow process, but there was no alternative. The conditions for reform had to be maintained, and this meant supporting the government with all its weaknesses. The revolutionaries believed that "reforms must be obtained by all means possible, except the one that can give them to us."[73] Turati claimed the support of a majority of Party members. He announced the results of a referendum held by *Avanti!*, in which 122 Party sections approved the conduct of the Socialist deputies, while only 24 opposed it. The revolutionaries, however, charged that the referendum was handled fraudulently, and the incident raised the temperature of the debate still further.[74]

The disagreement between revolutionaries and reformists had by this time moved beyond the purely theoretical sphere. A split occurred in Milan and quickly spread to other parts of the country. Turati himself led the Milanese reformists out of the Milanese Socialist Federation (FSM) and established his own Socialist Union (USM) in July 1901. The main reason for the dispute was the Socialist vote for Zanardelli. The heads of the anti-Turatian opposition in Milan, Costantino Lazzari and the Neapolitan Walter Mocchi, enjoyed national stature and were soon joined by Arturo Labriola. When Turati became convinced that he could no longer work in the same organization with the revolutionaries, he founded his own section and newspaper. The revolutionaries in Milan appealed to the Directorate, which temporarily resolved the quarrel. Within a short time, however, Turati resigned from the Directorate, the Chamber, and the Party to protest the Directorate's actions. The Milanese rallied to Turati, who refused reelection until April 1902, after he had demonstrated his enormous popularity in the city. In 1903, when his influence in the national organization was beginning to slip, Turati again took the reformists out of the official Party section. Reformists in other major cities followed his example, and the Party saw no peace until 1909, when Turati regained control of the national organization.[75]

The revolutionaries attacked Turati on practical as well as theoretical grounds. Their analysis of the political situation convinced them that the reformists would receive a few reforms of doubtful value in return for their collaboration, and they continuously challenged their adversaries to enumerate the concrete benefits of their policies. Turati was primarily interested in blocking reaction, and in this sense the Zanardelli-Giolitti government, and the "Giolittian Era," was a major improvement over nineteenth-century governments. With the aid of the Socialists, however, the new cabinet initiated a number of important reforms that helped solve some of the country's problems, although many were not adequately pursued by later governments.

Zanardelli outlined the cabinet's liberal program in a speech to the Chamber on 7 March 1901. He hoped to eliminate at once the excise taxes on flour, bread, and pasta in the smaller municipalities and more gradually in the larger cities. The Socialists had criticized these levies as being unfair to the poor. Zanardelli also pledged to temper the inequities of the fiscal system in the South and suggested an immediate reduction of the salt tax in the area. In order to improve the lot of agricultural workers throughout the country, Zanardelli said that he would seek legal recognition of workers' organizations. Finally, he committed his government to an active role in social legislation and in trying to improve education.[76]

The Socialist spokesman in the Chamber generally approved the program but objected to Zanardelli's failure to reduce military expenses and expressed doubts about the tariff. While the tariff structure remained intact, the Socialists believed that Zanardelli's promise to alleviate the poor's fiscal burdens would remain a pious hope.[77] In fact, a secret military convention with Germany committed Italy to send six army corps to Germany's defense in case of war and made it impossible to reduce the army below twelve corps.[78] And to attempt to lower the tariff would have meant political suicide for any government of the period; even the northern industrial workers, who constituted the base of the Socialist party, opposed such action.[79] The major achievement of the reformists and the Extreme Left was to obtain the government's agreement to "consolidate"— that is, stabilize—military expenses for a period of six years. The reformists claimed credit for halting the rise in expenditures, but the revolutionaries accused them of smoothing passage for the military appropriations by not attending the session in which they were adopted.[80]

Italy managed to stabilize expenditures at a time when all the big European powers were expanding their armed forces.[81] Several Socialist proposals for keeping military expenses down, however, were not adopted, and after 1905 Italian military spending rose dramatically, partly to make up deficiencies created during the stabilization.[82]

If Socialists influenced only minimally military spending and tariff policy, they influenced policy in other fields, such as labor, to a greater extent. Because Giolitti had refused to intervene in labor disputes on behalf of private entrepreneurs, the number of successful strikes rose dramatically as the workers became more organized.[83] The number of resistance leagues mushroomed, and in September 1901 representatives of the agricultural leagues declared the leagues both socialist and reformist. By the end of 1901, the National Federation of Land Workers was established. At its height this organization attracted 227,791 members, more than any industrial union.[84] The movement was growing too fast even for reformist leaders. The leagues became powerful enough to create friction with the chambers of labor in the cities, also under reformist influence.[85]

According to Gioacchino Volpe, in this period the political education of the workers really began.[86]

Although the growth of workers' organizations was most spectacular in rural areas, the workers of the North also organized. The year 1901 was important for establishing new national category federations and for strengthening existing ones. For example, the metalworkers' union (Metalmeccanici), destined to be one of Italy's most powerful unions, was established as a permanent organization in 1901. In Milan, the reformists reorganized the postal union, the first successful organization of government workers, and in February 1902 Turati became its president, assumed effective control, and championed it in Parliament. Within a year the union counted 10,000 members. It founded a newspaper and a cooperative and was very active in improving working conditions. It eventually nourished hopes of becoming the nucleus of a worldwide union of postal, telephone, and telegraph workers.[87] The number of chambers of labor also increased rapidly, from nineteen to fifty-eight in a year, a rate of growth that elicited a note of caution from Socialist labor leaders. In 1902 the category federations and the chambers of labor organized the Central Secretariat of Resistance to coordinate policy. Its director was a reformist, Angiolo Cabrini.

This organizational pace was too rapid to maintain, and in late 1902 the labor movement suffered a series of setbacks that caused a precipitous decline in union membership. Employers organized to resist the demands of their workers and pressured the government to stiffen its attitude toward strikes. The revolutionary-reformist dichotomy also began to affect the labor movement. Revolutionary influence made inroads among the category federations, while the reformists became entrenched in the chambers of labor.[88]

As the labor movement's momentum slowed, social legislation passed at the urging of the Socialist deputies began to take effect. In 1902 a Labor Office (Ufficio del lavoro) and a Superior Council of Labor (Consiglio superiore del lavoro) were established. Their functions were to collect statistics and to suggest specific legislation to alleviate working-class conditions. Turati was named a member of the Consiglio, which included representatives of all classes, while his friend, Giovanni Montemartini, became the first head of the Labor Office in 1903. The Chamber also passed legislation providing for or extending old-age, sickness, and accident insurance and maternity benefits. Turati and Kuliscioff organized rallies (more than 300 were held on a single Sunday) to pressure Parliament into passing a Turati-sponsored measure to protect women and children from industrial hazards. In those rallies the lower classes for the first time intervened directly, systematically, and successfully to support a bill pending in Parliament. During the same period the Chamber adopted measures protecting emigrants, aiding malaria- and pellagra-stricken areas of the country, promoting land reclamation, and instituting a medal rewarding labor. The impetus for social legislation continued after the end of the Zanardelli-Giolitti partnership and slowed only in 1904.[89]

There was activity in the South during this period also. The Neapolitan Socialist newspaper, *La propaganda*, drew national attention to the South with its stories of corruption in Naples. A parliamentary commission confirmed the allegations in October of 1901, and in December the Chamber debated special provisions on behalf of the city.[90] In September of 1902, the elderly Zanardelli dramatized the South's predicament by undertaking a fact-finding tour of Basilicata, often traveling in ox-drawn carts under a fierce sun.[91] To help the South, the government then sponsored measures to extend long-term credits, provide tax relief, and encourage the construction of aqueducts, roads, and rail lines. According to one deputy, this was more than had been accomplished in forty years, although much remained to be done.[92] The government and its Socialist supporters were not without critics on this issue. Arturo Labriola believed that what the South needed was not aid but a massive peasant revolution, whereas Salvemini argued that the aid was not enough. Turati, however, defended the government's actions.[93]

The government had scant success in implementing fiscal reform. Although Giolitti had been the main proponent of progressive taxation, political realities ruled out any real effort to change the tax system. The finance minister, Leone Wollemborg, proposed to lower the tariff on certain kinds of flour, to abolish the excise taxes on flour, bread, and pasta, and to make up the lost revenue by rendering the inheritance tax slightly progressive and by imposing taxes on sales of gold and on stock market transactions.[94] The Chamber gave these proposals a hostile reception, badly bruising them in committee. As the cabinet was particularly vulnerable, this reaction was more likely an attempt to bring down the government than an objection to the measures themselves. As a result, Giolitti pressured Wollemborg into withdrawing his proposals and presenting new ones. These, however, did not survive the cabinet's scrutiny, and Wollemborg resigned.[95] That the Socialist delegation did not protest Wollemborg's ouster has led to the modern charge that they were interested more in liberty than in reforms.[96] In fact, the Socialists were unwilling to defend Wollemborg because they did not wish to risk the life of the cabinet for reforms they considered fairly minor.

Indeed, Wollemborg's successor, Paolo Carcano, modified the proposals, and they passed the Chamber in January 1902.[97] The major disappointment was that Giolitti failed to follow up these measures with more meaningful changes.

The Zanardelli-Giolitti government created a liberal political atmosphere in the country and undertook reforms that led to the modernization of Italy. In this sense, Socialist support was necessary, but the results were disastrous for the Party. Turati's policy widened the schism already latent in 1894. Socialists considered Socialists their worst enemies, and the schism limited the Party's political effectiveness.

CHAPTER VI

The Rise of a New Opposition

IN A REPORT to the Socialist Congress of Imola in 1902, Giovanni Lerda, a moderate leftist, noted that Party membership had increased from 19,000 to 60,000 between 1900 and 1902. This rapid growth worried rather than elated Lerda because many people considered themselves Socialists simply because they opposed the local mayor or the parish priest. Too many Party members lacked "Socialist consciousness and morality." There were too many pseudo-Socialists in the organization.[1]

Although Lerda made this argument in a general sense, the revolutionaries blamed the situation on reformist policy, which promised wage hikes and shorter working hours, not socialism. Reformism was grossly materialistic and had nothing to do with revolution; the reformists were a new breed of aristocrats who exploited the Socialist party in order to wield power. Before the Socialists could lead the proletariat to socialist revolutionary principles, they had to end reformist domination of the Party. The revolutionaries made their first attempt to do this in 1902.

Indian Summer: The Congress of Imola

The Congress of Imola opened on 6 September 1902. Party officials read a telegram in which Jean Jaurès supported the reformists. Ivanoe Bonomi presented a motion for the reformists, and Claudio Treves and Arturo Labriola, seconds to Turati and Enrico Ferri, engaged in a verbal duel. The next day 10,000 Socialists marched through the streets of Imola to demonstrate their support for the Party.[2]

The climax of the meeting came on the third day with the speeches of Turati and Ferri, the champions of the opposing factions. Turati reiterated his practical approach to Socialist doctrine. In Milan, he said, results counted, not talk. He reviewed the organization and accomplishments of the Milanese working class and said that it was not interested in Ferri's rhetoric. Ferri and the revolutionaries intimated that they favored violence and said that revolution was not the raising of barricades or the rejection of reforms. Then what was it? Was it only "The manner in which some words are pronounced and certain phrases are accentuated"? Turati then attacked Ferri's ally, Labriola, who had challenged the usefulness of social legislation and reforms in general in changing the state's structure. Because Labriola considered the state the main exploiter of the masses, he advocated a frontal attack on it. But, Turati objected, capitalists controlled the state, and Parliament could be used to curb their power. Moreover, as Labriola did not believe in collectivization, Turati did not consider him a Socialist but saw him as some kind of hybrid anarchist–petty-bourgeois–liberal republican. Turati labeled the Ferri-Labriola coalition a complete misalliance.[3]

In this Turati was correct. Ferri and Labriola had in common only the desire to end Turati's predominance. Ferri had no ideological commitments, but he was a good orator and adopted the fashionable ideas of the moment. Having won a mass following in the Party, he seemed desirable as an ally and formidable as an enemy. Unlike Ferri's, Labriola's ideas were always interesting, even if he also changed them often. Labriola had both influenced and been influenced by Georges Sorel and was thus one of the originators of revolutionary syndicalism, which he himself imported into Italy.[4]

At Imola, Labriola challenged the reformists to produce the reforms they had promised. No doubt the bourgeoisie would grant social reforms, but not important ones. It would not lower the duty on grain, decrease military expenditures, or change the tax system. The government would not enforce outside the North even the reforms that did pass. He concluded that reformist method was ineffective.[5]

Ferri's objections were less concrete. One of his disciples had explained that Ferri believed in the "German method," as opposed to the "English method" of the reformists—that is, he believed that the proletariat should always demand more than it believed possible to attain at any given moment. It would then settle for less, but threats were the only means to achieve big reforms as opposed to the trivial riformette Turati was willing to accept. Socialists must push for reforms, but the actual proposals and concessions must issue from a frightened bourgeoisie without any cooperation from Socialists.[6] Thus the Party would infuse the proletariat with a revolutionary soul and a revolutionary aim (collectivization) while making use of a revolutionary method (class struggle). In this way the Party would achieve major reforms without corrupting the workers as the reformists had done.[7]

The motion by the Ferri group stressed these ideas. It paid homage to the "revolutionary character" of the Party and proposed that the organization remain "independent and separate" from all social classes or political parties.

The reformist motion introduced by Bonomi proclaimed useful to the development of socialism all reforms "that elevate the economic, political, and moral conditions of the proletariat or that block capitalist exploitation." It confirmed the full "autonomy" of local sections to contract political alliances and praised the Socialist deputies for successfully defending the proletariat against possible reaction, giving them the right to "the most absolute freedom of action." This stipulation ended the deputies' subordination to the Party. Bonomi's motion won over the revolutionary motion by a vote of 417 to 275.[8]

On the last day of the congress, Turati attempted to carry his victory further by proposing to abolish the Directorate, the only Party institution capable of challenging the deputies' supremacy. He accused the Directorate of being authoritarian and suggested replacing it with a three-man secretariat. Ferri pointed out that the effect of Turati's proposal would be to transfer all power to the deputies, and the vote resulted in a 266-to-266 tie, after which Turati withdrew the motion.[9]

A second important issue at the congress was Leonida Bissolati's management of *Avanti!*. The revolutionaries complained that Bissolati refused them access to the Party organ as a platform from which to criticize reformism, and Bissolati acknowledged that the paper expressed the opinions of its editor.[10] After the congress ended, the revolutionaries initiated a successful campaign to replace Bissolati.

In fact, the results of the Congress of Imola were temporary. The reformists were in an unassailable position because their policies had resulted in concrete gains for the workers and because a group capable of mounting an effective offensive against them had not yet been organized. The last two months of 1902 witnessed the opening of an offensive against Turati, by the revolutionaries with the charge that the reformists were interested only in local advantages for the industrial workers of the North and the organized peasants of the Romagna and Emilia and ignored basic reforms for the rest of the country, especially the South.[11] As the benefits from reformist policies began to wane, the left wing gained strength.

The Climate Changes

The critics of reformism were at least partially correct. Giolitti's liberal policies, on which reformist fortunes rested, were not applied uniformly. Where important Socialist leaders could pressure the government on behalf of their constituents, Giolitti instructed local government officials to tread softly. The Socialist deputies' leverage depended upon the precarious balance of forces in the Chamber, where they were in a position to undermine the government. In areas lacking Socialist representation, however, arbitrary government tactics continued. Even in the North, Giolitti imposed limits on labor agitation, carefully preventing strikes from getting out of hand and taking an inflexible position against strikes in public service industries.[12] Giolitti pursued this policy out of conviction and to protect himself against the charge that labor agitation was threatening the public order. When Socialist organizers began extending their activities to rural areas outside the Po Valley, to the South, and to the public service sector, the government stepped in, declaring law and order in danger. On the land, the number of *eccidi* increased.[13] Although Turati became convinced that the Socialist deputies had to review their commitment to the government, they continued to support it out of fear of Sonnino, who continued to attack the cabinet from the right.

The differences between the Socialists and the government over strikes in the public service industries came to a head in February 1902, when workers threatened to halt the nation's rail traffic. A rail strike paralyzing the country would have been politically disastrous for Giolitti and would have damaged the economy. On 23 February, as the railway workers prepared to strike, Giolitti militarized them and ordered them to run the trains.[14] Once he had averted the strike, however, Giolitti pressured the minister of public works and Zanardelli to find funds to help the railway workers, and he acknowledged their grievances in their dispute with the companies.[15] The government intervened in several other strikes that threatened public services in 1902. Giolitti averted a general strike in Leghorn by threatening to send warships into the harbor and troops into the city. In Turin the government sent soldiers to run the gas works during a strike in March. When the Socialists objected, Giolitti authorized the prefect to arrest the Socialist deputies Oddino Morgari and Quirino Nofri if they advocated a general strike.[16]

Turati disapproved of the extension of strikes into the public service sector and worked actively to convince the railway workers not to strike, although he castigated both the railway companies and the government for their handling of the dispute. A strike, he told the railwaymen, would harm the collective interests of the nation and "might cause the liberal government to fall and make way for a reactionary one." The Milanese radical daily, *Il secolo*, reported that Turati was anxious for the government to call a delegation of workers to help settle the railway dispute but was afraid to make the suggestion himself for fear of being branded as a traitor. Turati asked Giolitti to communicate any concessions to the workers through himself or other reformist leaders. He also sought to convince the government to abandon its hostility to the Federation of Postal and Telegraph Workers because he, as president, had given it "an orderly and temperate character."[17]

These developments had repercussions beyond the public service sector. Industrialists and landowners, stunned by the government's liberal attitudes, began to recover from their shock. They organized to resist the demands of the workers' leagues and in many cases became strong enough to rescind previous concessions. Economic factors also worked in their favor. On the land, higher wages spurred the introduction of more efficient machinery. In 1902 a worldwide recession in prices began to be felt in Italy, bringing greater unemployment and consequent improvement of the employers' position.[18]

Turati had foreseen the negative repercussions of the strike movement and had attempted to slow it down. He wrote that Socialist leaders frequently advocated strikes with little consideration or when the workers were inadequately prepared. For him the strike was a double-edged weapon, and he emphasized the more basic and difficult task of organization. City workers (Turati did not criticize the strikes on the land) seldom bothered to consider the timing of their actions, their aims, or whether their goal could be achieved by negotiation. If they were well organized, he believed, the threat of a successful strike would generally be sufficient to gain concessions, because employers would rather settle disputes than provoke strikes in which they would lose money. The workers, however, rushed into strikes when employers were willing to talk, when they had stockpiled goods, and when there was overproduction. Although Turati understood that the past repression of the workers helped account for their propensity to strike, he blamed the revolutionaries for subverting the workers. The leftists justified all strikes, whether successful or not, on the grounds that they cut into profits, which all Socialists were supposed to eliminate. This theory paralyzed industry, scared off investment, and would lead to defeat and humiliation for the workers' movement. He concluded: "Just let this orgy of disorderly, unprepared, and useless strikes continue, especially in the public service sector and transportation, and you will see, even under this liberal government, the passage of restrictive legislation under the guise of protecting the sanctity of contracts and of safeguarding the public interest."[19]

Turati's courageous criticism of the workers' strike movement and its more militant supporters in the Party weakened his own position, also worsened by his reluctance to withdraw his support from the cabinet despite its manifest hostility toward the workers after February 1902. The Socialist deputies' attitude caused an overwhelming reaction against them within the Party. The Directorate instructed the deputies to vote against the government, but they refused, citing the likelihood of a reactionary replacement. In 1903 matters rapidly worsened as Bissolati was ousted as editor of *Avanti!*, to be replaced by Ferri. In Milan Arturo Labriola had instituted a campaign that eventually succeeded in eliminating reformist control of the city's chamber of labor. In addition, the cabinet itself tottered when Zanardelli's preoccupation with a divorce law alienated conservatives still further and when the cancellation of the czar's visit undermined his influence in foreign affairs.[20]

In the wake of developments, the reformists began to move toward opposition, especially through the influence of Anna Kuliscioff, who chided Turati for supporting the government to such an extent that people believed he wished to become a minister. She wrote to him: "Your weakness is to adopt the government's point of view so often that you seem part of the cabinet." She was convinced that supporting the government in order to block reaction had been correct, but now, she claimed, even Sonnino and Rudinì admitted that Italy could be governed only by means of liberal policies. There was no longer any fear of reaction, and for this reason the masses wanted the Socialist deputies to cease collaborating with the government. She believed that the deputies had missed a great opportunity to garner support by failing to demand political, social, and fiscal reforms and failing to go into opposition when these were refused. Under the circumstances, they had to be content that the "experiment" had produced a greater respect for liberty and civil rights and must immediately join the opposition. If the deputies continued their support of the government much longer, she warned, the left wing would take over the Party.[21]

Turati was reluctant to move decisively against the government. When he sent Kuliscioff a draft of a motion he intended to present at a caucus of Socialist deputies scheduled for 25 March 1903, she responded: "Why this air of two lovers separating but already arranging future trysts?" She would not vote for the motion if she were present, she informed him. Turati modified his draft to meet his companion's criticisms, and she approved the changes, writing that now the motion defended cooperation only in principle while not repudiating the reformists' past policies or condemning old allies.[22]

At the caucus Enrico Ferri criticized the government for failing to press for reforms and called for a debate on fiscal reforms.[23] Aimed at Turati, this motion would not only have ended cooperation for the present but would have condemned it in the past and would have removed any justification for it in the future. Turati's motion stated that the Socialist goal of preserving liberty had been achieved but that the promise of major reforms, which had seemed so bright, had not been fulfilled. Turati's motion passed, and the principle of cooperation and its possibility in the future was saved. In a speech to the Chamber on 31 March, Turati criticized the recent actions of the government but said that it would "be blessed in our history." He praised Giolitti for having inspired the cabinet's real achievements, and the speech appeared to be an implicit promise of Socialist support for a future Giolitti government.[24]

Indeed, the greatest problem for Turati and Kuliscioff was how to disengage themselves from Zanardelli while preserving their close relations with Giolitti. The two Socialist leaders basically agreed with Giolitti's analysis of the country's predicament. There were limits to how fast the government could move in order to concede liberty to a people unused to freedom. Although Giolitti acted against what he (and the reformists) considered to be the excesses of the workers, he evinced a genuine concern for their welfare and resisted strong pressures to restrict the right to strike and to curb the independence of the workers' organizations.[25] Kuliscioff predicted that Giolitti would have "a future as a modern man in Italy, for at least twenty-five years." She noted with pleasure that the Socialists had succeeded in "isolating" Giolitti and that, therefore, he would survive the cabinet's demise with his prestige intact. She credited Turati with this achievement and judged that the Socialist party had become the arbiter of the political situation, because Giolitti would be unable to gain conservative support. Giolitti's great merit was to have understood "what we were doing and to go along."[26]

In fact, when Giolitti disassociated himself from the cabinet he was careful to strengthen the good impression the reformist Socialists had of him. In June 1903 Giolitti resigned, citing the opposition of his strongest supporters, the Socialists. In private, Giolitti blamed several of his fellow ministers for adopting measures that provoked agitation he was then bound to quell as minister of the interior.[27] Giolitti's resignation on this basis pleased the Socialists, who blamed the conservatives in the cabinet.[28]

Thus, Turati and Kuliscioff had prepared the groundwork for the Socialist deputies to support a Giolitti cabinet, but increasing opposition within the Party prevented them from doing so.

At the end of 1902 a group of young Neapolitan Socialists, including Arturo Labriola and Walter Mocchi, had moved to Milan in order to challenge Turati on his own turf and use the city as a base from which to take over the Party and the Socialist press. They denounced Turati for having transformed the Socialist party into a "monarchical" organization that served a worker's aristocracy while neglecting the masses of the South, the Center, and the poorer areas of the North.[29] They linked up with Turati's opponents, revolutionaries and old *operaisti* led by Costantino Lazzari, and founded a weekly newspaper, *Avanguardia socialista*, as a rival to the reformist *Il tempo*. Arturo Labriola recalled that the *Avanguardia* was very difficult to edit because of the lack of cohesiveness that was the fatal flaw of the anti-Turati group.[30]

The achievements of the left wing during this period derived primarily from the intellectual quality and energy of Arturo Labriola, the main Italian exponent of revolutionary syndicalism.[31] Revolutionary syndicalism was the antithesis of reformism. Whereas the reformists hoped to use parliaments to achieve reforms that could gradually change society, for revolutionary syndicalists parliaments "cannot become instruments of social revolution." All dominant social classes created their own specific institutions, and the bourgeoisie had produced parliaments to maintain its power and resolve internal disputes. Parliamentary mechanisms precluded the dominance of one class or party over any other. Socialist parliamentary action could be useful only for propaganda reasons.[32]

The syndicalists also dismissed reforms. No society had ever reformed itself by means of pressure brought to bear by an oppressed populace. Bourgeois society reforms itself every day but does not reform itself out of existence.[33] Accordingly, the bourgeoisie had blunted every attempt to pass meaningful reforms, and the Socialist deputies diverted attention by denouncing the lack of support from the masses.[34] Socialists undertook innocuous campaigns in favor of parliamentary measures instead of increasing the revolutionary fervor of the workers; they had become one more clique in the Chamber.[35]

Thus, the syndicalists rejected the reformist identification of revolution with the natural evolution of society speeded up by reforms. According to Labriola, revolution was the means by which to break the hold of a dominating class; it would bring about the destruction of the existing social and political order and the passing of power to a new social group. This necessarily meant violence, and to denounce violence was to bolster the existing order. In opposition to Turati's pacifism, Labriola advocated urban guerilla warfare against the government.[36] By preaching against violence and by "mediating" disputes between the workers and the government, the Socialist party, he thought, suppressed the revolutionary spirit of the workers.

For the syndicalists, the Party was a political class consisting of leaders of bourgeois origin who had corrupted socialist principles. They were Socialists for intellectual reasons or because they needed a job, and they had transformed the Party into an electoral organization that survived by manipulating the workers. The Party, therefore, was destined to disappear as the working class took charge of its own destinies.[37]

The proletariat would gradually determine its own policies through the institutions it had created: the trade unions. After the revolution, the trade unions would control the means of production. The workers would federate among themselves up to the national and international level and avoid the new elites they accused the reformists of fostering.[38]

The polemic against the "mediation" of disputes led the syndicalists to stress "direct action," especially strikes. As Turati was well aware, the syndicalists favored political strikes in order to damage capitalist interests. The strike as a method culminated in the "specific form of the proletarian revolution," the general strike.[39] The revolutionary syndicalists spoke of the general strike in romantic terms and did not see it as a mass work stoppage to achieve specific aims. They interpreted it as a "social myth," a "drama" that demonstrated the political maturity of the working class. The workers, however, persisted in seeing it as a coordinated, mass strike with concrete objectives. A disappointed Labriola later lamented the Italian workers' "positivistic" temperament, which prevented them from understanding the loftier concepts of the general strike.[40]

Ultimately, the idealistic nature of revolutionary syndicalism, its stress on strikes, and the weak organizational talents of its early adherents sealed its fate, but Labriola's faction achieved considerable success in Milan, "the fatherland of reformism."[41] The Socialist deputies' continued support for the government and Turati's campaign against excessive strikes facilitated his opponents' task. "We are the favorite target of the white-gloved revolutionaries," Anna Kuliscioff wrote to Turati.[42]

The first test of strength between the syndicalists and the reformists came over control of the local Party section, the Federazione socialista milanese (FSM). As previously mentioned, the reformists had seceded from this organization in 1901, but the Directorate had patched up the quarrel. During the local elections of July 1902, the rival factions fought again, and *Il tempo* commented: "The Socialist Federation is finished."[43]

In October 1903 Turati organized the Gruppi socialisti milanesi (GSM), independent of the FSM,[44] whereupon the Neapolitan Socialists demanded Turati's formal expulsion from the Party. The Roman Socialists did the same, although they later backed down.[45] The FSM contended that Turati was out of the Party, but when the Party hierarchy refused to issue a declaration to this effect, the syndicalists began agitating for a Party congress to expel the reformists.[46]

Besides the violation of formal Party rules, the syndicalists charged the reformists with sabotage of the workers' movement. Reformism had abandoned socialist ideals by fostering the political neutrality of workers' organizations and concentrating on purely economic aims. This had increased wages because employers were taken unaware by the growing agitation, but when they began offering resistance, the workers' leagues, on the land and in the cities, collapsed because they lacked an ideology to strengthen their resolve. Organizations such as the Silk Workers' League dropped from 800 to 26 workers practically overnight. It was time to end Turati's domination of the Party and to make the workers combative by imbuing them with true Socialist fervor.[47]

The revolutionary syndicalists hoped to achieve these aims by moving to eliminate reformist domination of the Milanese labor movement, the most important in Italy, and then using it as a base to extend their influence. In September of 1903 they formed a permanent committee whose announced aims were to oust the reformists from the chamber of labor, to deemphasize immediate material aims, and to make the workers class conscious.[48] In October a bitter strike against Ferrovie Nord, a local rail line, failed. The chamber of labor's reformist leaders had opposed the strike and had cooperated with Turati and Treves to dissuade the railway workers on the national lines from undertaking a sympathy strike. The incident had important repercussions. At a stormy meeeting in the chamber of labor's headquarters, the syndicalists charged Turati with betrayal. The campaign against Turati came too late to give the syndicalists control of the chamber in the elections of November 1903, but they succeeded in May of 1904. The revolutionary syndicalists also became the dominant influence in the National Federation of the Chambers of Labor.[49]

Perhaps even more spectacular than the assault on the labor movement was the successful coup against *Avanti!* brought off by Labriola and Ferri. The circulation of *Avanti!* had dropped, and the newspaper was in financial trouble. The revolutionaries blamed the decline on Bissolati's allegedly having transformed *Avanti!* into a reformist mouthpiece. When Bissolati appealed to the Socialist sections for financial aid, the *Avanguardia* called for his removal. The revolutionaries advised the local Party organizations to refuse the request for funds as long as Bissolati remained editor, and enough of them did so to force Bissolati's resignation in April of 1903. Ferri succeeded Bissolati and opened the door to syndicalist influence.[50]

It will be recalled that all this activity had forced the Socialist deputies to come out against the Zanardelli government in March of 1903.[51] At the same time, it was quite clear that Zanardelli was in poor health and that Giolitti would succeed him.[52] The Socialist deputies were prepared to support Giolitti, but the ascendance of the revolutionary wing was so rapid as to make this impossible.

The king asked Giolitti to form a cabinet in October 1903. In a surprise move, Giolitti began consultations by approaching the Socialists and the Radicals. He made an offer of a cabinet position to the Radicals, and rumors began circulating that he would ask Turati to join the government. Speculation as to Turati's possible participation had been heard for months, and now he was mentioned as the next minister for agriculture, industry, and commerce.[53]

Giolitti confirmed the rumors by asking Turati to consult with him in Rome. Because such a meeting would weaken his position in the Party, Turati believed it unwise to go. In his reply, Turati stated that conditions in the Party precluded his participation in a cabinet and blamed the left wing for subverting the formation of a truly liberal and reform-minded government. He believed that his position in the Party had been so undermined that he could give Giolitti only his personal opinions, which would be worth little to him. However, Turati authorized Bissolati to speak to Giolitti for him.[54] When Giolitti tried to persuade Bissolati that Turati should enter a cabinet that would guarantee liberty and be sympathetic to the lower classes, Bissolati was unconvinced. He agreed with Giolitti's arguments but said that the masses would not understand such a move.[55]

Giolitti was apparently genuinely disappointed by Turati's refusal to join his cabinet. He had written that Turati was "serious enough to realize that it is no longer sufficient to stand on the sidelines to applaud or jeer."[56] Responding to criticism that his offer to Turati had been a gesture, Giolitti said that Turati's participation would have been a boon for the country and that in turning to Turati he had intended to demonstrate his commitment to reforms.[57]

Because of his conviction that a split on the national level would result if he did so, Turati resisted the pressure to join a government.[58] He cited the "immaturity" of the masses as *the real reason why we should hasten to comfort them with more schools and aid* of every kind," but he believed that it would serve no purpose for Socialists to enter a cabinet that would be sabotaged by members of their own party. Socialist ministers could not function "in an atmosphere of suspicion . . . , where they must guard their backs from their friends even more than from their adversaries, where all fruitful action is rendered impossible for them."[59] He cited no ideological impediments, as the syndicalists duly noted.[60]

When the Socialists and the Radicals refused to participate in his government, Giolitti, after some hesitation, turned to the Right. A historian has commented: "Since the most visible negative aspects of Giolittianism (corruption, cynicism, etc.) can be dated as beginning in 1903–04, we may conclude that these aspects were the alternatives Giolitti was forced to choose in place of the failed support of the *Estrema* in the Chamber and in the country."[61] Giolitti made this shift to the right despite warnings from the incredulous Socialists that they would turn against him and despite his earlier assertion that their support was crucial for his liberal policies.[62] In fact, after a series of meetings, the Socialist deputies denied him their support.[63]

Although he pledged to continue the liberal policies of the Zanardelli government and promised more aid for the South, Giolitti's new program disappointed the Socialists.[64] Reflecting the influence of the economic expert, Luigi Luzzatti, it concentrated on narrow economic improvements such as reducing the interest on the public debt. In addition, the cabinet had close connections with well-heeled clerical circles through Tommaso Tittoni, the new (and totally inexperienced) foreign minister.[65] In answer to Socialist criticism that he had "sold out," Giolitti answered that his program would have been the same even if the Socialists had joined him.[66]

The reformists had hoped to penetrate the bourgeois fortress, wrote a hostile observer. When they finally reached it, "on their knees and their hands folded in prayer, a resounding slap knocked them back to where they had started."[67]

Bologna: The Syndicalist Bid Fails

These events strengthened the syndicalist demand for a special congress, at which they hoped to expel the reformists.[68] The Milanese group, however, needed Ferri's support to achieve their objectives. At first Ferri seemed to go along but then made known his unwillingness to precipitate a split at the national level. The differences among the leftists became public in December 1903, but Ferri refused to change his mind, probably because the reformist leaders retained a great deal of influence.[69] As a result, the syndicalists tried to win the greatest possible support before the congress opened by making a strong showing at the Lombard Regional Congress, called to determine the position of the Lombard Socialists at the upcoming national congress.[70]

Although the regional congress at Brescia ended in a formal victory for the revolutionary syndicalists, the reformists demonstrated that they still enjoyed a great deal of support. Preliminary skirmishes before the congress resulted in a number of successes for the reformists, and the final vote was not very conclusive—73 to 68, with two abstentions.[71]

The successful syndicalist motion, eventually presented for approval at the national congress, blamed the reformists for the "degeneration" of the Socialist spirit. It objected to the supposed transformation of the Party into a "prevalently parliamentary, opportunist, constitutional, and possibilist-monarchist" organization. It rejected participation in cabinets and support for governments as inconsistent with the class struggle. It declared reforms useless for altering the fundamental structure of bourgeois society, maintaining that parliamentary action was of no value in abolishing private property and in making gains outside the bounds of the Italian Constitution. Finally, the motion declared as legitimate all means of offense and defense against the state, including violence. The motion resoundingly rejected all the reformist principles and, according to Mocchi, reaffirmed the permanent revolutionary character of the Italian Socialist party.[72]

The syndicalists demanded that the reformists either submit or leave the Party, but it was quite clear that the reformists were unwilling to do either. The reformists abstained from any further participation in the meeting and cast doubt on the legitimacy of the majority. When Turati reported on Brescia to the GSM, that organization instructed its Executive Committee to disregard the motion.[73]

The regional congress failed to have the effect most desired by the syndicalists: it did not convince Ferri to support the syndicalist thesis that a split was necessary.[74] They continued to woo Ferri by downgrading the differences between him and themselves. According to Labriola, these differences consisted only "of *tone* and *measure*." The syndicalists argued that it was now the reformists who wished to break with the Party because they were no longer supreme. Ferri, however, was prepared to sponsor a compromise that would allow the reformists to remain in the Party. Asked what would happen at Bologna, Labriola answered: "I'm convinced— nothing serious. I suppose Ferri's middle road will win out. It will be difficult for us to put together a majority around the principles enunciated at Brescia." The syndicalists had decided, however, to

stay in the Party and continue their efforts to capture it, even if
Ferri robbed them of total victory at Bologna. Most syndicalists
believed their momentum would be strong enough to give them
control of the Party in a short time.[75]

Besides courting Ferri, the syndicalists tried to split the reformists by making overtures to reformist sympathizers unhappy with
Turati's willingness to support cabinets. Most, however, followed
the lead of the labor organizer, Rinaldo Rigola, who refused the
bait.[76] At the same time, the syndicalists attempted to mobilize
international Socialist opinion in their favor; they argued against
Turati's contention that they were "anarchists" and announced that
they would not compromise their principles at Bologna.[77]

Indeed, the syndicalists advocated structural changes in the Party's organization that would embody their successful Brescia motion. It would do no good to vote in new policies if the reformists
could continue to defy the Party as they did in Milan, so the syndicalists vowed to reestablish iron discipline. All groups would be subordinated to the Party, especially the Parliamentary Group. Thus,
they proposed strengthening the Directorate by giving it the right
to censure, suspend, or expel anyone violating party discipline.[78]
Ferri, however, refused to support this proposal, and it failed.

The reformists were as intransigent as their opponents. Turati
labeled the syndicalists illogical anarchists who urged workers to join
economic organizations but condemned their attempts to achieve
a better standard of living. He advocated their expulsion.[79]

The major reformist liability was the refusal to abandon the principle of voting for governments. Leonida Bissolati's report on socialism and governments reiterated the standard Turatian position,[80]
thus ensuring the reformists their "Ferri" in the person of Rinaldo
Rigola. At Bologna most votes on the right would gravitate toward
Rigola instead of Turati, just as on the left they went to Ferri rather
than to Labriola.[81] Labriola understood this when, a week before the
congress, he admitted that the majority was someplace between
himself and Turati and said he could count upon only 150 delegates
out of 800. He predicted that 500 votes would go to the Center,
grouped around Ferri. The main difference between the Center and
his group, Labriola said, was that the Center did not believe that
violence was necessary to establish socialism. On all other points,
he and Ferri agreed.[82]

At Bologna, Ferri presented a motion to end capitalist exploitation
by working for economic, political, and administrative reforms,
while rejecting Socialist participation in bourgeois cabinets and forbidding the Socialist deputies to support governments by their votes
or in any other manner and under any circumstances. Turati reject-

ed the motion because of this provision and objected to Rigola's milder Right Center motion for the same reason. Both proposals were moderate compared to Labriola's, the same one voted at the Lombard Regional Congress. In his speech, Labriola launched into a full-scale diatribe against Turati, calling reformism the "most violent negation" of socialism and asking for its condemnation. Labriola's discourse was a dissertation on revolutionary syndicalism, which stressed the role of violence. "The proletariat must never forget," he had written in his report to the congress, "that the source of all rights is . . . violence."[83]

Turati again condemned violence as irrelevant and accused the syndicalists of being crypto-anarchists. Violence could not elevate a proletariat crushed by centuries of exploitation. Only a patient struggle for reforms could do this, and democracy was the essential prerequisite for reform. If reformism had not yet achieved all the results it could, it was because the revolutionists had sabotaged it, had discredited the deputies' work in Parliament, and had deprived them of support among the masses. Although Turati conceded that it would be a "century" before any Socialist could honestly join a cabinet, the Party must vote for reform-minded governments.[84]

Turati was clearly on the defensive at Bologna. The syndicalists accused him not only of betraying Marxist principles but of wishing to retain the monarchy. According to them, Marx had demonstrated that the struggle for socialism could occur only in a republic, whereas the reformists strengthened the monarchy by participating in its politics, voting for its ministers, and arguing that the masses could achieve their goals without a revolution. Therefore, they asked the congress to make "clear and decisive republican affirmations."[85]

Turati's ideas on this issue had indeed gone through a long evolution. At first he took an orthodox Marxist stand, writing that the monarchy impeded the development of the bourgeoisie. Using the French revolutionary model, Turati predicted that the bourgeoisie would overthrow the monarchy and establish its own republic "of the monarchists, of the clericals, of the reactionaries, of the speculators." Conditions for the proletariat would then worsen, but the class struggle would be simplified and clarified. In due time, according to the early Turati, a social republic would emerge, *perhaps* by means of violence and the dictatorship of the proletariat. By 1901, however, Turati considered it possible to make real progress toward socialism even under the monarchy. The conditions under which the Zanardelli government came to power, for example, constituted a parliamentary revolution more significant than a change in the form of government "in the limited sense that non-Socialist republicans attribute to this phrase." Thus, Turati considered the monarchy merely a "setting" within which the struggle for socialism took place; he compared it to the frame of a painting.[86]

Although Turati believed that the country would eventually go through a republican phase, he rejected the syndicalists' contention that the Party should concentrate a great deal of energy in overthrowing the monarchy. Should the monarchy ever again attempt repression, the Socialists would move against it, but in the meantime, there was more to building a republic than abolishing the monarchy. "The most urgent task is to create a republican people," Turati said at Bologna, "not to change a coat of arms." The republic would mature within the monarchy and make it obsolete, just as socialism evolved from within capitalism.[87]

As the debate at Bologna proceeded, Ferri asked Labriola and Mocchi to come to see him. As Mocchi recalled several years later, Ferri told him:

> I will not vote for your Brescia motion, even if it were perfect [oro colato] because it has the taint [peccato originale] of being the motion presented at Brescia; I will not vote for Bissolati's motion [reformist] even if it were perfect, because it has the taint of being Bissolati's motion. I will wait and see. Meanwhile, is there any way to reach an agreement?

The syndicalist leaders declared that they would vote for any motion that affirmed "*the absolute incompatibility, always and everywhere*, between the class struggle and collaboration with governments, open or implied." Ferri refused his support. Labriola and Mocchi then stated that the syndicalists would vote for a motion simply prohibiting collaboration. When Ferri saw that the reformists had lost their majority but remained a very powerful minority, he presented the compromise Left Center motion previously described.[88]

On the floor of the congress the reformist and syndicalist motions were first pitted against each other. The reformists received 12,255 votes and the syndicalists 7,410, but there were 12,560 abstentions. A vote was then taken on the Ferri and Rigola (Right Center) motions. Ferri obtained 16,304 votes to Rigola's 14,844. Equivocation, Turati and Labriola agreed, had won out at Bologna.[89]

Turati and Labriola therefore concluded that they would remain in the Party and continue fighting for control. Turati wrote that the congress had demonstrated the existence of "two parties" within one but consoled himself with the thought that they had existed in the beginning and would always be there. The syndicalists concluded that Bologna had signaled the end of "electoral" socialism.

They predicted that Turati would continue moving toward a government-oriented social democracy and eventually separate from the
Party.[90]

The syndicalist interpretation was overly optimistic. The vote at
the congress had demonstrated that the reformists retained much
more support within the Party than the syndicalists, despite syndicalist inroads in the labor movement. The syndicalists understood
that their top priority now must be to eliminate reformist influence
from the workers' organizations,[91] but the reformists, while less
dramatic, were more patient and skilled labor organizers than they.
As for the coalition with Ferri, it was practically nonexistent, except
as a tactical union to oppose Turati. Ferri had no consistent ideology
and was motivated mainly by a desire for popularity and by political
opportunism. He let the syndicalists down at every crucial juncture
—as they should have expected—and within a year, Ferri and the
syndicalists were engaged in a bitter dispute.[92]

To their disappointment, the syndicalists discovered that the
Bologna congress had altered very little in the everyday life of the
Party. The deputies continued to flout Party discipline, and the autonomous reformist groups refused to rejoin the FSM, despite a referendum against them and despite an order from the newly elected
Directorate. The syndicalists were incensed when Turati asked his
fellow deputies if he should leave the Parliamentary Group and they
replied that the Directorate's order was of a "purely formal and
local nature."[93] There was little the syndicalists could do, however,
and they achieved success only outside the Party organization.

Their opportunity came during the fall of 1904 over the issue of
the eccidi, which continued throughout 1902, 1903, and 1904. The
syndicalists usually seized upon such incidents to denounce reformist "collaboration" with the government. In August 1904, Labriola
warned that the bankruptcy of parliamentary reformism had increased the chances of a general strike.[94] When on 3 September
soldiers fired on striking miners in the Sardinian town of Buggerru,
workers responded immediately and held protest meetings all over
Italy. In Milan, the chamber of labor, recently captured by the syndicalists, invited all Italian workers to begin a general strike within
eight days. Other camere also discussed a general strike, the one at
Monza declaring that it should take place automatically should another eccidio occur.[95]

In the meantime, Party officials worked to calm the waters.
Avanti! gave the events little prominence and instead urged the
Directorate to consider the matter. When it did meet, the Directorate opposed a general strike and specifically rejected the motion
by the Milan chamber of labor. This Directorate, the fruit of the

intransigent "coalition" at Bologna, included Ferri, who came out strongly against a strike.[96] The Directorate, however, did not make its opposition public, preferring to issue a vague statement while it dispatched a representative to explain the decision to the Milanese. The Directorate hoped that the agitation would subside, but on 14 September the police killed two more workers and wounded several others at Castelluzzo (Trapani). When the Directorate met again, the general strike had already begun at Monza and Milan, and its endorsement was only the recognition of a fait accompli.[97]

On the morning of 15 September, Milan took on the aspect of a deserted city, with the police remaining out of sight while workers' squads kept the peace. The strike quickly spread to those sections of the North, the Center, and the South where there were organized workers.[98]

Caught by surprise, the reformists had to accept the strike but attempted to keep it within its original bounds. Turati praised the generous protest of the proletariat and criticized the government but courageously said that he opposed the strike. He advised the workers to trust the deputies and a committee they were about to elect. This was an unpopular position, and when he tried to speak on another occasion he was shouted down.[99]

If the general strike had taken the reformists by surprise, it also caught the revolutionaries off guard. The spontaneity and the success of the strike prompted them to try to take advantage of it by extending its scope. Labriola and Lazzari advocated continuing the strike until Giolitti's cabinet fell. But its continuation required the cooperation of the railwaymen's federation, and that group, heeding reformist suggestions, had refused to join the strike. Turati, meanwhile, advised the strikers to end their action, now that they had made their point. Labriola later admitted that bringing down the cabinet had been an impossible goal.[100]

In the end the strike failed. It remained uncoordinated while reformists and syndicalists tried to exploit it for their own political purposes. Giolitti took the necessary precautions but did nothing else, concluding that the strike had not been called in response to a great national or economic question. He advised the prefects to remain calm and to wait for the strike to end, which it did as workers slowly drifted back to their jobs after four days. The Socialist deputies did little. They rejected suggestions that they resign in protest or resort to obstructionism and instead asked for the immediate reconvocation of the Chamber.[101] Giolitti preferred to dissolve it, as it was reaching the end of its five-year term. Exploiting the anti-Socialist reaction to the general strike, he asked the people "to judge those parties and men who had provoked that useless and damaging interruption in the normal life of the country."[102] The general strike failed to achieve even its more modest goals— for example, a law that would regulate the police during strikes and reduce the chances of more *eccidi*.[103]

But the strike had some indirect results. It demonstrated that the local workers' organizations were numerous and efficient but that they needed a central apparatus, which the reformists supplied in 1906. It also set the pattern of protest in Italy. Future *eccidi* would frequently be followed by general strikes, as this seemed to be the only method of influencing the authorities.[104]

The rival factions drew different conclusions in their analyses of the strike. Enrico Leone claimed a great success for the syndicalists and saw the general strike as a new method of achieving workers' rights.[105] Arturo Labriola informed the reformists that five minutes of "direct action" were worth as many years of parliamentary banter. The strike had been valuable because it had polarized Italian parties, had given the workers a sense of accomplishment, had destroyed the Turati-inspired illusions of the masses, and had united the proletariat of North and South in a common action.[106] The reformists thought the strike had demonstrated the bankruptcy of syndicalism. Although Turati condemned the strike's excesses, he sympathized with the initial protest. He drew the lesson that protest strikes must be short, have clear and attainable aims, be directed by authoritative leaders, and respect essential public services.[107] Another reformist leader, Garzia Cassola, pointed out that the general strike would never have been possible without the labor organizations the reformists had founded.[108] The reformists opposed all future general strikes and continued to stress organization. They especially feared the "polarization" of Italian politics produced by the strike, which Labriola considered one of its major achievements.

In fact, polarization caused liberal groups previously sympathetic to the Extreme Left to withdraw their support and provoked the entrance of Catholic forces into national politics during the elections of 1904. These elements swelled Giolitti's majority and made him less attentive to the Extreme Left. In short, polarization isolated the working class and made further economic and political gains difficult.[109]

The Revival of Reformism

$\mathbf{T}$HE GENERAL STRIKE of 1904 was the apogee of revolutionary syndicalist fortunes in Italy. The strike set into motion a series of events that eventually led to the reestablishment of the reformist hegemony.

The Decline of Revolutionary Syndicalism

One of the general strike's main political consequences was the participation of the Catholics in the elections of 1904. The Catholics were well organized and disciplined but had kept out of national politics because the *non expedit* forbade participation, although after the 1898 crisis a softer line replaced the Catholics' previously inflexible attitude.[1] After the 1904 general strike, Tommaso Tittoni, Giolitti's link to the Catholics, sought the help of a political ally of the powerful Catholic organizations of Bergamo, Count G. Suardi, to extend the moderate-Catholic alliances to the national level in the interests of preserving social order.[2] Suardi spoke to Paolo Bonomi, leader of the Bergamo Catholics, and Bonomi, in turn, saw Pope Pius X.[3] When Bonomi argued that the Catholic organizations would be destroyed if the Catholics failed to participate in the upcoming national elections, Pius gave his permission.[4] This decision improved the cordial relations with Giolitti and caused the defeat of a number of Extreme Left candidates.[5]

Apparently, the electorate struck out against the parties that had instigated or condoned the strike. The Socialists lost four seats in the Chamber, dropping from thirty-three to twenty-nine, while the Republicans lost five. The Radicals gained three seats, but more than half of the Radicals supported Giolitti. The Extreme Left could count on only sixty-seven votes instead of eighty-six. Seventy-six rightists and three Catholics opposed Giolitti, but his support in the Chamber had risen from 52.28 percent to 71.2 percent. In addition to the Catholic alliance and the conservative backlash, the lack of proportional representation helped Giolitti because it distorted the electoral results. In 1904, for example, the Socialist popular vote increased from 164,946 to 326,013, and proportional representation would have entitled them to 108 seats instead of 29. Government interference in the South also helped account for the victory.[6]

The Chamber of 1904 was so conservatively oriented that it embarrassed Giolitti. Turati saw him caught in a dilemma. He would either have to renounce his plans for democratic reform or resign to make way for a cabinet that reflected the overwhelming conservative nature of the Chamber.[7] Indeed, Giolitti felt the need to give some balance to the Chamber by sponsoring a Radical for the body's president over considerable opposition.[8] Anna Kuliscioff interpreted this as a hopeful sign, but Turati disagreed. The revolutionary syndicalists had ruined the labor organizations, poisoned the tone of political life, neutralized the most powerful liberal leader in the country, and made it impossible to implement the Socialist reform program. Socialist influence on the government was zero.[9]

There were signs, however, that revolutionary syndicalism was waning. In Milan the best-known syndicalists had run against the reformists and had received only 1,360 votes, as compared to 10,645 for the reformists.[10] The syndicalists recognized these results as a disaster, admitted they had made mistakes during the general strike, and resolved to tone down their most extreme statements.[11]

The syndicalists, however, had misinterpreted the lessons of the general strike. They assumed that their aggressive methods were basically sound, but in fact the "political" strike would continue to be ineffective. In 1905 syndicalist influence had increased among the railwaymen, who were agitating for job security, an eight-hour day, and ten days a year sick leave. At the time, the government was ending the conventions by which private companies ran the railroads. The Socialist deputies had pushed for the state takeover, but the syndicalists accused the companies, the banks, and the government of shady dealings at the expense of the taxpayer. Furthermore, the government wished to eliminate the railwaymen's right to strike, and when the minister of public works introduced a bill that provided for compulsory arbitration of disputes, the railwaymen obstructed the running of the trains. The reformists warned the railwaymen against a strike, arguing that special techniques had to be used to press workers' demands where state services were concerned. They suggested a combination of union agitation, mediation by the Socialist deputies, and mobilization of public opinion. As usual, however, the syndicalists called the reformists "counter-revolutionaries" and "collaborationists" and denounced their "mediation." They supported the rail workers' actions as a perfect example of how unions should take over the class struggle on behalf of the revolutionary proletariat.[12]

Several days after the obstruction began, Giolitti suddenly resigned, citing illness.[13] The syndicalists claimed a victory because, they said, their threat to transform the obstructionism into a general strike had caused the resignation.[14] In fact, however, "obstruction" was unsuccessful and was about to be called off before Giolitti resigned.[15] Giolitti's exit did not mean the end of his policies, and the Chamber elected his hand-picked successor, Alessandro Fortis. Fortis resubmitted Giolitti's railway project to the Chamber practically intact: railway workers could not strike.[16] On 17 April a committee of railwaymen called a protest strike. It was a dismal failure, with only 23,635 of 53,320 organized workers participating. The railwaymen appealed to the Secretariat of the Resistance to call a general strike, but it refused. Public opinion turned against them, a labor leader commenting that they "struck for their own particular reasons." After four days, the strikers returned to work without achieving their goals.[17]

Turati declared that this strike proved the bankruptcy of the syndicalist method. Not only had Giolitti easily outmaneuvered the syndicalists, he claimed, but the Socialist deputies alone had prevented retaliation. As further proof that cooperation worked, Turati also claimed that the parliamentary delegation had acted in concert with deputies of the Center to block a government scheme to renew the railway conventions. If the workers wished to improve their conditions, he wrote, they must return to the reformist fold and coordinate their actions with the Socialist deputies.[18]

Revolutionary syndicalist influence was, in fact, detrimental to the labor movement. An immediate result of the railway strike, for example, was the syndicalist sabotage of the Secretariat of the Resistance. In addition, the number of chambers of labor declined from ninety to eight-two, and total membership from 340,228 to 318,446, between 1904 and 1906; the number of organizations belonging to the camere dropped from 3,328 to 2,733 during the same years. Even the workers' combativeness, it has been maintained, decreased during the syndicalist period. In 1906 a workers' congress refused to sanction general strikes as a means of protesting eccidi, a principle that had the endorsement of a majority of the chambers

of labor. Probably the reason for these developments was that lost
strikes undertaken under syndicalist auspices "could be cited by the
dozen."[19] It is particularly ironic that few new labor organizations
were founded in Milan during these years and that fewer workers
participated in strikes during the heyday of the revolutionary syndicalists than did during the height of reformist influence.[20]

Turati's prodigious activity on behalf of the Milanese working
class accounted for his ability to defy the Party organization and
eventually to reconquer it. His development of the postal workers'
union into a powerful organization during this period has already
been mentioned, and the union provided moral, financial, and organizational support for the reformists.[21] He was also the major influence behind the Società Umanitaria in Milan. The Umanitaria
ran schools, investigated living and working conditions, and provided legal and other services for the poor. This institution resisted
all attempts by the syndicalists to take it over.[22] Through Turati's
auspices the Umanitaria also organized the opening of five free li-
braries in the working-class districts of Milan in 1904. Within six
months over 8,700 readers were using them, and the city and the
government were providing subsidies.[23] In 1906, again in Milan,
Turati helped found the Italian Union for Popular Education, which
published a journal, sponsored lectures, and pioneered in the use
of the cinema as an educational tool. He was the union's vice-
president and driving force for many years.[24] Reformists were also
prominent in staffing the "free universities," which provided important educational opportunities for persons who could not afford to
go to school.[25]

This activity began to show results in 1905, although it would
be another year before the reformists were able to win the struggle
for the labor movement. The reformist attempt to recapture the
Milan chamber of labor failed in 1905, but it set the stage for victory
in 1906.[26] Reformists also entered the elections for the Secretariat
of the Resistance, which had been paralyzed after the recent railway
strike. Reformist activity aroused the syndicalists, who took complete control of the organization but proved unable to revive it.[27]

In 1906 the reformists founded a centralized organization capable
of guiding the national labor movement, the General Confederation
of Labor (Confederazione generale del lavoro, CGL). In February of
that year, the Metalworkers' Federation had invited other federations to meet in Milan in March for the purpose of founding a national workers' organization.[28] About twenty trade unions accepted
the metalworkers' invitation, and the delegates met on 4 March.[29]
On the same day an article summarizing the problems of the labor

movement and the goals of the meeting appeared in Treves's *Il tempo*. (The secretary of the metalworkers' union was Ernesto Verzi, a reformist in close touch with Turati.)[30]

According to the article, the principal question plaguing the Italian labor movement was the relationship between the chambers of labor and the trade union federations. The local chambers of labor had attempted to substitute themselves for the trade union federations, thus blocking the growth of the federations, national organizations competent to deal with the complex problems of an entire industry. The chambers of labor were "local proletarian units" intended to assume the leadership of municipal politics, ensure the enforcement of social legislation, facilitate employment, and aid the pacific resolution of labor disputes. The article concluded that the federations and the chambers should act strictly within their respective spheres and organize a confederation to coordinate their activities.[31] These ideas were accepted by the delegates. They agreed to hold a congress representing all workers to determine the specific structure of the new confederation. Later, a planning committee scheduled the congress for 29 September and determined how the workers' organizations should be represented.[32] The syndicalists denounced the proposed confederation but decided to capture it.[33] Their strategy failed because between the spring and the fall of 1906 the initiative passed definitively into the hands of the reformists. Anna Kuliscioff reported from Milan that reformist meetings and lectures were always packed to overflowing while those of the syndicalists were poorly attended. She wrote that the workers supported reformism "with the loyalty of the best times." Even syndicalists praised Turati's coherence and sincerity.[34] Kuliscioff's judgment was confirmed in May when the reformists won the elections for the executive committee of the Milan chamber of labor.[35]

During this period, the revolutionary syndicalists went into a rapid decline on the national level as well. In February 1906, Fortis fell and was replaced by a Sonnino government that came to power with the aid of Socialist votes. A prime mover in this unusual experiment in class collaboration was Enrico Ferri, who had steadily been moving further away from the syndicalist group and who, in June of 1905, had removed most of the syndicalists from *Avanti!*.[36] The syndicalists denounced the vote for Sonnino, derided Ferri's attempts to rationalize the Socialist deputies' action, and accused him of being worse than Turati.[37] When the deputies ignored an order from the Directorate not to support Sonnino, the *Avanguardia* began a press campaign focused on Ferri.[38] In March Walter Mocchi stated that Ferri should have his head examined and announced the

definitive end of the "revolutionary concentration" formed at Bologna.[39] Mocchi also appealed to Ferri's followers to cross over to the
syndicalists, but this did not happen. Instead, Ferri eliminated what
syndicalist influence remained on *Avanti!*.[40] The break with Ferri
exposed the lack of support for revolutionary syndicalism within
the Party. A new majority was being formed around Oddino Morgari's "integralist" faction, to which Ferri transferred his support.[41]

The reformists observed the split on the left with mounting satisfaction. They had always thought of Ferri as more dangerous than
the Extreme Left because of his popularity. Kuliscioff believed that
only the Left could destroy Ferri, as Ferri was destroying syndicalism. Laissez-faire would be the reformist strategy—the left wing
would be allowed to destroy itself.[42]

It was within this context that the congress that founded the
General Confederation of Labor convened on 29 September 1906
in Milan. The reformists were extremely well organized, and the
syndicalists' only hope of defeating them was to ally with the anarchist and republican groups present, but this alliance failed to stop
the reformists. In a desperate effort to block reformist control of
the new organization, part of the opposition proposed submitting all
decisions to a referendum, but this move also failed.[43] As a result,
the syndicalists announced their intention to withdraw, draft their
own constitution, and submit it to the workers. The delegates greet-
ed their secession with "glacial silence."[44] According to one critic,
by walking out the syndicalists gave up any chance of taking over
the organization in the future. They created an independent labor
movement, but the CGL became the great pole of attraction for the
workers.[45]

The failure of the revolutionary syndicalists to gain control of the
nascent CGL ended their power within the Socialist party.[46] This
was obvious at the next Party congress, held in Rome shortly after
the foundation of the CGL. The syndicalists hardly mattered, as reformists and integralists battled for control of the Party.

The integralists had emerged between 1904 and 1906. Integralism
took its name from the "integral" socialism of Benoît Malon, who
had tried to combine the best of liberalism and socialism, but it
was practically indistinguishable from reformism. The integralists
repeated reformist themes. For example, they cautioned

the proletariat against the illusion that it could, whenever it
decided, "improvise" socialism with a stroke of insurrectional
audacity, and also against the ... illusion of being able to
achieve socialism only by means of electoral and parliamentary

action. Integralism considers the achievement of socialism to be the result of the varied and gradual action of many factors—agents which dissolve the fabric of the capitalist state and encourage the formation, in embryo, of socialist organs during the maturation of the capitalist economy itself.[47]

Morgari suggested steering a course between syndicalism and reformism, that is, rejecting "little" reforms and emphasizing the economic struggle and resistance to "absorption" by the radical bourgeoisie. Socialist deputies should be forbidden to vote for a cabinet unless a referendum were held on the question first. On the other hand, Socialists should accept alliances whenever necessary, as long as they continued fighting for their principles. The Party, Morgari believed, "must remain *intransigent in substance*, even in the act and above all in the act of *becoming cooperative in form*."[48]

Turati denounced integralism as "reformism without reforms, revolutionism without revolution, cooperation without opportunism, intransigence without excesses, concord without consent."[49] The reformists, however, were too astute not to make use of it. Although Turati professed that he would not join with the integralists to defeat the syndicalists,[50] Kuliscioff observed that Ferri had hitched his star to integralism and had thus become its appendage. This, she noted, served the reformists' cause. She suggested Claudio Treves as being particularly suited to approach the integralist leaders in order to bring them closer to reformism than they already were.[51] Clearly, the reformists would accept a union for tactical reasons once they had denounced integralist ideology.

At the Congress of Rome Turati argued that integralism was "reformism plus obscurity," lamenting the confusion integralism introduced into the Socialist party just when it needed to clarify its ideas. His real aim, however, was to finish off revolutionary syndicalism, to make the continued existence of the syndicalists within the Party impossible. He stated that the syndicalists were not socialist in theory or tactics. Syndicalist labor policy was akin to literary drama and had damaged the labor movement the reformists had created. "I say that wherever the workers' movement is serious, it is reformist." At the previous congress, Turati recalled, he had said that reformism and revolutionary syndicalism were mutually exclusive. Now he invited the syndicalists to be logical and leave the Party.[52]

Turati spoke from a position of strength because the reformists had the support of the organized labor movement and, through an irritating but necessary "integralism," a de facto majority at the congress. Turati and Labriola had intended to expel each other from the Party since 1904, and Turati had won the struggle.

In fact, Labriola planned to provoke the delegates. The reformists were de facto clericals, militarists, and monarchists, he said. "Do you want to make Filippo Turati mad as a beast? Say 'republic' to him." Reformist labor policy was akin to begging: "What difference does it make if the worker works half an hour more or less?" He agreed with Turati that at least the reformists were clear. Morgari, he said, did not even recognize himself for the reformist he was. Ferri was the "revolutionary socialist of the word." Labriola denounced the Socialist movement as artificial and informed the delegates that he had attended his last congress.[53]

The integralist motion condemned syndicalist tenets, including reliance on the general strike, violence, and direct action. It repudiated the concept of all power to the unions. It reaffirmed the gradualistic approach to socialism and defended social legislation. The motion did proclaim intransigence the rule and cooperation the exception and objected to "systematic" alliances, but very mildly. For example, it did not make voting for governments subject to a referendum, as Morgari had suggested, but left the decision up to a majority decision of the Directorate and the deputies meeting together. It came as no surprise when Ferri announced the reformists were prepared to vote for the integralist motion.[54]

Besides the integralist motion and a syndicalist proposal that defiantly summarized the faction's principal tenets, an intransigent motion presented by Giovanni Lerda prohibited voting for cabinets and all other kinds of collaboration. The triumph of the integralist motion, however, was devastating: integralist, 26,947; syndicalist, 5,278; intransigent, 1,101; abstaining, 757.[55]

Before disbanding, the congress elected a new Directorate, which reflected the various shadings of the integralist majority. In a weak attempt to restrain the parliamentary delegation, the congress enlarged the Directorate to ensure that the deputies would not have an automatic majority in plenary meetings.[56]

Although the reformists had achieved their major objective by isolating the syndicalists and hastening their departure from the Party, the congress of 1906 was not wholly satisfactory. The integralists had less enthusiasm for cooperation with the bourgeoisie, although they accepted it in principle. The reformists were also unhappy at the restrictions the congress had placed on the autonomy of the Socialist deputies. They believed that parliamentary maneuvering required instant decisions; the deputies could not consult with the Directorate every time there was a crisis in the Cham-

ber, nor did they wish to accept the risk of being outvoted. As a
result, the integralists and the reformists fought hard to gain control
of the Party over the next two years, and in doing so they had to
contend with an unexpected new rival, the General Confederation
of Labor.

Reformists, Integralists, and Labor Leaders

It is not surprising that the CGL challenged the Socialist party for
the political leadership of the working class. CGL leaders claimed
the allegiance of 300,000 persons, a number that dwarfed the steadily declining Party membership.[57] The internal fighting that continued within the Socialist party between integralists and reformists
also gave the labor leaders ample opportunity to advance their own
ideas at the expense of the Party.

The CGL's first step was to establish its authority, showing itself
especially anxious to centralize functions that hitherto had been
separate. The new organization founded its own newspaper, issued
identification cards, drafted programs of legislative proposals, entered into agreements with other organizations, and established
direct contact with the Socialist party Directorate. On 15 January
1907, Rinaldo Rigola became secretary-general.[58]

Under Rigola's leadership the CGL attempted to extend its activities into areas usually reserved to the Party. In November 1906,
Angiolo Cabrini, who favored a greater political role for the union,
summarized its legislative aspirations before the integralist-dominated Directorate. The Directorate, however, reasserted the Party's
traditional policy-making role and restricted the CGL's competence
to narrowly technical economic issues. Shortly afterward, the union
made use of a particularly bitter strike to exert its influence in
the political arena. At the end of 1906, the maritime workers of
Genoa, who had called a strike, discovered that they had taken on
more than they could handle. The workers appealed to the CGL
to declare a general strike in sympathy but were refused. The union's
executive committee stated that the CGL would become involved
only if and when the employers threatened the workers' right of
organization—a clearly political function. In addition, the CGL reserved for itself the right to appeal for national solidarity during
strikes; and it moved further into the political arena by blocking
the Party's support of strikers who did not belong to the CGL.[59]

CGL leaders initiated a policy designed to establish hegemony over
the Party or, failing this, to establish a "labor party" of their own.
The ideological component for this attempt was provided by a faction of reformist politicians, notably Bissolati, Ivanoe Bonomi, and

Antonio Graziadei. Turati opposed the appearance of this new tendency within his ranks and had already condemned its early ideological manifestations, but his need for CGL support allowed the
movement to progress further than it otherwise would have done
and eventually contributed to a reformist split.[60]

At the end of 1906, Turati attempted to work out a clear understanding with the CGL by proposing close cooperation between the
Socialist Parliamentary Group and the CGL. He attributed the Party's stagnation to its inability to organize the masses to support
rigorous action by the deputies, a lack the CGL could remedy. Turati
frankly admitted the poor performance of the parliamentary delegation and suggested that the CGL join in a national effort to obtain
salaries for the deputies, thus enabling them to spend more time in
the Chamber. The arrangement suited both Turati and Rigola, because it isolated the integralist-dominated Directorate. In addition,
salaries for deputies would make it possible for worker representatives to serve in the Chamber, an important step in the direction
of a labor party. Rigola jumped at the opportunity. He published
the results of a poll favorable to salaries, offered his own plan, and
placed the whole issue on the agenda of an important meeting of
labor federations scheduled for April 1907. Turati also refurbished
the tactic of parliamentary alliances by calling for the "most progressive and enlightened" factions of the bourgeoisie to support the
reform program of organized labor and the Socialist deputies. This
suited the CGL, which was interested in lessening its exclusive dependence on the Party, and further weakened the Directorate.[61]

On 3 April the CGL's executive council requested a meeting of
Extreme Left deputies to discuss joint policies. The CGL hoped to
hammer out a minimum program of reforms it considered especially
urgent. Fully aware of how much the deputies needed its support
in the country, the CGL framed its proposals in a "take it or leave
it" manner. At the meeting the participants agreed to oppose a bill
then before the Chamber because it was prejudiced against the rice
workers; to introduce a measure abolishing night work for bakers;
to establish a committee, headed by Turati, to propose abolition
of night work for women and children; and to campaign for remuneration for deputies. The CGL had demonstrated its power to
such a degree that the integralists denounced Turati for placing the
union's "direct action" above Parliament.[62]

The CGL was now ready to pose the question of independence
from Socialist party control. The union leadership argued that the
CGL must remain above Socialist ideological squabbles and be free
to cooperate with sympathetic parties if it wished to engage in politics to best advantage. The union had been wooing non-Socialist

workers and parties, as demonstrated at the recent meeting. Any
relationship with the Socialist party had to be clearly defined. Moreover, the CGL was unhappy with the Directorate's neutrality toward
the inroads the revolutionary syndicalists were making in the labor
movement. Fausto Pagliari, who had close connections with Turati,
informed the integralists that they must choose either the reformist
concept of gradual elevation of the workers or the "adventuristic
and catastrophic revolutionary method." At the same time, the
CGL's executive committee warned the Party to follow policies more
in line with the desires of the CGL. On 18 June the committee drafted a series of proposals to be placed before the Directorate. The
most important would have required the Directorate to obtain the
consent of the CGL before supporting strikes or other labor agitation.
Taken as a package, they would have established the CGL's exclusive
authority over the labor movement and eliminated Party interference in the confederation's affairs. Rigola stated that the CGL could
no longer accept a junior partnership with the Party. He argued that
the Party included nonproletarians and that the CGL was the only
legitimate representative of the proletariat. Indeed, the secretary-
general intimated that the Party should become an arm of the labor
movement, an idea very clearly expressed by Ivanoe Bonomi in his
Le vie nuove del socialismo. In July the CGL's council strongly endorsed Rigola's positions. It demanded the supreme command of all
future strikes and exhorted "the Party, the Directorate, the newspaper [Avanti!], and the Parliamentary Group" to gear all of their
activities to that of the CGL. If successful, the council's position
would have subordinated the Party to the labor organization, something the Directorate's standing committee duly noted when it rejected the council's claims on 13 August. The standing committee
proposed coordinating the actions of the Party and the CGL and suggested joint meetings of the Directorate, the CGL leadership, representatives of Avanti!, and the Socialist deputies. The meeting was
scheduled for 7 October in Florence.[63]

   The CGL's executive committee announced its objectives in advance of the meeting. It aimed for Party recognition of its predominant role in the labor movement and agreement on a common legislative program. Rigola informed Turati that the purpose of the
Florence meeting was to define the different "spheres of action"
of the Party and the CGL, an objective that had the endorsement
of the reformist leader.[64] The strong criticism of the integralists,
which always accompanied the CGL's declarations, also pleased
Turati. CGL policy, however, tended to relegate the Party to a subordinate role, something Turati either failed to realize or chose to

ignore. The joint meeting, in fact, greatly weakened the Party. The Directorate agreed to one of Rigola's major objectives: using the Party's resources to encourage the formation of national industrial unions under the aegis of the CGL. The Directorate also relinquished to the CGL control over all strikes arising from economic issues and accepted severe restrictions of its own role in political strikes. The Directorate agreed to secure the consent of the CGL before it called any strike for political reasons, thus giving the CGL a de facto veto. Furthermore, the Party pledged to withhold its support from any union that undertook a strike contrary to the orders of the CGL. This allowed the CGL to establish strict discipline over the labor movement. Other arrangements certified the Party's subsidiary role during strikes. In return, the CGL promised to endorse Socialist principles.[65]

The agreement with the Directorate allowed the CGL to continue its policy of taming unruly elements in the labor movement. In 1907 there were a number of bitter strikes punctuated by violence and by demands on the CGL to call general strikes in protest or sympathy. The CGL refused and withdrew all support from rebellious strikers. The Directorate scrupulously adhered to the arrangements that had been worked out at Florence, despite protests from the Party's left wing.[66] The establishment of the CGL's authority was crucial in light of another development—the formation of a corresponding employer's organization that would negotiate directly with the CGL in an effort to guarantee peace on the labor front.[67]

The CGL's hostility toward strikes pleased Turati, whose opinions on the subject coincided with those of the labor leaders.[68] Turati soon discovered, however, that the CGL's success against the Party, which he had supported, had an ironic effect. He always conceived of the Party and the labor movement as equals, but the labor leaders and some reformists of the Right considered the workers' movement to be superior. Turati opposed this as the pernicious revival of *corporativismo*, which he had defeated in 1892. Now the integralists had entered into agreements that, in effect, recognized the auxiliary role of the Party. The labor leaders were satisfied with the existing situation and proved reluctant to alter it.

This reluctance became clear when Turati went on the political initiative and asked the CGL to play a supporting role. When the Chamber reopened at the end of 1907, he called for maximum CGL support for an ambitious legislative reform program.[69] The confederation, unwilling to accept a secondary role but unable to ignore Turati's specific requests, stalled for time, saying that an answer would be given at its congress scheduled for the end of 1908. In

February, however, Turati tried to force the CGL's hand by suggesting the admission of Catholic elements into the Socialist-democratic alliance. He suggested a specific program on which all participants could agree and again advocated the maximum use of CGL resources to build support in the country.[70] Rigola, however, countered that there had been many violations of the workers' right to organize, including arrests, and that the CGL's main objective was defense. The confederation's National Council accepted Rigola's thesis and ordered preparations for a conference on this theme in March. Representatives of all the economic associations and of the democratic political parties would be invited.[71]

Rigola's strategy was aimed at restoring the initiative to the CGL. Not only did the confederation reject Turati's suggestions and focus on a less controversial theme, but by inviting representatives from all parties to attend, it reinforced its autonomy. In fact, Rigola had already had contacts with Republican party leaders, had accepted non-Socialist workers' organizations into the CGL, and had made strong statements in favor of the workers' movement having its own independent political apparatus.[72]

Turati appealed to the CGL to include discussion of a well-defined program for the new elections, and he promised the confederation a major voice. He had hardly made this suggestion, however, when the CGL executive committee set the date of the meeting for 31 March, not enough time to work out the complex program suggested by Turati.[73] Turati complained that it was unreasonable to mobilize deputies, executive organs of the Extreme Left parties, and officials of labor organizations to discuss the defense of workers' rights, which, he maintained, were not being threatened. He again emphasized the importance of working out a program "that could become the platform of a real popular bloc" and tried to persuade Rigola to postpone the meeting until May. In the meantime Turati promised to work closely with the secretary-general on the details of the program.[74]

Rigola's refusal was polite but firm. He argued that the true purpose of the meeting was to deemphasize the general strike, by which the immature Italian workers were too frequently seduced. Agitation for workers' rights was an issue that members of the CGL could understand and would be the starting point of the complex program that Turati wanted and that the next CGL congress would certainly produce.[75] Turati replied curtly that the CGL had arranged for the meeting to have no value whatsoever beyond the theme it had announced. There would be no political agreement with the other popular parties.[76]

Rigola's maneuvers were aimed at preventing any faction of the Socialist party from seizing the political initiative from the CGL. The CGL congress was sovereign and could put together a coalition of the country's democratic forces independently if it wished. Rigola had nothing against Turati's new bloc, but it "had to be born under the aegis of the confederation and as the instrument not only of its economic but of its political hegemony."[77]

Rigola's maneuvers also alerted the integralists to the CGL's real intentions. The Directorate was happy to attend the Rome convention to discuss workers' rights; its great fear was the possible discussion of political issues, an obvious intrusion upon its political space. The Directorate became alarmed when the CGL, in an effort to soothe Turati, said that the participants would begin preliminary consideration of a program along the lines Turati had suggested. The Directorate's standing committee objected to this overt usurpation of the Party's function and claimed a violation of the Florence agreements. The CGL's executive committee concluded that nothing prohibited alliances between the confederation and other parties and accused the Directorate of interference in its affairs. In response, the Directorate denounced the Florence pact.[78]

The inability of the integralists to deal with the CGL had more immediate consequences for them than for the reformists. Overwhelmed by their failures as leaders and deprived of their function as the balance of power by the disappearance of a viable left wing from the Party, they lost their dominant position at the next Party congress.

Little resulted from the convention on behalf of workers' rights, which finally met in April 1908, but it signaled an intensification of the CGL's campaign to establish its political supremacy. When Turati accused the CGL of having a limited vision of the role of the proletariat and focusing solely on economic issues,[79] Pagliari admonished the Party to accept an increasingly subordinate role or the CGL would break off relations. In an interview with *La stampa*, Rigola openly raised the possibility of founding a "labor party" on the English model but backed off when he was accused of "depoliticizing" the workers' movement.[80]

Despite Turati's continuing disagreements with Rigola, the link between them remained strong.[81] They were in agreement on curbing unruly workers and reducing strikes, and hence the unions deemphasized strikes and helped keep the Party on a reformist course, as they did in Germany.[82]

It Italy, however, the unions exercised less control over the workers. Inefficient organization on the local level and high dues produced dissatisfaction.[83] The strike became the focal point of tensions within the labor movement, and frequently the workers struck to protest their leaders' policies. In 1907 a recession touched off serious labor unrest resulting in strikes, despite the CGL's efforts at restraint.[84]

These strikes produced new suggestions for attaining labor peace. The most important of these suggestions was compulsory arbitration, which Turati strongly endorsed, and several collective contracts with no-strike clauses were negotiated by some unions. The Superior Council of Labor drafted legislation along these lines, and the reformists pushed for it.[85] Because these plans required the unions not only to refrain from strikes, but to post deposits as a guarantee against wildcat strikes, the rank and file generally opposed all such initiatives. As a result, the CGL came out against compulsory arbitration, the bill to institute it died, and contracts of this type were not renewed.[86]

The difficulties the CGL encountered in restraining its member organizations made a restructuring of its administrative apparatus necessary at the Congress of Modena in September 1908.[87] Another major concern was political autonomy. A motion before the congress sanctioned political alliances with all parties that did not hamper the class struggle. CGL leaders aimed for complete freedom to negotiate support for workers' benefits without regard to ideological considerations. An amendment restricting agreements to groups that "accepted" the class struggle passed, but the leaders noted that it placed no limits on the CGL because political parties interpreted the class struggle in their own way. They did not wish to block the amendment, which was endorsed by the Turati group. In order to ensure the confederation's autonomy, however, the delegates authorized a national campaign for reforms of the kind Turati had suggested but for which the Party would normally have had primary responsibility.[88]

Although Turati remained uneasy about the CGL's push toward political independence, he needed its support to regain control of the Party apparatus. Because the CGL was fighting off a strong challenge from the revolutionary syndicalists during this period, Turati and Rigola promised each other mutual aid at the Socialist party congress scheduled for Florence on 19 September 1908.[89] In his comments on Modena, Turati overlooked the issue of CGL independence and praised the delegates for steering a precise course between "revolutionary" and "traditionalist" tendencies. He insisted that the Party end the revolutionary syndicalist "perplexity" at its upcoming congress. The revolutionary syndicalists had already seceded from the Party but continued to plague the labor movement. They had recently led a series of bitter strikes and had criticized CGL policy at Modena.[90] The Party's formal excommunication of the revolutionary syndicalists would, therefore, benefit the confederation's leaders, and the reformists could use the measure to rally the Party.

Rigola was determined to defend the CGL's prerogatives despite his pact with Turati. The secretary-general devoted much of his speech at the congress to the general strike, synonymous with revolutionary syndicalism, but he also warned the delegates to elect a Directorate that accepted the CGL's policies. Otherwise, he threatened, the CGL would break off relations with the Party.[91]

If Turati took offense at this tone, he did not show it. For him the workers' movement represented "reality," he said, and the confederation was the greatest force of the organized proletariat. The Party and the CGL had different, but complementary, functions. Difficulties in defining the precise role of each existed and would remain, "but we cannot, if we seriously wish to be Socialist, stand apart from the workers' movement." Turati admitted that the CGL's pragmatism corrected the theoretical quibblings of Socialist intellectuals, but he reaffirmed the Party's guiding role in the class struggle. With the disappearance of revolutionary syndicalism, the dissolution of integralism, and the Party's acceptance of reformist positions, "only socialism remains."[92]

In fact, reformists, labor leaders, and integralists, except for Morgari, agreed on a resolution that formally condemned revolutionary syndicalism and general strikes.[93] It relinquished full control of strikes to the CGL and gave it a substantial voice in determining the Party's policies in elections, Parliament, and municipal governments. The motion also listed a series of reforms to serve as an electoral platform during the national elections of 1909: social legislation, abolition of the grain tariff, reduction of the length of military service, and a progressive income tax. Reflecting concern over the increasingly close relationship with bourgeois reformists, the motion allowed support for non-Socialist candidates only in exceptional cases and instructed Party members to emphasize the "inevitability of class antagonism." This resolution received a majority vote of 18,251. A motion by Morgari gathered 5,957 votes, while the left wing received 5,384; there were 144 abstentions.[94]

Turati's victory at the Congress of Florence prevented the CGL's supremacy. In his assessment of the congress, the reformist leader reaffirmed the Party's directing role in the class struggle.[95] In 1909 and 1910, Rigola, backed by Bissolati, tried to found a "labor party" but discovered that he lacked the support of the rank and file and of some influential labor leaders.[96] In addition, a split developed between Turati and Bissolati on this and other issues, and Bissolati found himself isolated.

E. C. Longobardi, spokesman for the revolutionaries at the Congress of Florence, pointed out the reason for the CGL's ultimate failure: it represented only 7 percent of Italian workers.[97]

CHAPTER VIII

The Reformist Suicide: Turati,
Bissolati, and Salvemini

$\mathbb{A}$FTER A FIVE-YEAR struggle, Turati's doctrines were again official Party policy as a result of the Congress
of Florence. The revolutionaries remaining in the Party could mus-
ter little support, Ferri's influence had vanished, and the revolutionary syndicalists had seceded. The Left had collapsed, and the reformists were more powerful than at any time since 1901. Ironically,
however, the waning of the Left contributed to the dissolution of
the reformist coalition.

The ideological basis for a schism was inherent in Turati's thought.
Rival reformist solutions to such important questions as universal
suffrage, militarism, parliamentarianism, and clericalism emerged,
advocated by persons who freely acknowledged their debt to Turati.
Between 1908 and 1911 a full-blown anti-Turati group that claimed
to make Turati consistent took shape—the "reformists of the Right."
At the same time other dissident reformists fought Turati on these
and other issues.

The Reformists of the Right

The ideological dispute among the reformists began on 1 July 1905,
when the revisionist thinker, Antonio Graziadei, distinguished between revolutionary syndicalism and ordinary or reformist "syndicalism."[1] He equated the latter with the English trade-unionism
Marx had admired. In the "English" model of socialism political
parties were the workers' instruments, whereas in the "German"
model prevalent on the Continent parties dominated the workers.
According to Graziadei, after the Socialists had helped the workers
to become politically conscious, the parties would disappear, leav-

ing the proletariat to conduct its own liberation struggle. The "true" syndicalists were, therefore, the Turatian reformists, that is, the best organizers of the working class, who favored practical English methods of educating the proletariat over the strikes and violence of the revolutionary syndicalists.[2]

Turati disputed Graziadei's thesis. Graziadei's stress on the Party's disappearance likened him to the revolutionary syndicalists, and his emphasis on economic rather than political priorities was a throwback to the *operaismo* of the 1880s, Turati argued.[3] Graziadei protested but confirmed Turati's position by making the same objection the *operaisti* had made in 1892, that the Socialist party was not *"the most appropriate instrument for the political action of the working class."*

Graziadei's arguments revealed an even more serious incompatibility with Turati, his ill-concealed eagerness for class collaboration. This attitude did not coincide with Turati's championship of political alliances, because Turati approved of transitory political agreements among parties for tactical reasons, whereas Graziadei seemingly advocated permanent deals among classes. Graziadei accused Socialists of all persuasions of overemphasizing the maximum program and of considering workers the only productive members of society, although the bourgeoisie was just as productive. He advised the Party to stop attacking the bourgeoisie as the "ruling class" and to foster a greater understanding between workers and entrepreneurs for the general benefit of society. Again, Graziadei cited England, where cooperation produced benefits for everyone.

Turati rejected "class collaboration" on a heroic scale, dismissing it with an ironic commentary to Graziadei's article. "Even the boldest revisionism does not scare us," he wrote; but Graziadei had chosen principles and methods from different schools of thought, ignored their consequences, and pasted them together by playing on words.[4]

Graziadei, however, was not so easily dismissed. Within two years an important group of reformists subscribed to the ideas he had expressed, endorsed their acceptance by the CGL's high command, and issued an ideological statement aimed at making them official Party policy. This faction, the "reformists of the Right," included Leonida Bissolati, Ivanoe Bonomi, and Angiolo Cabrini, who favored the CGL's efforts to found a "labor party."

In 1907 Ivanoe Bonomi issued the group's ideological statement, *Le vie nuove del socialismo*, which tried to make Turati "logical." It bore a laudatory dedication to Anna Kuliscioff, to which Bonomi added Turati's name in a new printing in 1944. *Critica sociale* reproduced part of the book, noting that it was "to a certain extent also ours, and we must not only deal with it but return to it whenever we wish to find or rethink ourselves." Significantly, however, the journal did not comment on it further.[5]

Openly revisionist, Le vie nuove was influenced by Eduard Bernstein and Graziadei. Bonomi cited the radical alterations that had occurred in capitalist society since publication of the Communist Manifesto. Progressive democratization of bourgeois regimes had led to coalition governments that were no longer defense committees for capitalist interests. The demands that Marx believed could be attained only by means of the dictatorship of the proletariat were being implemented through normal political channels in the democratic countries. He granted that this could not happen in politically backward countries such as Germany, where the political intransigence of the German Socialist party was justified. In other countries, Bonomi implied the regular participation of Socialists in cabinets, something Bissolati had already advocated.[6]

Such participation was inevitable because, after a long period of increasingly significant social legislation the European parliaments were confronting the most important problem of the future—the collective organization of labor and the collective resistance by capital to the workers' demands. All over Europe, legislation introducing collective contracts was being drafted (the Superior Council of Labor was in the process of doing this in Italy).[7] Bonomi considered the collective contract especially significant because he interpreted it as the juridical crystallization of the class struggle. It brought legal recognition to the proletariat and would create a body of law suited to the future organization of society. As labor became "collectivized," the workers would make greater demands for which their increased productivity would pay. Eventually, however, society would reach the point of no return, and the bourgeoisie would face the dilemma of halting the progress of the working class or doing away with capitalism. Because Bonomi believed that the first alternative was impossible in a democratic society, the second would prevail. The socialist revolution would thus be the result of gradual conquests by the workers, which, "grown beyond the limits within which . . . many believed they could be contained, will burst the narrow frame of capitalist economy and, expanding, will destroy it."[8]

Bonomi believed that the workers would be in charge of this process. He repeated Graziadei's advocacy of the English model of trade-union supremacy against the German system of Party dominance. The Party could have an auxiliary political role, but the proletariat did not have to rely exclusively on the Socialist party for aid; several parties could represent its interests, as was the case with capitalists. In short, Bonomi also believed in the eventual disappearance of the Socialist party.[9]

Bonomi envisioned the proletariat as a pressure group making requests of a liberal democratic state that had the general interest at heart. He viewed Giolittian Italy as a democratic state evolving in a straight line toward socialism. Moreover, he believed the process to be irreversible. As a result, he had become the first authoritative Socialist leader to repudiate Marxism: The proletariat would come to power, not for any dialectical reason but because it constituted a majority in a democratic society that could never become undemocratic.[10] Bonomi's thesis involved a massive dose of optimism.

The impact of these ideas on Turati, who believed reaction to be inherent in Italian society, was negligible, and he would resist the efforts of the reformists of the Right to woo him. They failed to convince him, Bonomi recalled twenty years later, because he remained a Marxist.[11]

The reformists of the Right presented their ideas as a logical extension of Turati's ideology. Although Turati denied this, the roots of the new movement can be traced to him. There were differences in degree, however, which led to qualitative modifications of his thought. Turati's doctrines were always tempered by reality, but he did not identify reality with the political situation and allow it to alter his basic principles. Thus, divisions between Turati and other reformists occurred on a number of key issues before his friends coalesced into a solid separate group. For example, Bonomi advocated normal Socialist participation in politics with no preconceived ideas about intransigence or joining cabinets. Turati had no theoretical objections, provided conditions were right, but after 1905 he found it difficult to prevent his colleagues from supporting or joining governments at practically every opportunity. Turati had opened a Pandora's box when he successfully justified voting for governments in 1901. Turati's principles had to be applied *con giudizio*, something the different factions found it difficult to do.

Probably the first symptom of serious disagreements among the reformists appeared in December 1904. In that year, a caucus of the Parliamentary Group selected Enrico Ferri as its spokesman to answer the crown's address to the Chamber. Turati fumed because he believed that the reformist majority had chosen Ferri out of fear of the revolutionary syndicalists. When the other deputies agreed with him privately, he boycotted the next meeting of the group, denouncing the cowardice of the reformist deputies for not supporting him and singling out Bissolati for special criticism.[12] Anna

Kuliscioff accused the deputies of exploiting Turati's prestige and urged him to withdraw from the group and publicly announce his reasons for doing so. Indeed, she pressed him to leave politics entirely and devote his efforts to *Critica sociale* and theoretical considerations, a suggestion she often repeated.[13]

In 1906 the reformist deputies quarreled over the question of Socialist policy toward the Sonnino cabinet. The first Sonnino government was an attempt by the Extreme Left and the Right Center to break Giolitti's hold on the Chamber of Deputies. To the deputies who were not part of Giolitti's majority, his system had come to mean one-man domination of Parliament, corruption, electoral fraud in the South, and clerical alliances. In 1906 Giolitti's opponents on all sides of the Chamber, including Turati, combined against him.

Turati still believed Giolitti to be the most effective Italian politician,[14] and he explained his opposition in the Chamber of Deputies in January 1906. He praised Giolitti for his past efforts to grant liberty to the Italian masses but accused him of neglecting reforms that would have given meaning to this freedom. First, Giolitti had renounced divorce; then he gave up on other reforms. His five years in power represented "a great bankruptcy of hopes and expectations." The southern problem had not begun to be solved, despite the adoption of legislation to start irrigation projects, develop electric power, and eliminate malaria. The government nominated official candidates, interfered in elections, and depended upon shady local power brokers for support. Giolitti cited social legislation, but much of it remained a dead letter. The government enforced bad laws and neglected good ones. In Giolitti's area of expertise, fiscal reform, nothing had been done, except to fire those who took it seriously. At the same time the funds needed to finance reforms were going to the armed forces, whose budgets had increased tremendously. Finally, Giolitti deliberately failed to enforce existing anticlerical legislation, thus allowing the Catholics to infiltrate the schools. This failure, Turati said, had led to a resurgence of clericalism and had made the Catholics into a great force in the educational and economic life of the country. In short, Giolitti was responsible for Parliament's "confusion, impatience, political disintegration."[15]

The Catholic issue was a sore point with the Extreme Left during this period. Giolitti had proclaimed state and Church two parallels that would never meet, but strict application of the Law of Guarantees and selective nonenforcement of other legislation set the Catholic hierarchy above ordinary Italian citizens and favored the Catholics in other ways. As a result, the Catholics attained a monopoly over private education, a great influence in public primary education, and an increasingly important role in the economic life of the country. The Extreme Left's concern about the numerous banks the Catholics had founded and the growing number of industrial enterprises in which they were engaged led to an anticlerical campaign and coalition, which, however, had scarce results beyond electing a grand master of the Freemasons as mayor of Rome.[16] In national politics the growing influence of the Catholics was a major factor leading to Socialist support of Sonnino.[17]

Although Turati was not enthusiastic about Sonnino, he agreed to support him to break Giolitti's hold on the Chamber. Turati suggested that the Socialists attach conditions to their aid, specifically a commitment to present a divorce bill, to provide aid for the South, and to appoint the Radical Ettore Sacchi as minister of the interior.[18] Sonnino, however, made few concrete commitments. He favored action to help the South, fiscal and scholastic reforms, and, less clearly, universal suffrage. With regard to the Church, he promised to maintain all the state's rights. Above all, he promised to provide honest government.[19]

This last promise apparently explains the extraordinary wave of enthusiasm for Sonnino that swept the Extreme Left. In 1906 Sonnino became the symbol of probity and ability while Giolitti turned into the purest embodiment of corruption and inefficiency. Sonnino's honesty and supposed technical expertise would open a new era in Italian politics, according to Ivanoe Bonomi, spokesman for the emerging reformists of the Right. Bonomi praised Sonnino as an honest conservative, an eternal "loner," an independent statesman who rose above the crass interests of his class. Sonnino had understood that the old Right of Rudinì had splintered and that Giolitti's flirtation with the Church and his inability to deal with economic problems had left only two viable groups within the Chamber, his own and the Extreme Left. By boldly joining with the Extreme Left, he avoided clerical influence as the leftist parties dissociated themselves from Giolitti. Together the two groups could solve the country's most pressing "technical" problems: government dishonesty, bureaucratic incompetence, postal and railway inefficiency, increasing Church power, high interest payments on the public debt. The coalition would break up after these "neutral" questions had been resolved, leaving a new conservative class and a proletarian-dominated Left to contend for power. Thus, an important legacy of the alliance, according to Bonomi, would be the disappearance of the intermediate political groups, with the resultant simplification of the class struggle. Another benefit would be the greater unity of the Socialist party, which the question of support for Giolitti kept divided. When Turati disagreed with this euphoric assessment, Bonomi accused him of standing aside, "diffident and angry," because of his unreasonable attachment to Giolitti—a view scholars still accept.[20]

As we have seen, Turati supported the Sonnino experiment in order to find an alternative to Giolitti, but he wished to keep Socialist options open. In private he informed Anna Kuliscioff that he favored a Sonnino-Sacchi cabinet. Indeed, his intimate knowledge of the future cabinet's composition, which he described to her, suggests communication between Turati and Sonnino, as does a letter in which Turati described Sonnino's program five days before it was presented in the Chamber.[21] Confronted with Bonomi's unbridled enthusiasm and the knowledge that Bissolati was of the same opinion, Turati attempted to put the situation in perspective.[22] He could not understand his colleagues' excessive enthusiasm for Sonnino. Conditions were not so favorable as they had been in 1901, but the Socialists were already counting their reforms. Sonnino's promises were nice but vague, and the Socialists would be foolish not to remain vigilant.[23]

The Sonnino "experiment" proved more complicated than the deputies expected. In March 1906 the Socialist Parliamentary Group met jointly with the Directorate to discuss the situation because the Directorate opposed voting for Sonnino. Ferri, who strongly supported Sonnino, was in an embarrassing position because of his formerly rigid intransigence. He introduced a motion that prohibited voting for governments but excluded a return to the prior parliamentary equilibrium. Turati objected that if the Socialists opposed the restoration of the previous situation they had to vote for Sonnino, whereupon the deputies decided to wait until Sonnino presented his government to the Chamber.[24]

Sonnino's debut generally pleased the Socialists. His program included tax relief and other measures favoring the South, decentralization, abolition of prior censorship, social legislation, reform of the bureaucracy, the judiciary, the military administration, and the schools, and looked forward to the eventual establishment of a ministry of labor. In addition, his cabinet included the Radical leader Ettore Sacchi and the Republican Edoardo Pantano. Kuliscioff considered this program modest but favorable to the proletariat and small property holders. She believed Sonnino's pledges of honest government and praised him for taking the first step toward civilian control of the military and for challenging the Church.[25]

The revolutionaries, on the other hand, denounced Sonnino's program, initiating action that had serious results for the Socialist party. One immediate effect was the end of the coalition with Ferri, who justified his position by arguing that the intransigent policy adopted at the Congress of Bologna allowed voting for the government *caso per caso*.[26] As this formula by definition allowed favorable votes for individual pieces of legislation while mandating no-confidence votes against cabinets, Ferri's erstwhile revolutionary syndicalist allies objected to his "comical" behavior, and he replaced Turati as *Avanguardia socialista*'s preferred villain.[27] When, at a caucus of the Socialist deputies, Ferri sponsored a motion clearing the way for them to vote for Sonnino, the revolutionaries were even more infuriated and asked the Party sections to repudiate their deputies.[28] At an emergency meeting of left-wing leaders in Milan, the participants endorsed the Directorate's opposition to voting for Sonnino and accused the deputies of violating Party discipline and the instructions of the Congress of Bologna. They requested a special meeting of the Directorate to censure the deputies and to express no confidence in Ferri as editor of *Avanti!*.[29] According to the leftists, the Party had become a powdery collection of sections with a feeble executive on top, a "political expression" that could not control its own representatives. They demanded the complete restructuring of the Party's executive organs.[30]

Despite this accurate analysis, the revolutionaries' attempt to discipline the deputies resulted in further weakening the Directorate. Rather than debate the issue of the "autonomy" of the Parliamentary Group, Ferri's supporters on the Directorate resigned. Because the Directorate had been elected at the Congress of Bologna by a coalition that had included Ferri, his supporters now contended that the Directorate no longer represented a majority of the Party.[31] By implication, the Directorate's decisions were null and void. The Directorate reacted by blasting Ferri and the deputies.[32] The Parliamentary Group, however, counterattacked. According to a statement issued by the deputies, it was useless for the Directorate to claim to interpret policies adopted by congresses because no congress, *past, present, or future*, could infringe upon their right to judge events as they unfolded and to take action as they pleased.[33] For the first time the deputies claimed not only autonomy but independence. Unless the Party curbed the deputies, an observer commented, they would dismantle the Party.[34]

The principles enunciated by the deputies had repercussions on the Parliamentary Group itself. If the group was not subject to any higher authority, individual deputies or factions need not submit to the group. This situation brought about the group's eventual fragmentation and the erosion of an important base of influence for Turati. All the same, he approved of the deputies' declaration of independence and cited pragmatic reasons for doing so.[35]

The fall of Sonnino's cabinet after only a hundred days and the debate over the events that led to the fall caused great animosity between Turati and Bissolati and illustrate the widening rift between the reformists in the Parliamentary Group. On 6 May 1906, police in Turin fired into a crowd of workers, killing one and wounding several. Preparations began for a protest general strike, and although a majority of the Socialist deputies apparently opposed the strike, they failed to agree on a statement when asked their opinion by the labor leaders. As a result, Turati explained in an open letter to his constituents, the unions called the strike. To Anna Kuliscioff, Turati explained that only two deputies had disagreed with his contention that immediate action was necessary to avert a general strike, but the group lacked the courage to oppose Ferri, who favored one.[36] At the next caucus, Turati introduced a formal motion opposing the general strike, calling for reforms, and pledging to work for general elections. The proposal passed by a nine-to-five vote but only served "to make absurdity more absurd and cowardice more cowardly." After having adopted Turati's motion, the group agreed to ask the Chamber to pass a resolution condemning the Turin shootings. If their proposal failed, the Socialists would obstruct proceedings and encourage violence in the streets; and at Ferri's urging, the deputies also agreed to resign en masse.

This turn of events incensed Turati because his motion had affirmed confidence in Sonnino whereas Ferri's did the opposite. The Socialists sabotaged the cabinet they had sponsored just when part of its program stood a chance of passage. Why oppose a general strike and then advocate violence and obstructionism? Turati stormed out of the meeting and resolved not to attend any others.[37]

The group initiated an obstructionist campaign, but it fizzled when the Radicals and Republicans refused to join it. The Socialist deputies thereupon resigned from the Chamber, bringing Sonnino down.[38] Turati went along, but he refused to sign a letter of protest his colleagues sent the president of the Chamber and instead published an open letter criticizing them. Turati directed his full fury at Bissolati, who passively accepted Ferri's demagogy. Kuliscioff agreed with her companion, calling the resignations a "joke" and castigating Bissolati. Bissolati blamed Sonnino for the failure of important reform measures, but Kuliscioff held the Socialists responsible.[39] The Bissolati faction reacted to this criticism through Bonomi, who published an indignant but confused statement accusing Turati of heading a Milanese "workers' elite" and of being soft on revolutionary syndicalism.[40]

Sonnino's failure prepared the way for Giolitti's return, as Turati had already informed his constituents and as Kuliscioff admitted. Indeed, there was no alternative to Giolitti as the Chamber was then constituted.[41] The chances of breaking Giolitti's domination had been slight, and the heterogeneity of the opposition had confirmed the supremacy of the Piedmontese politician. After Sonnino's fall, Giolitti formed the "long ministry," which had the second longest tenure in Italian history. The lesson of the "Hundred Days" was not lost on the Socialist deputies. When Giolitti had been friendly to them they had won significant reforms; the way to achieve others was to cooperate with him. The question was: What form would this cooperation assume, and for which reforms would the deputies trade it? These problems caused more debate and more serious splits.

Salvemini, the South, and Universal Suffrage

The desire of some reformists to cooperate with governments on a regular basis was only one major cause of dissension. The demand of other reformists for universal suffrage as a means of solving the southern question caused another important rift.

The champion of universal suffrage was the historian Gaetano Salvemini. Salvemini charged that the North-South dichotomy permeated the Socialist party, in addition to the rest of Italian society. Unified Italy exploited the South, he said, collecting a higher proportion of taxes there in relation to the region's wealth and appropriating less for schools, railroads, aqueducts, and other public works, but the North-dominated Socialist party ignored Marxist principles and accepted the myth of southern "laziness" as the explanation of the South's backwardness. According to Salvemini, the North and South could not pursue identical policies. The North had attained its political freedom after the 1890s, but the South had not. In consequence, northern Socialists could concentrate on economic and social reforms while southerners had to fight for political liberty. Salvemini attributed the decline of reformism after 1902 to Turati's infatuation with social and economic reforms that were impossible to attain, thus making him vulnerable to the more politics-oriented, South-led left wing.[42]

Salvemini then undertook a general critique of Turati's reformism. Turati failed to recognize the essentially political nexus of the alliances he advocated with the industrial bourgeoisie, which was not interested in social reforms. A comprehensive program of political reform, however, would strengthen the industrial bourgeoisie and gain the support of southerners instead of dividing the Party. It was necessary to turn against Giolitti, however, because he interfered in southern elections. This interference ensured him a majority in the Chamber, which allowed him to defeat the reforms for which Turati hoped.[43]

Salvemini vividly described the stuffing of ballot boxes, the cooperation between police and criminals, and the terrorizing of political opponents in his *Ministro della mala vita*. These tactics, he said, resulted in the South's returning 150 of Giolitti's 250 staunch parliamentary supporters. Giolitti refrained from using these methods in the North because the larger number of voters made such techniques more difficult to apply than in the South, where the literacy requirement excluded most people from voting and where a change of a few hundred ballots could decide an election. In the North, Giolitti tolerated Socialist organizations, appropriated funds for public works in areas where the Extreme Left was strong, and gave government contracts to Socialist cooperatives. As a result, the northerners either ignored government repression in the South, denied it existed, or blamed it on the victims.[44]

In general, Salvemini advocated greater independence for the Party and renunciation of the strictly legalitarian role it had assumed, accepting violence if the masses consciously decided on it. These opinions reflected the desperate conditions in the South and clashed with Turati's pacifism.[45]

Turati viewed the southern question from what he considered an orthodox Marxist perspective. Socialism was supposed to issue from a highly industrialized society. He had written very early that the South would have to await the development of industry before the Socialists could be successful there, and he never changed his mind.[46] He attributed the repression about which Salvemini complained to local political cliques that reflected the backward economic and social conditions of the region. As for universal suffrage, Turati opposed giving illiterates the vote, suggesting at one point that seats in the Chamber be distributed on the basis of the voting population of an area as a means of preventing southern deputies from stopping reforms.[47] He also rejected Salvemini's appeal to focus on "political" reforms because he opposed gearing the action of the country's advanced sections to the needs of the most backward.[48]

Salvemini objected to this passive attitude and stressed the national ramifications of the southern problem. A coalition of southern landowners and northern industrialists controlled the Chamber. The only way to defeat the coalition and clear the way for reforms was to make it difficult for the government to elect so many supporters in the South, and this meant increasing the number of voters through universal suffrage. Abolishing the literacy requirement would bring new groups interested in changing the status quo into politics—for example, emigrants returning from America and members of rural leagues. Happily, Salvemini believed, universal suffrage was the only major reform that stood a chance of being enacted into law, for it had widespread support, cost nothing, and could be easily implemented. He was certain of success if the Socialists concentrated their resources on a campaign for the vote and if the Socialist deputies opposed the government in Parliament. It was time for the Party to agree on one well-defined issued capable of changing the country's fortunes and to stick to it.[49]

As we have seen, Turati objected to concentrating Party resources on universal suffrage for the South, but he also feared that, once given the vote, the southern peasant would cast it for the Catholics. Salvemini objected that in the South the priest was considered a member of the ruling class and that the Catholics would get less support than in the rural areas of the North. The Party might adopt more imaginative policies than denying the rights of the southern peasant because he might come under Catholic influence, he wrote.[50]

Anticlericalism was not the real reason for the Party's lukewarm attitude toward universal suffrage, Salvemini charged; the real reason was the entente between northern Socialists and the industrialists, whose interests Giolitti represented. The Socialists and their constituents profited from the continued exploitation of the South through the tariff, which favored the industrialists and their workers, the backbone of the Socialist party. The tariff kept out foreign manufactured goods, making southern Italy a captive market for expensive northern industrial products and guaranteeing wages and profits for the North. Countries hurt by Italian protectionist policies retaliated against southern agricultural exports. This economic system perpetuated poverty in the South, but the Socialist deputies supported it, despite their theoretical commitment to free trade, because they feared the reaction of their constituents.[51]

When Salvemini's arguments failed to produce any modifications in the Party's policies, he lost faith in the Socialists' professed interest in justice for the South.[52] The Party had lost touch with reality and was not only dead but a ghost—and the Parliamentary Group was "the ghost of a ghost." The old idealism of the Socialists was gone. Party workers cared only about jobs, and the deputies served the special interests of northern workers' elites, not the proletariat. Turati countered weakly that progress would always be uneven.[53]

The debate became more heated, however, when Salvemini released an interview strongly critical of the Parliamentary Group in June 1910. Asked his opinion of the deputies' favorable vote for Luigi Luzzatti, ostensibly because he had promised to enlarge the suffrage, Salvemini cited the pressure of Socialist consumers' and producers' cooperatives in the North. The cooperatives hoped to be rewarded with government contracts, after which the Socialist deputies would give the government a free hand in the South.[54]

The interview earned Salvemini the rebuke of the Socialist deputies, but Salvemini argued that the well-organized cooperatives of the North elected a compact group of deputies who looked after their interests within the Socialist Parliamentary Group and the Chamber. Because southern workers had no representation, the deputies defended not the "proletariat" but a workers' elite. No government could ignore such powerful groups; it contented them by awarding lucrative contracts and by favoring social legislation benefiting northern industrial workers. The northerners thus accepted the lion's share of public works funds and supported the government even if it repressed the South, accusing workers who did not share in the benefits of being politically "immature" for criticizing cabinets friendly to the "proletariat." Salvemini branded the Socialist deputies the main culprits in this process. They forced the poorest part of the working class to subsidize the richest, killed Socialist idealism by emphasizing "practical" results that favored the workers' elites, and compromised the general interests of the proletariat.[55]

The reformists of the Right were the main object of this attack, since they were most anxious to cooperate with the government and championed the interests of organized labor. Bissolati indignantly denied Salvemini's thesis, calling the cooperatives an integral part of a democratic resistance movement. The Socialist deputy was a "product and exponent" of the whole proletariat, not certain parts of it. Northern Socialists had initiated campaigns for reforms that would primarily benefit the South, Bissolati insisted, citing the agitation for universal suffrage then taking place in the country. This concern for the South had also prompted the deputies to vote for Luzzatti, who sincerely wished to expand the suffrage. Although it was true that social legislation had its major application in industry, this was because of the special problems that arose with industrialization. The Party, however, was studying its possible application in the South. Bissolati admitted the special problems the tariff raised but refused to endorse free trade, even though this violated Socialist principles, because the deputies had to study any immediate practical effects of such a policy on the masses.[56]

Bissolati chose to interpret Salvemini's criticisms very narrowly. He failed to rebut Salvemini's points on the tariff, and his reply on social legislation was unsatisfactory. Finally, the Socialists were conducting a campaign for universal suffrage, but, as we shall see, it was the least they could do. In fact, Bissolati (at this time) and Turati had serious doubts about universal suffrage and accepted a Luzzatti compromise that Salvemini considered worthless.

Turati's position on the South was more complex than Bissolati's. The government, Turati agreed, "always cultivated the political and social *cammore* in the South, instead of weakening them, to win support against the modern consciousness of North and Central Italy." Because the North had always treated the South as a conquered territory, it had toward that depressed region a special obligation that could be fulfilled by tapping the economic resources of the North. Only technically skilled northerners operating within the ambit of a democratic government could alter these economic conditions, and this alone could break the power of the old ruling classes in the South.[57] Turati offered this solution in 1900, when he assumed the rapid increase of democratic representation in the legislature, but he illogically clung to it when this failed to occur. To Salvemini, however, Turati's suggestions smacked of paternalism.[58]

Although Turati remained cool toward Salvemini's campaign for universal suffrage, he did make concessions. In 1905 the *Gruppi socialisti milanesi* passed a Turati motion endorsing universal suffrage for the South as an important goal. Turati understood that the Socialists must support agitation on behalf of universal suffrage, but he expressed his reservations clearly. He disapproved of the excessive enthusiasm generated around the question. In Italy, the Socialists expected increased liberty and reforms as the natural consequences of universal suffrage, whereas it had been the other way around in other countries.[59]

After 1905 Turati seemed even less convinced of the usefulness of universal suffrage. Kuliscioff believed that the ballot would cause "half a revolution" in the South, but Turati dismissed her contention. The southern problem was historical, not political, he said. For example, the Socialists had offered the southerners aid, but they had not demonstrated any interest. To change his mind on the historical causes of the southern problem would mean to renounce his gradualist beliefs. Socialist gradualism had even greater validity in the South than in the North:

> To me it seems difficult to propose universal suffrage when it is generally admitted, even by Socialists, . . . that even the present system is too advanced for the South. It is necessary to treat the region as the British treat their colonies, i.e., to concede a "semiconstitution," which gradually becomes more comprehensive as people learn to apply it.[60]

Kuliscioff strongly disagreed with Turati. Whereas Turati believed that the Party was doing the best it could, Kuliscioff believed that Salvemini was correct about the North-South dichotomy in the Socialist party and that it was inappropriate to apply the same methods to both regions. Turati's tactics perpetuated the existing situation in the South, whereas revolt and violence offered the only hope for change. She favored the foundation by Salvemini of a revolutionary Socialist organization that would operate exclusively in the South.[61]

Turati preferred a more "reformist" alternative to the southern problem. Along with the Neapolitan Socialist, Ettore Ciccotti, Turati cosponsored a plan for obligatory voting. According to this idea, at age twenty-one, men would be called up to vote in the same way they were summoned for military service. Illiteracy would be considered a temporary disability to be corrected at special state-run schools. This would remedy what Turati considered a major drawback to giving illiterates the vote, namely, the removal of an important educational incentive for the lower classes. "Electoral conscription" would improve the proletariat's cultural level, thus decreasing the Church's influence, increasing the turnout in elections, and making universal suffrage a reality within a few years. Few people accepted these ideas, and a bill embodying them received little support in the Chamber.[62]

Faced with increasing evidence of Salvemini's appropriation of the issue, Turati again endorsed universal suffrage in August 1908, but his ideas on the subject seemed to have changed little. In September 1909, he again made a case for economic reforms over universal suffrage, which he called the "least suitable" measure for priority action.[63]

As time went on, however, Turati's position became less tenable even among the reformists. Bissolati and Bonomi endorsed universal suffrage because it bolstered their hopes for closer cooperation with Giolitti. Kuliscioff broadened the discussion to include women, and when Turati contradicted her the debate hit the front pages of Critica sociale.[64] Other members of Turati's inner circle succumbed to the enthusiasm generated by Salvemini. Treves, for instance, advocated convening the 1910 national congress ahead of time to debate the issue. Turati blocked the attempt, but the Directorate did initiate a campaign in favor of the South. Turati served on the coordinating committee, but the effort encountered many difficulties.[65] He still resisted making universal suffrage the focus of Party action, and when a close ally of Salvemini, Turati's friend, Giuseppe Emanuele Modigliani, attempted to do so, Turati opposed him. Anna Kuliscioff continued her efforts to change his mind, but universal suffrage "won't work, won't work, won't work," Turati answered her, "especially in the South, for which it was created and brought into the world."[66]

By July 1910, however, there appeared signs of a softening in Turati's attitude toward universal suffrage, which he perhaps began to consider a prerequisite for other reforms. Unfortunately, as so often in the past, the transition from theory to action was difficult. Most of the Parliamentary Group by now was clamoring for universal suffrage, but few deputies were willing to put in the time a strenuous campaign required.[67]

In October of 1910 universal suffrage was thoroughly debated at the Socialist party congress held in Milan. Salvemini delivered a long, hard-hitting speech in which he amplified his ideas on the subject. He blamed the deputies for failing to generate national enthusiasm for universal suffrage, saying that northern workers had no idea of the plight of the South and pressed only for measures that benefited themselves. The Party had not fulfilled its duty to help the South, which he had counseled to be patient until the northerners gained enough strength to practice what they preached. "Instead," Salvemini concluded, "as you grow stronger, your indifference and selfishness grow."[68]

The Party, Turati conceded, should pay more attention to the South, but it should continue to concentrate its efforts on the industrial workers, the advance guard of socialism. This was a Marxist tenet to which the Party must adhere, or else it would become a philanthropic institution. Turati attributed the failure to achieve major reforms, including universal suffrage, to a general collapse of the local organizations, something the deputies could not control. The Party should revitalize the local sections so it could mobilize the masses behind the initiatives of the Parliamentary Group.[69]

Having reiterated his position, Turati made an effort to incorporate Salvemini's ideas into his resolution. Responding to Salvemini's accusation that the northern Socialists upheld only the special interests of their region, Turati's motion committed the Party to consider the requirements of the regional organizations in terms of the general interests of the proletariat. The Party was "not to damage or retard the major reforms necessary for the political and economic awakening of the class consciousness" of the South. According to Turati's resolution, the Party's action would revolve around four aims: universal suffrage for both sexes and proportional representation; an end to increasing military expenditures; more funds for education; social legislation. Furthermore, although Turati's motion preserved the local autonomy of the sections, it went very far

in endorsing the political intransigence Salvemini favored. Turati
warned against the dangers of political "blocs," which created illusions, adulterated the class struggle, and gave the Directorate veto
power over political alliances. Turati thus asked the national congress to sanction the political intransigence he had recently instituted in Milan.[70]

Salvemini appreciated Turati's gestures but did not vote for his
motion. He distrusted the Bissolati faction and disagreed with the
motion's full confidence in the Parliamentary Group. Salvemini endorsed a motion by Modigliani which split the reformist vote. The
result of the voting was: Turati, 13,006; Modigliani, 4,547; Lazzari
(revolutionary), 5,928; abstaining, 932.[71]

Socialists and Governments

Salvemini distrusted the reformists of the Right because they exploited the suffrage issue to argue in favor of Socialist participation
in governments, which both Salvemini and Turati opposed. Indeed,
Turati kept his fellow reformists from becoming part of the government only with great difficulty.

In April 1910 the Socialist deputies overrode Turati's opposition
to voting for the new Luzzatti government. Turati had moved toward intransigence in 1909, but Luzzatti's promise to enlarge the
suffrage had aroused the sympathy of a majority of the Gruppo parlamentare. Turati managed only to preface the Socialist deputies'
positive vote with a very critical declaration in which he expressed
skepticism about the probabilities of obtaining significant reforms
and made clear his own hostility.[72]

Socialist endorsement of yet another cabinet angered many Socialists, including Kuliscioff. She scolded Turati and refused to be
placated by his own opposition to the maneuver. Bissolati had been
the prime mover behind the vote for Luzzatti, and she accused
Turati of having reacted too mildly against his friend for fear of a
split with the reformists of the Right. They quarreled over this issue
until the end of Luzzatti's term.[73]

Dissension among the reformists increased as the relationship
between the Socialists and Luzzatti proved unsatisfactory. Turati
continually complained about Luzzatti, and the Directorate was
cool, although it could do little but complain and defer to the
"autonomy" of the deputies.[74] In December 1910 Treves tried to
bring the Socialist deputies into opposition, but, surprisingly, Turati
blocked the attempt. A declaration of no confidence, he believed,
would provide Luzzatti with an excuse to renege on his promises.
Turati made a final effort to reach an accommodation with Luz-

zatti, but the understanding quickly fell apart. At this point, Turati publicly attacked the cabinet, much to Kuliscioff's satisfaction. In January 1911, Turati led the Socialists into opposition, and Kuliscioff expressed the hope that they would remain there for a while.[75]

At the same time Salvemini vigorously objected to the manner in which the reformists of the Right exploited the franchise to elicit support for governments. In a series of blistering attacks published in Treves's *Avanti!* and Turati's *Critica*, Salvemini demonstrated how Luzzatti's proposed reform prostituted Socialist ideas for automatic registration and obligatory voting, ignored the basic issue of illiteracy, and was not a step toward universal suffrage. Because illiterates would still be ineligible to vote, the bill would have no impact in the South, for which it was supposedly designed. Salvemini dismissed Bissolati's contention that Luzzatti's reform would increase the number of voters by 2 million, and he was particularly incensed with Bonomi, whom he accused of deliberately distorting the facts in Luzzatti's favor. Salvemini published a savage attack on Bonomi in the *Critica*, denouncing him for suggesting that only organized workers in the North could appreciate the right to vote. The reformists of the Right would accept anything, Salvemini wrote, provided it was not universal suffrage.[76]

Despite the hard attitude that Salvemini and Turati adopted toward the reformists of the Right, there was no rapprochement between them. Turati remained closely linked to the companions of his youth and, furthermore, opposed Salvemini's suggestions for aggressive action by the Party on behalf of universal suffrage. Salvemini wished him to mount an all-out political offensive, including complete intransigence in the Chamber, an exposition of illegal government methods in the South, and a vigorous educational campaign to explain why present political conditions rendered reforms impossible. Because Socialist representation was miniscule compared with the Party's real strength, the struggle must be fought in the country, with the Socialist deputies preventing the Chamber from functioning and coordinating their obstruction with general strikes and "insurrectional disorder" in the piazzas. The Socialists should refuse to settle for anything less than universal suffrage, a clear demand that would allow them to win national support and resist the government. They would win, Salvemini predicted, because the government majority lacked principles and would break under pressure.[77]

Turati responded by criticizing the southerner for his dogmatism and intransigence, which distorted reality and damaged his own effectiveness. Salvemini exaggerated the probable results of universal suffrage, Turati maintained, and argued as if the reform would have cataclysmic effects. His denunciation of compromise and advocacy of insurrection rested upon two invalid assumptions: a revolutionary situation in the country and a monolithic bourgeoisie. Gradual improvement of the South was the only certain course, and this meant making compromises and ensuring greater coordination between Socialist deputies and Party organizations. Turati accused Salvemini of having lost his sense of balance. Besides his philosophical objections to violence, Turati said, he had little faith in the Socialist organizations' ability to undertake the combat Salvemini advocated.[78]

Rebuffed by the Party, Salvemini left the organization in 1911, thus further weakening the reformists' position. In 1902 Turati had written that, if Salvemini was right, "socialism of the North and socialism of the South, incapable of understanding each other, must follow different roads."[79] Almost forty years later, ironically, Salvemini reached conclusions on the southern question that were close to Turati's, namely, that the historical factor was paramount, that lack of natural resources seriously limited the region's potential, that universal suffrage was not a panacea, and that gradual improvement was the only course possible.[80]

Another ironic aspect of Salvemini's exit was the usurpation of the universal suffrage issue by the reformists of the Right. They continued to use the debate over the franchise as a tool to encourage Socialist participation in cabinets. Their support of Luzzatti had backfired, but Giolitti was a different matter because he offered universal suffrage rather than timid extension of the franchise. Salvemini could object to this only on procedural grounds—receiving universal suffrage as government largesse—and because the person he had denounced as the worst of the corrupt oppressors of the South would taint the reform.[81]

In March 1911, during the discussion of Luzzatti's bill to enlarge the franchise, Giolitti announced his intention to support universal suffrage, whereupon the Radicals withdrew from the cabinet and forced its resignation. Giolitti supported Luzzatti, Turati commented, "like the rope that holds the hanged man." Actually, Luzzatti had never had a majority of his own but had been brought in to solve the thorny problem of the maritime conventions.[82] Turati called the Luzzatti experience a joke.[83] From Turati's correspondence it appears that Giolitti had left the political scene in 1909 in order to loosen his ties with the Right and to return in two years oriented toward the Left, which had demonstrated renewed vigor in the elections of that year. Already in 1910 Bissolati expected Giolitti to offer the Socialists some positions in his next government.[84] Indeed, in early 1910 a periodical published the results of a survey of

Socialist leaders on the question of joining cabinets, which revealed the Party's tolerant attitude toward availability of Socialists for government coalitions.[85] Giolitti would attempt to entice Bissolati or one of his friends into his cabinet using universal suffrage as bait, Kuliscioff predicted immediately upon Luzzatti's fall.[86]

Turati chided her for jumping to conclusions, but no sooner had he mailed the letter than he was writing to confirm her prediction. His letter, marked "extremely confidential," informed Kuliscioff that Giolitti had called Bissolati to his office for negotiations. If several Socialists would enter his cabinet, Giolitti promised to press for quasiuniversal suffrage—the vote for all males over twenty-one who had completed elementary school, who had served in the army, or who were over thirty, regardless of literacy. Giolitti also informed Bissolati of his plan to institute pensions for workers, which would be funded by nationalizing the life insurance industry. Bissolati asked about the status of the military budget and what attitude Giolitti intended to take toward the Church, both hotly debated issues among the Socialists. Giolitti responded that the program he had outlined would force dissolution of the Chamber and would be impossible to implement without Socialist aid; prudence dictated caution on other issues. There is no indication that a colonial war was mentioned. Bissolati asked why Giolitti had not consulted Turati, rather than himself, and Giolitti said Bissolati was a more appropriate choice.[87]

Soon after the talk, Giolitti arranged a meeting between Bissolati and the king, who accepted "with pleasure." On 23 March Bissolati paid a visit to the monarch dressed in a gray suit and wearing a soft hat because, as he explained, he did not possess formal dress. Bissolati was the first leader of the Socialist party openly to consult with the king, and an uproar followed, notwithstanding the Socialist's informal dress.[88] Rumors circulated that Bissolati had succeeded in overcoming Turati's opposition to Socialist participation in the new cabinet and that the Milanese leader would also confer with the king, but these rumors were false. Bissolati had not consulted with Turati before the audience, dramatic evidence of the deteriorating relationship between the two men.[89]

As usual, Turati had no theoretical objection to participation in cabinets; he simply distrusted Giolitti. Giolitti wanted some individual Socialists in his cabinet, Turati believed, not sponsors of an organic reform program. Bissolati was the only leader of stature willing to accept this condition. Of course Bissolati's interpretation was different: he favored joining the cabinet in order to obtain universal suffrage. According to Giolitti, his program had Bissolati's complete approbation.[90]

Turati dissuaded Bissolati from accepting Giolitti's proposal only with great difficulty. There was no valid reason for Bissolati to associate himself with the government, because the Party could not profit any more from such a dangerous step than it already had, Turati argued. Giolitti could not back out of his commitment to universal suffrage and had acknowledged the maturity of the Socialists. Bissolati objected that the Extreme Left wished him to join the cabinet, but Turati countered that at least part of it would vote against him. This last piece of information, Bissolati later admitted, forced him to change his mind.[91] When Turati telephoned him to learn his decision, Bissolati promised to turn Giolitti down, and Turati suggested he mention serious programmatic impediments as the reason for his refusal. Bissolati, however, cited purely personal reasons, praised Giolitti's program, and pledged his full support. Turati, infuriated, judged the letter more of an acceptance than a refusal, but, mercifully, Giolitti did not publish it, despite Bissolati's invitation to do so.[92]

Anna Kuliscioff's reaction to the whole affair was quite different from that of Turati, who wished to preserve Party unity at all costs. She saw Bissolati as the leader of a de facto party within the Party. The differences between Bissolati and Turati were irreconcilable, she believed. It would therefore be more sensible to encourage Bissolati and his friends to join the government and to form their own organization separate from the Socialist party. If Bissolati could infuse the government with his own democratic ideals, honesty, and efficiency, the Socialists would profit. With Bissolati defending democratic institutions, a "liberated" Socialist party could direct its full attention to helping the proletariat.[93]

Kuliscioff's chances of convincing Turati to cut himself off voluntarily from Bissolati were slim, and, as we have seen, he talked Bissolati out of joining Giolitti. In the *Critica*, however, Turati criticized Bissolati for consulting with the king, presenting him as a symbol of the doubts that afflicted the Socialist party, but he opposed the call for a special Socialist congress that came in response to Bissolati's actions.[94] The political attitudes of the reformists of the Right, the mounting debate over military expenses, and the imminent outbreak of the Libyan War had stimulated an alarming revival of the left wing. The Socialist deputies' failure to censure Bissolati and their vigorous support of Giolitti's new government further encouraged the growth of the Left.[95]

By 1911 the reformists of the Right had achieved the consistency of a separate organization. In 1909 Graziadei and Bonomi had launched a new campaign to win converts, predicting the imminent demise of the Socialist party and the takeover of its political func-

tion by organized labor.[96] Bissolati made the same arguments at the
national congress in 1910, comparing the Party to the dying branch
of a tree, which, having fulfilled its function, would shrivel and
make way for new shoots.[97] It is true that the reformists of the Right
had already lost this battle because the CGL had backed away from
its idea of a separate "labor party,"[98] but this ideological split remained serious, as did the divergence on more practical issues, such
as power sharing, military expenses, and foreign affairs. Turati, however, formally refused to recognize the existence of the reformists
of the Right as a faction.[99] Sentimentalism accounted for Turati's
reluctance to confront the situation. Events, however, would soon
force him to take a stand against his old friends, no matter how
painful this confrontation would be.

CHAPTER IX

War and Revolutionaries: The End of Party Unity

T̲HE ISSUES DIVIDING the reformists probably would not have produced a definitive break between Turati and Bissolati had it not been for the debate over escalating military expenses and the Libyan War. As the reformist leaders quarreled, Italy attacked Turkey and seized its North African possession. Internal divisions reduced the capacity of the Party to prevent this action, and the Party's weakness contrasted unfavorably with the Nationalists' energy in mobilizing public opinion in favor of the war. Given Italian socialism's strong antimilitarist tradition, it is not surprising that the Party membership attacked its reformist leadership.

The Debate over Military Expenses and Foreign Policy

Traditional opposition to Italian military expenses within the Socialist party ranged from complete refusal to sanction them—"Né un uomo, né un soldo"—to reformist desires to proportion them to the country's wealth. To proportion them meant to limit the army to a strictly defensive role and to renounce all expansionistic dreams. Turati rejected automatic opposition to all military appropriations because such a stand would deprive the Socialists of all influence in foreign affairs. Kuliscioff had a clearer policy; she advised the Socialist deputies to formulate specific guidelines on the containment of future appropriations and to agree upon a figure beyond which they would not go. The armed forces could not be allowed to consume a large percentage of the country's meager wealth, leaving nothing to finance urgent domestic reforms. She advocated a campaign to explain this position to the nation, and Turati carried

the theme to the Chamber and the *Critica*. Until 1908 the Bissolati
faction generally agreed with this view. In June of that year, for
example, Bissolati himself was the spokesman for the Socialist deputies in opposing an extraordinary appropriation of 223 million lire
for the army.[1] This occasion was the last time Bissolati and Turati
substantially agreed on this issue.

A change in Bissolati's views had been germinating for a number
of years. At least since 1905 Bissolati had begun to doubt the classic
Socialist disbelief in the possibility of big wars, supposedly made
unlikely because of the overwhelmingly peasant and proletarian
composition of all belligerent armies. In May of 1905, Austrian and
Italian Socialists had met at a "summit" conference in Trieste to
discuss mutual problems.[2] Bissolati pledged Italian Socialist resistance to "militaristic bourgeois irredentism," while Viktor Adler
promised to support autonomy for the Italian-speaking areas of the
empire and to oppose Austrian expansion in the Balkans. The Socialist leaders failed, however, to reach an understanding on a practical
response to a declaration of war by either country. The Italians
promised to call an immediate general strike and to sabotage mobilization, but their Austrian colleagues refused to undertake a similar
commitment. The Italians thereupon withdrew their pledge.[3]

Although the Turatians emphasized the convention's positive aspects, Bissolati was disturbed at the outcome and attempted to reduce the likelihood of a war he suspected the Socialists could not
prevent. In the Chamber of Deputies on 15 December 1906, he
spoke in favor of a direct understanding between Italy and the dual
monarchy. Because public opinion would never permit Italy to fight
on the side of the Austro-Germans, the Italian government should
strive to replace the Triple Alliance with a bilateral agreement.[4]

In the meantime, relations between Italy and Austria hit new
lows, as did Bissolati's confidence in international Socialist solidarity. In September 1908, a diplomatic crisis arose over Austria's annexation of Bosnia and Herzegovina. In the wake of this affair, about
a thousand Austrian students at the University of Vienna attacked
Italian-speaking students demonstrating for an Italian university at
Trieste, killing two of them. Bissolati denounced the inaction of
the Austrian Socialists, citing their failure to oppose their government's policies as proof that Italian Socialists placed too much faith
in internationalism.[5] At the end of the year an earthquake destroyed
Messina and killed an estimated 100,000 people. The chief of the
Austrian General Staff and newspapers with government connections advocated attacking Italy while the nation was preoccupied
with the disaster. Bissolati replied in a violent article denouncing

the "Austrian jackals."[6] It was clear that he no longer believed in the traditional reformist foreign policy assumptions.

The result was a clash with Turati. The Milanese leader accused the Italian government of exploiting the Bosnia-Herzegovina affair to increase military spending. He cited this issue as one on which all reformists could unite and called upon them to organize a national campaign to fight the proposed increments.[7] Bissolati's response came in the form of a comment appended to an article in *Avanti!* which asked whether it was legitimate for the proletariat to defend the Fatherland. Bissolati argued in the affirmative, claiming that the poor showing of the Austrian Socialists during the Bosnian crisis disproved Socialist theories on the likelihood of war. Far from opposing the expenditures, as Turati suggested, the proletariat should favor them to protect its stake in the survival of the state. Bissolati then criticized the Party's "best brains," who made demagogic appeals to resist further spending.[8]

Stunned by Bissolati's reaction, Turati wrote an open letter asking him to state his views clearly. All Socialists agreed on the necessity of resisting attack, Turati maintained, but the Party did not believe the government's requests for new funds was justified. Turati was mistaken if he believed in the willingness of Socialists to defend the nation, Bissolati replied. He also dismissed Turati's hopes that Italy would pursue a foreign policy proportionate to its economic strength, because Italians would never accept a role similar to that of Belgium, Switzerland, or Holland. In short, for Bissolati defense had become more important than reforms because reforms were useless without independence.[9] Turati concluded that Bissolati condoned the spending of vast sums for defense. Later he would recall Bissolati's change in attitude as the "first sign of the disappearance of Socialist sentiment" among his friends.[10]

Turati was fighting a losing battle against his old friend. The Extreme Left supported Bissolati, generally recognized as the Party's foreign policy expert, and apparently believed that Turati lacked technical expertise on the subject. The prestigious *Corriere della sera* made this argument, and Kuliscioff reported that similar doubts existed among many persons who otherwise sympathized with his thesis. This contention seems unjustified, given the obstacles to anyone outside the government gaining access to critical military information, as Kuliscioff admitted.[11] Turati made few converts because his moderate ideas on foreign policy and military expenses were unpalatable to most Italians.

For reasons completely unrelated to Socialist theory, Turati did not sense the imminent threat to the Fatherland that concerned

Bissolati and the government. No one threatened vital Italian interests, Turati believed, and the country could stay out of any conflict if it renounced its expansionist aims. Even the Triple Alliance placed only limited obligations on the nation.[12] If a European war broke out, Italy's geographical location would allow the country to remain neutral. "I believe," Turati wrote, "that the risks of war and invasion stem from our own participation in intrigues, plots, or alliances that expose us to reprisals which are directly proportional to this participation." If Italy chose to withdraw from the arms race then taking place, the country would be strengthened because the savings could be applied to domestic reforms, which would create a society people would defend. Turati believed that increases in the military budget were suicidal. In relation to its wealth, Italy already spent more on arms than any other great power, taxed its people more heavily than any other country in Europe, and was still unable to keep up. The army provided a safeguard only against internal revolution. Its police role and policy of social discrimination assured its defeat in case of war but made impossible the reforms that were the best defense against internal violence and foreign attack. Turati recommended tailoring foreign policy objectives to the country's economic potential, abandoning claims to the irredenta, and renouncing colonial pretensions.[13]

Given the military-industrial-political context of the times, Turati's views were idealistic. Italian statesmen and industrialists embarked upon an adventurous foreign policy during the early twentieth century, encouraging economic penetration in the Balkans, Turkey, and North Africa. Massive arms expenditures favored heavy industry and other sectors of the economy that resisted curtailment of the military budget. Modern scholarship confirms Turati's views and demonstrates that his warnings of external and domestic disaster were hardly exaggerated.[14]

For a brief moment it seemed that on these issues there could be a rapprochement between the reformists of the Right and the Left. In June 1909, Bissolati voted with Turati against another government request for funds and advocated a policy of neutrality. Bissolati, however, was motivated by fear of being labeled a "militarist" and by his objection to renewal of the Triple Alliance. Indeed, a caucus held before the vote disclosed the existence of three factions among the eleven Socialist deputies present, a state of affairs that encouraged government arrogance.[15]

The fractures among the reformists, which had become obvious in 1909, worsened during the next two years. In June 1911, scarcely three months before the Libyan War, Bissolati flatly refused to join the other Socialist deputies in voting against further military appropriations. His political allies Bonomi and Cabrini openly defended the government, and the whole faction refused to attend a session of the Chamber at which the rest of the Gruppo opposed the government's request.[16]

The divisions among the reformists, therefore, were already very serious before the Libyan War definitively split them by driving Turati further from Giolitti, and Bissolati closer to him.

With the imminent dispatch of Italian troops to Libya in September 1911, the Socialists responded to grass-roots pressure for a general strike.[17] The CGL's Executive Council asked the union's executive committee, the Socialist party Directorate, and the Parliamentary Group to set the date, and after considerable wrangling, the Gruppo approved a twenty-four-hour strike, as recommended by the CGL.[18] Then Turati touched off a serious altercation by attempting to have the deputies issue a strong condemnation of Giolitti, accusing the government of "betrayal." This word offended the sensibilities of most deputies, and when Turati resisted attempts to delete it from his motion, a majority voted against him, thus refusing to take a strong stand against the cabinet.[19]

These divisions reduced the Party to impotence. Giolitti wired the king: "In my opinion, Socialist movement of no importance. Many favor undertaking. This morning [Salvatore] Barzilai told me Republicans disapprove Socialist attitude [on the general strike] and will not cause embarrassment."[20]

Turati felt betrayed not only by Giolitti but by Bissolati. The war confirmed the misgivings he had had about Giolitti during the negotiations for his most recent ministry. Turati accused Giolitti of using universal suffrage and workers' pensions as bait to trick the Socialists into supporting a war he had planned all along.[21] In a series of sharp articles Turati destroyed the moral and strategic basis for the government's action in Libya. Furthermore, he severely criticized Bissolati and his allies for condoning the war and pledged to continue his opposition to the conflict. To Kuliscioff he wrote that the cabinet should be shot for high treason.[22]

Turati's antiwar position provoked a violent backlash, and it required considerable courage to stand firm. Demonstrations against the Socialists took place in Rome, Milan, and other cities, a mob attacked the offices of Treves's *Avanti!* in an attempt to stop the newspaper's antiwar campaign, and a crowd threatened Turati in a Rome restaurant. Turati accused Bissolati of condoning the demonstrations against him.[23]

Turati's charge illustrates how rapidly relations between Turati and the reformists of the Right had deteriorated. Bissolati pointedly used the "bourgeois" press to make a case for Socialist support of the war effort. Taking care to cite only strategic reasons, Bissolati argued that the government should not have invaded Libya because the conflict would weaken Italy's position in the Balkans, but once war had erupted the Socialists could not protest idefinitely.[24] Continued opposition would render them incapable of helping Giolitti resist the demands for a wider war made by the fanatic Nationalists.[25] Bonomi also rejected Turati's arguments against Giolitti and hinted that the question of joining the cabinet was still open for the reformists of the Right. Invited by Turati to explain himself, Bonomi asserted that Italy had been forced to occupy Tripoli for international reasons Giolitti could not discuss publicly. The Socialists were obliged to help Giolitti achieve his limited war aims against increasing pressure to expand the conflict. Bonomi could not understand how Turati, the major architect of the alliance with Giolitti, could turn against it and leave Giolitti to the mercy of the conservatives. In an ironic commentary, Turati explained that the Socialists had supported Giolitti because he promised reforms, and now he wanted them to endorse a colonial war; that was too high a price to pay.[26]

Ironically, Giolitti's liberal program and the unswerving support of the reformists of the Right for Giolitti himself probably contributed to the war's outbreak. Such conservatives as Luigi Albertini, editor of the *Corriere della sera*, feared Giolitti's overtures to the Estrema, his reforms, and the offer of a cabinet position to Bissolati.[27] The *Corriere* represented powerful industrial interests, and according to Giolitti's confidant, Gaetano Natale, the "conservative currents were mortified and isolated" by Giolitti's program. Natale states that the Piedmontese statesman's program was influenced by Bissolati and Salvatore Barzilai, the Republican leader. The "substantially social democratic" Giolitti government of 1911, Natale maintains, struck terror into the hearts of conservatives, who then encouraged the war, hoping that a Socialist reaction would break the entente between Giolitti and Bissolati.[28] Albertini charged one of his best reporters to write a series of articles explaining "the political economic and moral reasons why Italy must occupy Libya" in order to inflame public opinion before the season favorable to a military campaign closed.[29] The *Corriere* also assailed Turati on the war and praised Bissolati and Bonomi.[30]

In addition to the *Corriere*, the Nationalist Association also pressed for war.[31] The Nationalists projected the Marxist class struggle onto the international plane, with Italy leading the "proletarian" nations in a revolutionary war against their capitalist counterparts.[32] In 1911 the Nationalists began a major propaganda campaign for

war by presenting Libya as the promised land and by vilifying Giolitti's domestic and foreign policies. The economic activities of the
Banca Romana in Libya and the institution's Vatican connections
also were important causes of the war. The Libyan conflict apparently sealed the alliance between Giolitti and the Church as Socialist
influence declined.[33]

Groups on the Left also supported the war. Oddino Morgari, for
example, cited Italy's "civilizing" mission in Libya, while Guido
Podrecca believed that the Italian proletariat would benefit in a
variety of ways.[34] Arturo Labriola's position was practically indistinguishable from that of the Nationalists.[35] The reformists of the
Right gave Giolitti even more support as the war continued.[36]

Turati's strong antiwar and antigovernment stance therefore made
a rapprochement with Bissolati impossible, a point Kuliscioff understood but Turati avoided. Despite growing militance on his left and
the erosion of his own position due to his continued identification
with Bissolati, Turati glossed over the substantial differences among
the reformists at the National Congress of Modena in October 1911.

Turati reported to Kuliscioff that Bissolati, though reluctant to
participate in the Modena proceedings, would defend the war on
strategic grounds.[37] In fact, Bissolati defended himself in a very
forceful speech to the congress. He praised Vittorio Emanuele for
consulting with Socialists, who should be flattered by this public
recognition. The Libyan War had not changed his own attitude toward joining cabinets, and he confirmed that he would have joined
Giolitti's if Turati had not intervened. Bissolati did not consider
the Libyan War sufficient reason to condemn Giolitti and throw
away universal suffrage. Indeed, the Socialists could avoid a big-
ger war only by their continued support of the cabinet. He would
not go along if the Party turned against the government: "I would
rather let myself be broken in half," he said, than oppose Giolitti's government.[38]

This position conflicted with that of Turati, who wished to use
the congress to force the deputies to vote against Giolitti when the
Chamber reopened. From now on, opposition must be the normal
Socialist policy, he emphasized in a speech denouncing the government. He did not exclude cooperation absolutely, but it must be
the exception to the rule.[39]

Turati authored a very long motion that stated this principle but
handled the reformists of the Right very gingerly. It disapproved
of Bissolati's actions, but couched this disapproval in nebulous and
polite terms so as not to provoke Bissolati's exit from the Party.
Kuliscioff considered it a confused statement, which deliberately

hid Turati's indecision, and berated him for his eternal attempts at conciliation.[40]

Turati's motion failed to receive a majority, or even the greatest number of votes, on the first ballot because of further splits among the reformists. Modigliani insisted on offering a resolution differing from Turati's by one word. The "integralists," who bore only a superficial resemblance to the old faction, also presented a motion that did not differ significantly from Turati's. The Bissolati-inspired motion proposed unlimited independence for the Socialist deputies. The result of the vote was: Lerda (left wing), 8,634; Treves-Bussi (Turati), 7,409; Modigliani, 2,095; Basile (Bissolati), 1,956; Pescetti (integralist), 1,023. Lerda withdrew his motion from consideration on the second ballot because the votes for the other motions would switch to the Treves-Bussi resolution.[41] Turati had won at a national congress for the last time, but a satirical newspaper summarized his role thus: "Io nel congresso, impavido, / fui chimico e orator / ed or (pare impossibile) ritorno vincitor: / Ritorno a'miei dominii / trombato e trombator."[42]

After the congress an interesting relationship developed between Turati and the Party's reviving left wing. The leftists were divided into a number of factions, of which Giovanni Lerda's was the most moderate, the most active, and the best organized. Lerda and Turati were not very far apart, and their interaction during this period can be described as a true *incontro mancato*. Lerda, for example, believed in the necessity for the proletariat "to work for its own education and elevation since these are the principal prerequisites for the real task of social renewal," as his Modena motion stated. Indeed, while he endorsed the Congress of Bologna's deliberations, he focused upon the imposition of political intransigence, which Turati had espoused, at least in the present situation. In an editorial discussing the Congress of Modena, Turati urged that the party was not as divided as it seemed because Lerda's position illustrated the "disappearance" of extreme revolutionary elements from the organization.[43] Lerda, in turn, approvingly acknowledged Turati's shift to political intransigence and his staunch opposition to Giolitti and the war. As a result, Turati offered Lerda an alliance on several occasions after the congress closed. This "entente," however, never materialized. Lerda demanded a complete break with Bissolati, a step Turati did not take, and other factions of the left wing resisted any accommodation with Turati. The reformist leader's editorial was wishful thinking. Far from having disappeared, the left-wing extremists would succeed in defeating Lerda and in ousting him from the Party.

Turati discovered soon enough the failure of the Modena conclave to bring unity to the divided Socialists. Bissolati came out of the confrontation defeated but defiant, and the left wing denounced Turati for leaving the door open for future collaboration with governments. The reformists of the Right accused Turati of being a "revolutionary," and the revolutionaries denounced him for being a "reformist of the Right," while Turati attacked both as extremists.[44]

Of the two groups, however, the reformists of the Right caused Turati greater problems. In January of 1912, Bissolati paid a second visit to Giolitti and asked him to call the Chamber of Deputies into session. Turati was furious, because he considered the meeting a further endorsement of the war, another opportunity for Giolitti to exploit Socialist divisions, and a likely cause of a backlash within the Party. Turati decided to take action, and the Chamber's reopening in late February produced a clamorous result—the formal division of the Gruppo.[45]

The process that led to this event commenced at a meeting of the Socialist deputies to determine their common response to the government. Quite clearly, Parliament's reopening would occasion an outpouring of patriotic sentiment and the endorsement of the nation's fighting men. Turati's group, the "reformists of the Left," wished to criticize the expedition, but the Bissolati faction refused to consider action that might appear unpatriotic. In violation of the recent congress, Bissolati again proposed cooperation with Giolitti to assure the success of his liberal program. Given these divisions, some participants suggested doing nothing, but this course of action was rejected on the grounds that it might appear to endorse the government. Eventually, over Turati's objections, a compromise motion passed. The Socialist deputies would stand in homage to the soldiers "who had done their duty," after which a spokesman would summarize the Gruppo's position. It was not possible to implement the compromise, however, because there was no position, and the only acceptable spokesman, Prampolini, opposed the whole idea. In the end the deputies came to no decision, and each remained free to attend the session or not as he wished. It was the most dismal possible result, Treves and Kuliscioff agreed.[46]

Despite this disappointing performance, Turati considered the Parliamentary Group the only Party institution capable of action against the war, since the CGL leadership and the Directorate had done nothing. The group, however, would remain paralyzed as long as the reformists of the Right obstructed it, and Turati therefore decided that it should be split. The result would be a smaller but more unified and effective organization. Kuliscioff applauded his plan and encouraged him to remain fast.[47]

Serving as a pretext for the schism was a speech by Bissolati on a bill converting into law the royal decrees proclaiming the annexation of Tripolitania and Cyrinaica. Although all the Socialist deputies but Enrico Ferri voted against the legislation, Bissolati praised the government on behalf of "a part of" the Socialist delegation. He accepted the cabinet's explanation that it had moved to prevent another great power from seizing Libya and acknowledged that Giolitti had acted in conformity with the will of the nation, "with the exception of a portion of the proletariat which is tied to the Socialist party." Bissolati said that he was faithful to Italy's supreme interests but felt obliged to vote against conversion of the decrees only because they unduly complicated the diplomacy of the war.[48]

Following the speech, an article in the *Critica* announced the fracture of the Gruppo and explained the reasons. For ten years, Turati wrote, "nonsensical" criticism of reformism from the Party's Extreme Left had caused some reformists to react by advocating greater collaboration with the government. This had resulted in an excessive dependence on parliamentary maneuvers, growing reformist paralysis, and an "involution toward bourgeois democracy" by the reformists of the Right. The latest example of these tendencies had been Bissolati's discourse in the Chamber, which Turati considered the last straw.[49]

Turati, however, proved unable to maintain this strong position because of the unwillingness of the reformists of the Left to sanction a definitive break. The disturbing unreliability of the Socialist deputies had already been evident in the vote on the annexation decrees, and now they proceeded to restore "unity" over Turati's protests.[50] The entire Gruppo and the Directorate met jointly and engaged in a protracted debate in an effort to resolve the crisis. At 2:00 AM, Bissolati offered to withdraw from the Gruppo in order to give it freedom of action. According to Turati, Bissolati's friends knew they were in for a beating on the issue of Party discipline and sought to avoid it by sacrificing Bissolati. Turati objected to having the Bissolatians without Bissolati in a superficially united delegation. He tried to postpone the vote until the next day, but all the Turatians, except Turati, abstained, and Bissolati's motion passed. Turati fumed but could do nothing except heed his companion's advice to boycott future meetings. He stayed away for a while but eventually drifted back. A different problem now confronted Turati and Kuliscioff—the imminent Congress of Reggio Emilia and the probability of being crushed between the right and left wings.[51]

The Libyan War and the Party's demonstrated impotence had given the left wing a tremendous impetus. The Turati-Kuliscioff correspondence of this period illustrates a growing awareness of the dwindling support for the left reformists. Only in March 1912 were

the Socialist deputies able to obey the injunction of Modena to oppose the government. However, the narrowness of the deputies' vote
—nineteen to fifteen with two abstentions—removed much of the
force from this decision and proved ineffective in changing the political destiny of the reformists because it failed to demonstrate
their resolute opposition to Giolitti.[52]

The Revival of the Left Wing

The left wing had begun reorganizing itself after the national congress of 1910, at the height of Turati's power. Turati's opponents
established a Central Committee to unify the scattered elements
of the Left and to coordinate the struggle against reformist dominance. The Central Committee initiated an organizing campaign
and, on 1 May 1911, began publishing a biweekly newspaper in
Rome, La soffitta. This official organ of "the revolutionary intransigent faction of the Socialist party" became the focus of left-wing
activity. Giovanni Lerda, an old-time leftist leader, became editor,
and his wife Oda, Francesco Ciccotti, Adolfo Zerbini, Arturo Vella,
Alceste della Seta, and Angelica Balabanoff, most of whom served
on the Central Committee, were its most assiduous contributors.

On May Day 1911, the Central Committee issued a nationwide
appeal, accusing the reformists of having demoralized the Party.
Reformist illusions of achieving socialism piecemeal and of overthrowing the middle class with the "gracious" collaboration of the
bourgeoisie itself had degenerated to such an extent that reformists
now

> approved and encouraged the participation of the Hon. Bissolati
> in the royal and bourgeois government, thus renouncing the
> simulation and tergiversation with which they tricked the Party
> in the congresses. They are prepared to become the tools of the
> regime they once fought, and which is the instrument of the
> bourgeoisie's conservative interests.

For purposes of winning support, therefore, the committee preferred
not to distinguish between reformists of the Right and of the Left
but vowed to unseat them all.[53]

In his first editorial, Lerda detailed the "depression, discomfort,
and confusion" into which reformism had led the Party and predicted that the Congress of Modena would endorse joining cabinets.
Many revolutionaries were seriously considering secession in such
an eventuality, but Lerda discouraged withdrawal, stating that it
would be more appropriate for Bissolati to leave the Party.[54]

The Soffitta group was ambivalent toward Turati. Like Turati,

it opposed violence, believed in social legislation, and agreed that
Socialist parliamentary action could have an important role in the
proletariat's elevation. Turati, on the other hand, had moved toward
political intransigence and strenuously opposed the war. These similarities caused Turati to argue that the *Soffitta* revolutionaries were
really crypto-reformists reduced to splitting hairs to distinguish
themselves from him. The revolutionaries responded that they rejected class collaboration in principle, whereas a specific situation
(the war), not ideological considerations, had driven Turati to the
left and closer to their position.[55] As time went on, the left wing
advocated expulsion of Bissolati, strict discipline, and a close watch
on the Turati group, but these conclusions evolved only after considerable internal disputation and consolidation. In 1911 the Central
Committee focused upon ideological clarification, tight local organization, discipline, and propaganda.

The left wing had always suffered from the lack of a coherent
ideology, and *La soffitta* did not resolve this problem. Angelica
Balabanoff attempted to clarify the faction's ideas, but her attempt
resulted in a charge by *Avanti!* that she was a reformist. Surprisingly, she agreed, although with a reservation. For her, acceptable reforms contributed to the formation of a Socialist conscience, whereas reformists believed that all reforms "mechanically" prepared the
way for socialism.[56] This attitude repeated the old, unsolvable arguments on the nature of reforms and clarified nothing. In general,
the terms of the ideological debate initiated by *La soffitta* were
trite, a fact that only Lerda would eventually have the courage to
recognize publicly, much to the dismay of his friends. Complete
rejection of the system and outright appeals to violence as an ideal
were not major issues in 1911, although they were later. In effect,
the revolutionaries criticized reformist practice because it had not
produced important reforms, to which Turati replied that the revolutionaries had not made the smallest revolution. Even the intervention of foreign Socialists, which the revolutionaries actively
sought, failed to alter the terms of the debate beyond stressing the
political intransigence on which most of the Party already agreed.[57]

The Central Committee was more successful in welding the diverse leftist groups into a political force. The committee prevented
the hemmorhage of left-wing strength, even though a "great majority" of revolutionaries favored a split if the reformists triumphed
at the Congress of Modena.[58] The Forlì Socialists, led by Benito
Mussolini, caused the most trouble, threatening in March 1911 to
leave the Party if the Directorate did not expel Bissolati for visiting
the king. Mussolini declared his section's "autonomy" after the
Directorate refused his demand and attempted to lead a revolt but

was stopped by the Central Committee. His actions cost the leftists 2,000 votes at the Congress of Modena.[59]

The revolutionaries also mounted a major campaign against the CGL leadership.[60] The Central Committee established a task force, headed by Oda Lerda, to plan revolutionary activity at the CGL's next congress, scheduled for Padua between 24 May and 28 May. *La soffitta* attacked the union's reformist policies, and the revolutionaries demanded the end of "class collaboration," energetic action to achieve workers' goals, and an end to "Germanic" bureaucratic methods. This "revolutionary-intransigent" position lost at Padua, but the *Soffitta* group achieved its main purpose, to make its presence felt and to gain experience for the next Socialist congress.[61]

The Central Committee created an infrastructure for this purpose when the CGL congress ended. In June 1911, it established a secretariat, through which it communicated with its local supporters and issued detailed instructions to them, and an information committee, consisting of speakers who could travel around the country rebutting the reformists. Finally, the Central Committee voted a resolution condemning Bissolati, initiated a campaign to force the Directorate to endorse it, and enjoined the revolutionaries to do the same on the local level.[62]

In order to avoid the disorganization that had plagued the revolutionaries in the past, the Central Committee consulted widely on the motion to be presented at the Congress of Modena and sent out the completed draft with directions to present it for debate in the local sections. The committee instructed the revolutionary sections to choose only experienced delegates and appointed fiduciaries to organize its local supporters and to collect proxies from sections too poor to send delegates to Modena.[63] These efforts paid off in leftist victories in Rome and other cities.[64] *La soffitta* became a weekly, and the Central Committee scheduled a series of meetings on the eve of the congress in order to coordinate left-wing actions. Finally, the committee opened an office in Modena where the delegates could obtain vital information.[65]

The revolutionaries smelled victory, but their leaders understood the need for more time to end reformist domination of the Party. The crucial question was whether the revolutionary faction would break up in the absence of a clear-cut victory. A member of the Central Committee, Arturo Vella, pleaded against secession in case of an equivocal outcome. The revolutionaries had barely completed their organizational base, and the Central Committee's efforts needed more time to come to fruition.[66] After September 1911, the revolutionaries could use the war issue to undermine the reformists. The Left held them responsible for the war, arguing that the Party's

138   CHAPTER IX

inability to organize effective resistance had encouraged the government to act with impunity.[67]

The revolutionaries were pleased with the results of the Congress
of Modena. Vella claimed that they could have won a run-off vote
but preferred not to enter into any deals that might confuse the
issues—a clear hint of talks with Turati. "Our campaign," Vella
said, had forced the deputies to cease supporting Giolitti. Bissolati
was now on an open collision course with the Party, and Vella suggested a motion to the Unione socialista romana endorsing strict
discipline and expulsion for anyone who disobeyed the injunctions
of Modena. The section under whose jurisdiction Bissolati came
passed the resolution.[68] Finally, the revolutionary faction named
a new Central Committee to coordinate the final drive against
reformism.[69]

At this point, however, Giovanni Lerda touched off an ideological
crisis. He issued a declaration criticizing the left wing's confusion
and its lack of a program capable of inspiring its practical political
action. The "revolutionary-intransigent" bloc, Lerda maintained,
was an inorganic mass composed of different theorists who had
united for a host of reasons. He urged the revolutionaries to work
out a comprehensive ideology but warned them against rigid dogmatism. "I do not believe in dogmas or formulas," he wrote, "not even
in those of so-called scientific socialism." Unfortunately, Lerda
could not provide a solution to the ideological problem he raised,
nor could it be solved in the ensuing discussion.[70]

The reaction to Lerda's statement was sharp. Angelica Balabanoff
called it a renunciation of Marxism but preferred not to probe any
deeper, emphasizing instead the successes the faction had already
achieved. Another writer, Vittorio Badaloni, issued a lengthy rebut-
tal warning Lerda not to slide any deeper into reformism because
this led directly to ministerialism and *ministeriabilismo* of the
Bissolati type. Leftists, Badaloni believed, must return to traditional
Marxism. These arguments had little effect on Lerda, who, as early
as 1897, had repudiated dogmatism. He was primarily interested
in educating and elevating the workers so as to achieve socialism
gradually and was thus very close to Turati, although he emphasized
political intransigence to a greater extent than did the reformist
leader.[71]

As previously mentioned, Lerda's outlook raised interesting possibilities of an understanding with Turati, who tried to exploit the
differences among the revolutionaries by making overtures to Lerda.[72] Lerda's wife acknowledged Turati's flexibility and his hostility
to Giolitti and the war; nonetheless, she discerned a fundamental
difference between the two groups. The left wing, unlike Turati,

believed in profound and continued antagonism between working class and bourgeoisie. Because there could be no lulls in this battle, electoral and parliamentary alignments were impossible at all times. Thus, the conjunction between Turati and the left wing was transitory because their premises were different. Lerda confirmed his wife's stance by deliberately making an entente impossible. If Bissolati voted for the government, he announced, the revolutionaries would demand his expulsion on the grounds of violation of Party discipline.[73] The "amputation" of the Bissolati faction became a prerequisite for the restoration of Party harmony and discipline, and Bissolati's head was the only pledge the revolutionaries would accept from Turati.[74]

Revolutionary propaganda now focused on reformism as a "major contribution" to the war and denounced the lukewarm support Party organs gave to antiwar activities.[75] Whereas the Socialist International had organized demonstrations in all the major cities of Europe, the revolutionaries complained, the reformist Party Directorate had sent a telegram of support to Brussels.[76] The Central Committee pressured the Directorate to organize nationwide protests but failed, although the Roman Socialists rioted in City Hall. The Directorate responded by publishing a pamphlet against the war, a step the Central Committee condemned as inadequate.[77]

As time went on, the Libyan War engendered conditions that favored the rapid growth of the left wing. In the North, credit restrictions imposed as a result of the conflict blocked industrial growth. On the land, cuts in public works projects also produced unemployment, especially in the Po Valley. Incomplete recovery from the severe recession of 1907 and the interruption of trade with Turkey and the Middle East aggravated the situation. Turati estimated that 40,000 persons were unemployed in Milan, and an additional 20,000 had no work in its province. According to Turati, 50 percent of the day laborers in the province of Ferrara lacked employment during the height of the agricultural season. Furthermore, in a process comparable to industry, employers on the land were introducing more sophisticated machinery. At the same time, prices increased, and real wages declined. Worsening conditions led to strikes that provoked brutal police repression. Workers linked the poor economic conditions to the war and objected to squandering the country's meager resources for the "Libyan desert." In response, the government imposed censorship, curtailed demonstrations, and increased arrests.[78] These developments alienated the rank and file from the reformist leadership, perceived as being too closely associated with the government or as having weakened the Party.

The left wing addressed itself to this latter issue very forcefully, promising to restore discipline and to centralize the Party. The Central Committee denounced the deputies for reducing the Gruppo to a collection of individuals. It also objected to the reported establishment of an anonymous committee in Milan to coordinate action against the war, a job that rightly belonged to the Directorate and that Lerda saw as a plot to sabotage the executive organs in anticipation of a left-wing victory.[79] By March of 1912, the revolutionaries officially announced their goal of expelling Bissolati at the next Party congress.[80]

Turati's response to the left-wing challenge was surprisingly inadequate. His sense of the strains within the faction was accurate, but he misjudged the possibilities for an understanding with Lerda. When Kuliscioff informed him that his ideas had little chance of being endorsed at the next congress, he upbraided her for her pessimism. His primary concern was to retain Treves as editor of *Avanti!*, he informed her. The delegates would reshuffle the Directorate, but otherwise the congress would have little significance. "The revolutionaries do not have anybody to govern the Party or publish the newspaper," he wrote, "and the rightists have almost no following."[81] Turati believed that the congress's sole purpose was to rebuke Bissolati.[82] Turati had a long history of defying congresses and had undoubtedly resolved to do so again. At a time when the Party Directorate was weak, continued control of the newspaper, close cooperation with the CGL, and influence in the local sections provided the basis for a comeback. This was a miscalculation, however, because the war and continued identification with Bissolati undermined Turati on all these fronts.

Bissolati especially damaged him. As previously mentioned, the Gruppo voted to oppose Giolitti only in February 1912, but the vote's closeness displeased Turati and Kuliscioff.[83] On 15 March an attempt on the lives of the sovereigns took place. Bissolati, Bonomi, and Cabrini joined other deputies in a visit to the Quirinale to congratulate the king on his escape, despite the refusal of the rest of the Parliamentary Group. This provided the revolutionaries with another opportunity to denounce reformism.[84] Even Turati's friends took exception to the behavior of the reformists of the Right. Modigliani had already come out for separation, and Kuliscioff believed that the *destri* had condemned themselves by their actions.[85]

Anna Kuliscioff tried to initiate steps that would dissociate Turati from Bissolati. After consultation with reformist leaders, she suggested the establishment of a national committee, based upon the Milanese Socialist Section (SSM), to prepare for the congress. Turati expressed disbelief that a committee could generate enthusiasm in the country, especially if dominated by the Milanese. He lamented the lack of young, militant workers, whom the reformists had once had "and who we once were ourselves."[86] Kuliscioff, however, met with Modigliani in order to patch up the differences between him and the reformists of the Left. Because Modigliani had a more intransigent image than Turati and had clearly expressed his willingness to break politically with Bissolati, they agreed that he should take the initiative against the revolutionaries. Turati and Modigliani would agree on a report and motion to present to the congress, have it endorsed by the Milanese and Reggio Emilia Socialists, and have copies printed "by the thousands" for distribution. According to Kuliscioff, this was the only chance Turati had of blocking a revolutionary victory at Reggio.[87]

Turati and Modigliani, however, could not agree. Critica sociale published Modigliani's report but criticized it in an editorial. Despite areas of agreement, Turati did not accept Modigliani's rigid political intransigence, his endorsement of Bissolati's expulsion, and his belief in the death of "political-democratic" reformism or in the birth of so-called social-economic reformism. Kuliscioff also defined Modigliani's proposed resolution as "much redder than that of the red revolutionaries."[88]

It is difficult to understand the strategy of the reformists of the Left. It would have been more profitable for Turati to concentrate on organization, the area in which he generally excelled but where he was being beaten. The revolutionaries were extremely active in the local sections. For example, the Reggio Socialists, the congress's hosts upon whom Kuliscioff had counted to begin building momentum for Turati, politely listened to their leaders, Turati's good friends Giovanni Zibordi and Prampolini, then converted Zibordi's motion into an "ultraintransigent" statement favoring the expulsion of the destri. This development was repeated in section after section. By June of 1912, visitors regularly came by to console Kuliscioff for the inevitable revolutionary victory at the upcoming Congress.[89] Without careful organization it proved impossible to reverse the trend toward the left unleashed by the war. Even though Turati's own antiwar activities aroused admiration among the Socialists, the lack of careful organizational work, the refusal to admit political intransigence as a principle, and the burden of Bissolati cost Turati control of the Party. Indeed, Turati's closest collaborators began asking the same questions regarding discipline, Party structure, and the problems of the Gruppo as did the left wing—and came to similar conclusions.[90]

Even Avanti! threatened to slip from Turati's control. Treves had taken over the newspaper from Bissolati in 1910 in poor financial shape, its reputation damaged, and its circulation down considerably. Treves restored its reputation, but urgent technical improvements required funds. In January 1911, Treves estimated that without the immediate infusion of 100,000 lire the newspaper would fold. On 9 April 1911, the Directorate established a joint-stock company and authorized issuance of 1 million lire in stock.[91] This operation brought financial stability, but Turati wished to achieve political stability as well, and by October of 1911 he had succeeded in moving the newspaper to Milan.[92]

These maneuvers provided the revolutionaries with ammunition against Turati. Criticism of the administration of *Avanti!* became a major theme. The revolutionaries objected to the joint-stock company as a typically capitalist institution whose shares would be purchased by workers' cooperatives of the North. Charges of poor administration, mounting deficits, corruption, and excessive remuneration for the editor continued until the congress, Lerda even charging Treves with censorship.[93]

The campaign against Treves eventually succeeded. By June of 1912, he was convinced that he would have to relinquish the editorship.[94] The Congress of Reggio Emilia named an interim editor, although Treves retained considerable influence until Mussolini became editor.[95]

At the same time *Critica sociale* was also in trouble. The review was in poor financial shape, and in May 1911 Kuliscioff raised the possibility of its demise. Turati made a number of suggestions to improve the financial health of the journal but focused on the lack of liveliness as the main problem. Kuliscioff remained pessimistic about the magazine's future because the reformists had lost the youth, and old relationships had changed. "At age twenty-two," she wrote, the *Critica* had become eccentric—too revolutionary for the reformists and too reformist for the revolutionaries. Nor were the editors prepared to alter their views in order to increase circulation. After considering seriously whether publication should cease, Turati and Kuliscioff kept the review alive as a sort of "refuge" from the political vicissitudes of the day.[96]

The political situation had worsened for the reformists. In March 1912, a committee named by the Directorate reported that the workers had indeed been "disorganized, disoriented, and unprepared" when the Libyan War began. Significantly, reformists composed a majority of the committee.[97] In its May Day proclamation for 1912, the revolutionary faction's Central Committee again linked the conflict with reformism, and Lerda accused the labor organizations of continuing to cooperate with the government.[98] Costantino Lazzari accused Turati and Treves of plotting the Socialist party's transformation into a government-oriented organization.[99] In order to restore the integrity of the Party, the revolutionaries demanded the expulsion of the Bissolati faction, and probation for the reformists of the Left.[100] They further returned to the policy of strict control over the deputies adopted at the Congress of Reggio Emilia of 1893.[101] At the same time, the Central Committee extended its own control in preparation for the congress by raising funds, publicizing a "model" motion, and making certain their people would attend.[102] The revolutionaries also solidified their position in the local sections by gaining control of the Milanese Socialist Section. A number of factors explain the takeover—poor attendance, Turati's apparent failure to appear, reluctance to dump Bissolati—all of which reflected reformist dispiritedness.[103] On the eve of the congress, the Central Committee claimed certain victory, warning only against the fresh offers of an alliance being made by Turati.[104]

When Socialist party delegates met at Reggio Emilia on 7 July 1912, the success of left-wing organization became immediately clear.[105] The hostile reception accorded a speech detailing the Directorate's activities set the tone from the beginning. Modigliani tried to moderate the attack of three revolutionary spokesmen in vain, and the congress passed a motion merely receiving the Directorate's report.[106]

Next the revolutionaries assailed the Parliamentary Group, inflamed by the report of its spokesman, Giovanni Montemartini. Montemartini had read his report to Turati, who had criticized it but had failed to foresee the rage it would arouse.[107] Despite Turati's attempts to head off criticism of the group, Montemartini provoked the congress by making an impassioned argument for complete independence from the Party. Congresses could discuss the deputies' actions as much as they wished, he said, but it would make no difference. The Gruppo could have no consistent "policy" because it was not possible to coordinate forty deputies when only five or six of them could be in Rome for any length of time. "Organic action" had been feasible only during the early days of socialism.[108] This direct and unreasonable challenge to the left wing was a political blunder of major proportions.

Mussolini's response was hard-hitting and brutal. He denounced the widespread parliamentary "cretinism" and said that Parliament was a bourgeois instrument designed to maintain the supremacy of the ruling class and useless for Socialists. Universal suffrage, which the Socialist deputies extolled, had merely extended the life of the pernicious institution. Mussolini simply dismissed all of Montemartini's contentions. Socialist deputies were not supposed to have any political autonomy, only "technical" autonomy. They had to execute the will of the Party sections, transmitted through the Directorate. Mussolini then criticized the specific action of the deputies, whom he accused of indifference and indiscipline. Bissolati, Bonomi, and Cabrini had congratulated the king on his escape from assassination, whereas he deserved the guillotine. He proposed the expulsion of all three, plus Podrecca, whose name was called out from the audience.[109]

Turati pleaded against the expulsions. He chastized the reformists of the Right for their attitude toward the Libyan War and the government but believed the differences with Bissolati could be worked out. The Party was in mortal danger if it had no room for persons with different opinions. "As heretics and rebels," he said, "we must recognize the value of heresy . . . even within the Party." Furthermore, Turati argued, it would damage the proletariat to force Bissolati to found a competing socialist party. Finally, Turati concluded, Bissolati's expulsion would not resolve the ideological debate within the Socialist party.[110]

Turati was also fighting for himself. The Party was striking at all the deputies through Bissolati, and at reformism as well. The focus of Socialist action, Turati feared, was about to pass from Parliament and from the labor organizations to the streets—and there the Socialist party could only lose. He fought a losing battle, especially since the reformists of the Right restated their positions.[111]

Two other motions competed with Mussolini's. One, presented by Ettore Reina, recapitulated Bissolati's actions but did not call for expulsion; and Modigliani's motion was identical to Reina's except for the conclusion that the reformists of the Right had "put themselves out of the Party." The results of the vote were as follows: Mussolini, 12,566; Reina, 5,633; Modigliani, 3,250; abstaining, 2,027.[112]

Modigliani announced that the remaining reformists would refrain from presenting a motion on the future policies of the Party, thus leaving a clear field to the intransigent wing. The victorious faction's concept of the Party's future, however, was moderate and predominantly reflected Lerda's influence. The motion reaffirmed traditional revolutionary concepts but ignored the question of violence, which for years had been the central dispute in the revolutionary-reformist dichotomy and which Mussolini favored. Another issue deliberately neglected by Lerda was Socialist cooperation during local elections, which Mussolini and the Extreme Left wished to prohibit. In general elections, Lerda's motion forbade alliances on the first ballot but commissioned the Party Directorate to authorize Socialist cooperation with bourgeois parties during run-off elections.[113]

For the reformists, the most significant part of the resolution was the theoretical end of the deputies' independence. The congress declared participation in cabinets and support of the Libyan War "incompatible" with Party membership and specifically entrusted the Directorate with "interpretation and execution of the deliberations of the Congress." The deputies could vote only for specific pieces of legislation, not confidence.[114]

Despite this prohibition, the motion of the left wing was mild, the result of a struggle between Lerda and the more radical elements of his faction. At a meeting before the congress, revolutionary leaders adopted a much harsher position than Lerda eventually took during the assembly. The motion, drafted by Francesco Ciccotti, was watered down because of differences among the leaders, much to the disappointment of Ciccotti, who believed that the congress was prepared to endorse a much more radical stance than the one Lerda presented. After the congress, a disgruntled Ciccotti complained of the "reformism" that had crept into Lerda's motion and stated ominously that the issue would have to be resolved.[115]

Prior to the congress, Claudio Treves had made a fresh attempt to establish links with the moderate revolutionaries. Writing in Avanti!, Treves interpreted the revolutionaries as divided into two incompatible groups: "rivoluzionari-riformisti" and "rivoluzionari-rivoluzionari." According to Treves, the latter group, best represented by Mussolini, propagated the "old-fashioned" concept of revolution as the overthrow of capitalism by violence. On the other hand, Lerda's "rivoluzionari-riformisti" and the Turatians believed in the attainment of socialism through reforms. There was disagreement as to "whether reforms should be obtained by cooperation or intransigence," but this could be discussed.[116] Treves's analysis was accurate, at least where it concerned the divisions among the revolutionaries.

Developments within the left wing seemed to confirm Treves's analysis and raised hopes for an eventual reformist comeback. During the debate, Modigliani publicly expressed pleasure that the most extreme faction had "surrendered" to Lerda; indeed, Modigliani himself appeared more radical.[117] Turati mourned Bissolati's expulsion but, in light of his own conflicts with him, could hardly be shocked. The political intransigence voted by the congress was not more extreme than that which Turati himself had already adopted in Milan and was not a throwback to 1893.[118] The limitation on the deputies' autonomy was the most serious aspect of the left wing's victory, but it seemed unlikely that the Party could wield any more actual control in this respect than in proved able to do after similar pronouncements in 1893, 1901, and 1904.

In addition to these considerations, the reformists retained de facto control of *Avanti!*, despite Treves's official removal as editor. The revolutionaries' choice, Giovanni Bacci, was in poor health and became editor in name only. Treves remained in charge and seemed likely to keep the editorship by default when the revolutionaries could not agree on a successor. Only after considerable debate did the Directorate make Mussolini editor in December 1912. At this point the reformists lost effective control of the newspaper.[119]

The victory of the left-wing moderates over the extremists, and their continued control of *Avanti!*, convinced the reformists that they had weathered the attack. After the congress, Turati could still ask, "Whose was the victory?" The victors of Reggio Emilia were not revolutionists, Turati wrote, but "intransigent reformists." Thus, for him, the great majority of the Party remained reformist and would formally recognize the fact.[120]

Turati was probably correct, but unforeseen circumstances intervened: World War I and its aftermath. Given the radically altered conditions and the loss of the Bissolati group, Turati was no longer able to put together a stable majority, although one author has argued that this inability was due to the intervention of workers from large, modern enterprises.[121] The innate contradictions of Socialist theory ensured continuation of the ideological divisions between reformists and revolutionaries. The Party remained evenly divided and unable to choose among the different courses of action open to it, especially during times of crisis. Despite his weaknesses and mistakes, Turati had the virtues of consistency, clarity, compassion, and, above all, a sense of the limits of political action. Had these elements been more widespread in the Socialist party hierarchy, some of the tragedies of Italian history might have been avoided.

THE 1912 SPLIT in the Socialist party marked a profound change in Socialist and Italian history. The divisions that had weakened the Party and prevented it from becoming a dominant political force were exacerbated. Turati had hoped to regain control of the Party and bring it once more onto a course that took account of Italian realities, but he failed to do so. After 1912 the Party stressed violence and intransigence, and its political influence declined. This policy prevented the Party from exploiting the increased support it received after World War I. Indeed, the revolutionaries caused the Party's splintering and defeat because they repudiated parliamentary action but failed to organize themselves for revolution. They failed to resolve the classic dilemma of democratic socialism, but, given their precarious position after World War I, it is astounding that they went so long without implementing either parliamentary or revolutionary tactics.

A brief overview of events from the Congress of Reggio Emilia to Turati's death in 1932 will illustrate the results of the Socialist party's inability to resolve the issues debated between 1892 and 1912.

Although the old-time revolutionaries still controlled the Party after 1912, Mussolini exploited his editorship of *Avanti!* to move Socialist action into the streets, the development Turati had most feared. Mussolini egged the crowd on to violence, scorning all peaceful methods of increasing Socialist influence. Turati repudiated but failed to dislodge Mussolini, who, on the contrary, gained strength at the Congress of Ancona in 1914. "Mussolinismo"—the attainment of power by demogogic appeals to the mob—became entrenched in the Socialist party and, fueled by the World War and the Communist revolution in Russia, produced the rhetoric of the "biennio rosso," the years immediately following World War I when the Socialists refused to discuss any means of coming to power other than violent revolution.

In 1914 Italy declared its neutrality in the war. The nation's top leaders, nevertheless, engineered Italy's intervention by promoting violent street demonstrations and by suppressing neutralist counter-demonstrations. The equivalent of "mussolinismo" had invaded the highest levels of government. Government promotion of violence and clever political maneuvering by the Right caused the Giolittian majority that had opposed intervention to do a complete turnabout in May 1915. Turati denounced the Chamber's cowardice and spelled out the grave implications of these developments for Italian democratic institutions. The "historic compromise" between Giolitti and Turati, established in 1901 and gravely weakened by the Libyan War, was now buried. The conservatives, who had resented Giolitti's moderate reformism, used the war to end the Piedmontese statesman's political authority, just as Mussolini had seized upon the Libyan War to destroy Socialist reformism.

The strains produced by World War I and the myth of the Russian Revolution pumped up the left wing—now called "maximalists" because they would settle only for the Party's maximum program—and greatly decreased reformist influence in the Party. In 1919, the Congress of Bologna rejected any compromise with the bourgeois system and called for violent revolution according to the Russian model. This call remained empty because the maximalists did not seriously organize for a revolution, apparently believing that their statements and the "revolutionary situation" would automatically bring about socialism. Instead, sporadic atrocities, strikes, and the wild maximalist rhetoric alarmed the lower middle classes that Turati had previously cultivated and caused the most reactionary groups within the bourgeoisie to support fascist attacks against Socialist organizations, institutions, and leaders. The inability of the maximalists to defend socialism from the brutality they had provoked stimulated the growth of the Party's Communist wing. Led by Antonio Gramsci and Amedeo Bordiga, the Communists advocated acceptance of Moscow's Twenty-One Demands, a break with the Turatian reformists, abstention from participation in the bourgeois political system, and serious planning for violent revolution. Unable to convince the maximalist leadership to adopt their viewpoint, the Communists formed their own party in 1921.

Turati realistically and acutely analyzed the postwar political situation. In 1919 he warned the maximalists that their empty threats against well-armed adversaries would provoke a ferocious reaction and would "ruin . . . the movement for half a century."

Unlike the Russian Revolution, an Italian revolution would immediately be starved out by the country's suppliers and creditors.

Turati applied the same criticisms to the Communists. Like the
old-time revolutionaries, he said, they wished to force communism
down the throat of a society that was not ready for it. As a result,
they advocated the importation into Italy of the Soviets, which he
considered undemocratic institutions. He warned the Italians not
to become the tools of bolshevism, "an eminently oriental imperial-
istic force." He also attacked Communist emphasis on violence,
the dictatorship of the proletariat, and thought control. The Communists, he predicted, would eventually abandon these ideas and
return to the social democratic methods of the reformists.

In the 1920s, however, the Communists were unwilling to accept
social democracy and attacked the reformists as their main villains,
thus further weakening and dividing the Left. In 1924, Turati's
"spiritual son," Giacomo Matteotti, complained that Italian communism had become the "involuntary accomplice" of fascism. The
historian Gaetano Arfé has written that the schism at the 1921
Congress of Livorno was a major cause of the decline of the Italian
working class.

The Socialist position worsened considerably in 1921. Fascist brutality, supported directly by large landowners and industrialists, and
indirectly by the government, increased with dramatic effect. The
maximalist and Communist rhetoric of violence provided the pretext for Fascist atrocities against the working class, and maximalist
control of the Party prevented the political solutions to the crisis
advocated by Turati and the reformists. Turati wished to collaborate
with other antifascists—the development Mussolini most feared—
but he could not do so because it would have undermined his position and split the Socialist party. Kuliscioff advised him to go ahead
anyway, but Turati refused to take the risk. The unity of all Socialist
groups, which had enabled the Extreme Left to defeat the reaction
of 1898–1900, failed to materialize. Continued Socialist intransigence in the Chamber made all ruling coalitions unstable, and this
instability exacerbated the political situation. The Socialist Parliamentary Group defied the maximalist Directorate only in June 1922,
when it proclaimed its willingness to support and join an anti-
Fascist government coalition. The Partito popolare italiano appeared
ready to collaborate, and in July Turati consulted with the king.
For a brief moment an anti-Fascist cabinet based upon Socialists
and Catholics seemed certain, but Giolitti, who was feuding with
the Partito popolare, refused to support the coalition. Vatican intervention and Fascist attacks on workers during a "legalitarian" general strike designed by Turati to support the political agreement

ended all possibility of success. From now on, a parliamentary coalition against, or even without, the Fascists appeared impossible. Moreover, the initiative of the Socialist parliamentarians caused another schism in the Socialist party in October 1922, when the maximalists expelled the reformists from the Party. Turati formed the Partito socialista unitario, which, with Matteotti as its secretary, became the strongest Marxist party. Finally "liberated" to cooperate with other anti-Fascist groups, the reformists were too late. At the end of the month, the March on Rome took place and culminated in a Mussolini cabinet.

Because Mussolini depended upon a non-Fascist majority, the possibility of voting him out of office existed. Turati worked hard toward that goal, but in 1923 the Fascists introduced the Acerbo bill, that would give 65 percent of the seats in the Chamber to the party receiving the most votes in the next elections, provided it was 25 percent of the total. Turati denounced this bill as the "most atrocious and strangest jest which has ever been conceived against a parliament and a people, . . . who are asked to sanction their own abdication and degradation." Attempting to redress previous government instability, the Chamber passed the bill, and unprecedented Fascist brutality against the populace produced a majority for Mussolini in the elections of 1924.

The Partito socialista unitario continued to resist the Fascists. Matteotti exposed the Fascist electoral atrocities in Parliament and demanded new elections. In June 1924, he disappeared and was later found murdered.

The resulting disgust and indignation in the country touched off a crisis that appeared impossible for Mussolini to survive. In the week after the discovery of Matteotti's body, the duce's isolation seemed complete, and even his own followers began deserting him. Turati and others discussed the possibility of breaking into his office and arresting him. Because he realized no one would defend him, Mussolini kept several "good revolvers" handy and then apparently wavered. He summoned Turati's friend, Carlo Silvestri, to an audience, but Silvestri declined. In a 1945 interview, Mussolini informed Silvestri that he had written letters to Turati and the king. The undelivered letters proffered his resignation and informed Vittorio Emanuele of the nation's wish for Turati to take over the government.

Political action against Mussolini took the form of boycotting the Chamber—the Aventine Secession. The anti-Fascist deputies hoped for an internal breakdown of fascism, which was not unlikely, but it failed to occur because liberal and conservative support for Mussolini remained steady. The possibility of a Turati cabinet caused

the king to cling to Mussolini even as he gave vague assurances
to anti-Fascist monarchists of his intention to curb him. Giolitti
and Pope Pius XI vetoed plans for a coalition cabinet to include
Giovanni Amendola, a monarchist leader of the Aventine, Don
Luigi Sturzo, founder of the Partito popolare, and Turati. Giolitti
considered the Socialists and the Catholics more dangerous than the
Fascists, and the pope would not hear of cooperation with the Socialists. As the crisis dragged on, Turati recognized the need for
stronger action, such as creating an "antiparliament" or appealing
to the nation, but the representatives of the constitutional opposition and the Catholics resisted such action.

The Aventine Secession's failure allowed Mussolini to transform
his government into a dictatorship in 1925 and 1926. The opposition
deputies lost their seats, non-Fascist political organizations were
dissolved, the press was muzzled, and opposition leaders were kept
under strict police surveillance. Freedom disappeared.

At the end of 1925, Anna Kuliscioff died, and her funeral occa-
sioned a violent anti-Socialist demonstration by the Fascists. Turati
was the object of continual Fascist harrassment, and he fled to Paris
in 1926, aided by the young anti-Fascist leaders, Carlo Rosselli,
Ferruccio Parri, and Sandro Pertini.

In exile Turati became the moral leader of Italy, inspiring the
formation of the Anti-Fascist Concentration, an organization that
coordinated the activities of the disparate exile groups. Through
his foreign-language newsletter, his articles, his international prestige, and his speeches, he warned a skeptical Europe that fascism
was a worldwide phenomenon that would inevitably lead to war.
Carlo Rosselli wrote: "He confronted the problem of interpreting
fascism . . . with a breadth of vision and a modern outlook which
were astounding in a man as old as he and which make us lament
the fact that Turati did not dedicate more time to the study of
theoretical problems." Turati lived to see verification of his prediction of fascism's spread beyond Italy.

During his last years Turati remained particularly concerned with
the problem of freedom within socialism. He saw similarities between communism and fascism, except for the different goals of
Lenin and Mussolini. Social democracy was the only alternative to
both, he insisted.

For Turati, violence and dictatorship were hallmarks of fascism,
no matter what it was called. The terms changed in the 1920s,
but these ideas were the same ones Turati had denounced in the
socialist movement since the 1890s. After his death on 29 March
1932, they continued to be debated within the Socialist party, notably between Pietro Nenni and Giuseppe Saragat, causing further

splits after the Party had been reunified in exile. Furthermore, discussion of revolution versus reform, dictatorship of the proletariat versus social democracy, began in the Communist party. With reformism apparently winning a de facto victory in the 1970s, the Italian Communist party has joined the Italian Marxist tradition created by Filippo Turati.

NOTES

Chapter I

1. For this period of Turati's life, see Alessandro Schiavi, *Esilio e morte di Filippo Turati;* Filippo Turati, *Le vie maestre del socialismo,* pp. 443–81; and Franco Catalano, *Filippo Turati,* pp. 303–15.
2. See Pier Carlo Masini, ed., *La scapigliatura democratica: Carteggi di Arcangelo Ghisleri, 1875–1890* (Milan: Feltrinelli, 1961), p. 110.
3. Filippo Turati, *Strofe.*
4. The poem has been published in Masini, *La scapigliatura,* pp. 64–66.
5. See Alessandro Schiavi, *Filippo Turati attraverso le lettere di corrispondenti (1880–1925),* pp. 13–29; and Masini, *La scapigliatura,* p. 16.
6. See Alessandro Schiavi, *Leonida Bissolati* (Rome: Opere Nuove, 1955).
7. Masini, *La scapigliatura,* p. 21; Catalano, *Turati,* pp. 9–11.
8. Luigi Cortesi, ed., *Turati Giovane,* pp. 7–8.
9. Ibid., p. 10.
10. See Biblioteca G. G. Feltrinelli, *I periodici di Milano: Bibliografia e storia,* 2 vols. (Milan: Feltrinelli, 1956), 1:70–74, 87–89.
11. Catalano, *Turati,* pp. 14–16.
12. See Masini, *La scapigliatura,* pp. 76–78, 82–83, 89; see also pp. 16–17.
13. Ibid., pp. 38–39.
14. Ibid., p. 20. Unless otherwise indicated, all translations are the author's.
15. See Cortesi, *Turati Giovane,* pp. 20–23.
16. Masini, *La scapigliatura,* pp. 27, 255–72. See also Cortesi, *Turati Giovane,* pp. 25–29; Catalano, *Turati,* pp. 29–38; and Biblioteca Feltrinelli, *I periodici di Milano,* 1:74–75.
17. Masini, *La scapigliatura,* pp. 18–20.
18. See Catalano, *Turati,* p. 14.
19. Ibid., pp. 15–16.
20. Cortesi, *Turati Giovane,* pp. 10–11, 77–83. See also Masini, *La scapigliatura,* pp. 66–71.
21. Masini, *La scapigliatura,* p. 79; see also pp. 64–66.
22. Ibid., pp. 76–78.
23. Ibid., pp. 85, 92–95.
24. Ibid., pp. 70, 77; see also p. 18.

25. Ibid., pp. 20, 98. The Italian transliteration (Kuliscioff) will be used throughout.
26. This is earlier than usually supposed.
27. Filippo Turati, "Il delitto e la questione sociale," *La plebe*, 12, 19, 26 November and 3, 10, 24, 31 December 1882. These articles were published as a separate work and went into several editions. They may be found in Cortesi, *Turati Giovane*, pp. 138–213; see also pp. 32–39; Catalano, *Turati*, pp. 41–46; and Schiavi, *Lettere di corrispondenti*, pp. 26–33.
28. The letter is in Masini, *La scapigliatura*, pp. 76–78; see also pp. 18–19.
29. Ibid., p. 77. An effort has been made throughout this section on Turati's thought to make reference to sources dating from the 1890s, that is, around the time the Socialist party was founded. This is to show that Turati's basic ideas were already set by then and that the decisions for which he was later attacked were not the result of any "change" in his ideology but simply an application of ideas he had expressed much earlier.
30. Filippo Turati, "Rivolta e rivoluzione," *Critica sociale*, 16 June 1893.
31. Ibid.
32. La critica sociale, "Necessità di un programma pratico," *Critica sociale*, 1 August 1892.
33. Filippo Turati, "Dove andiamo?" *Critica sociale*, 16 October 1892.
34. See Cortesi, *Turati Giovane*, p. 389; and Gaetano Arfé, *Storia del socialismo italiano*, pp. 32–33. See also J. L. Talmon, *The Origins of Totalitarian Democracy* (New York: Praeger, 1960). This is a more plausible explanation than the one given by Lelio Basso, who wrote that Turati was, essentially, not interested in politics as a means of gaining power. See Basso's "Turati, il riformismo, e la via democratica," *Problemi del socialismo* (Milan) 1, no. 1 (February 1958): 103.
35. La critica sociale, "Congresso operaio," *Critica sociale*, 16 August 1892. See also Schiavi, *Lettere di corrispondenti*, pp. 8–9.
36. Filippo Turati, "L'azione parlamentare dei socialisti in Italia," *Critica sociale*, 16 March 1892.
37. Filippo Turati, *L'organizzazione socialista* (Rome: Chilleni, 1950). This is a reprint of Turati's article, which appeared in the *Rivista italiana del socialismo* in November 1886 under the title "Organizzazione, studii, propaganda."
38. La critica sociale, "Il primo maggio in Italia," *Critica sociale*, 16 May 1892.
39. Turati, "Dove andiamo?"
40. La critica sociale, "Congresso operaio."
41. La critica sociale, "Una nuova fase della lotta," *Critica sociale*, 1 July 1892.
42. Filippo Turati, "Il momento attuale del socialismo in Italia," *Critica sociale*, 16 September 1892.
43. A detailed consideration of revisionism in Italy during this period is beyond the scope of this chapter, which is concerned with Turati's general ideology insofar as it affected his practical politics. Italian revisionism is examined by Enzo Santarelli, *La revisione del marxismo in Italia*. For other relevant material, see, Arfé, *Storia del socialismo*, pp. 83–97; Eric J. Hobsbawm, "La diffusione del marxismo (1890–1905)," *Studi storici* 15, no. 2 (April–June 1974): 241–69; Roberto Michels, *Storia del marxismo in Italia*, pp. 112–13, 156; Antonio Graziadei, *La produzione capitalistica*, pp. 65–66; Giorgio Gattei, "L'economia senza valore di Antonio Graziadei," *Studi storici* 12, no. 1 (January–March 1971): 38–63; Claudio Treves, "Socialismo ottimista," *Critica sociale*, 16 August 1899; and Catalano, *Turati*, pp. 136–38. On Bernstein, see Peter Gay, *The Dilemma of Democratic Socialism* (New York: Collier, 1962).
44. See Cortesi, *Turati Giovane*, pp. 42–47, 255–57; Catalano, *Turati*, pp. 57–59; and Masini, *La scapigliatura*, p. 55. Before Turati met Anna Kuliscioff he had

apparently been in love with an Austrian woman whose name remains unknown; on this, see Masini, *La scapigliatura*, pp. 88–89.

45. See Anna Kuliscioff, *Lettere d'amore a Andrea Costa, 1880–1909*, especially the introductory essay by Pietro Albonetti, pp. 13–128. The essay also provides a rather complete bibliography.

46. *Anna Kuliscioff, in memoria*, pp. 344–46. See also Richard Hostetter, *The Italian Socialist Movement*, 1:401–402.

47. Hostetter, *Italian Socialist Movement*, 1:407.

48. *Anna Kuliscioff, in memoria*, p. 346.

49. Antonio Graziadei, *Memorie di trent'anni*, p. 41.

50. See the speeches in *Filippo Turati: Discorsi commemorativi di Mondolfo, Gonzales, Nenni*; and Benedetto Croce, *Storia d'Italia* (Bari: Laterza, 1962), p. 161. See also the secret report in the Archivio centrale dello stato (Rome), Casellario politico centrale, ufficio riservato, busta 5241.

51. See Cortesi, *Turati Giovane*, p. 46.

52. Ibid., pp. 43–44, 46.

53. On this point, see ibid., p. 47.

54. Anna Kuliscioff to Filippo Turati, 27 May 1907. In Italy I was able to consult copies of the letters exchanged between Turati and Kuliscioff for the period 1900–12 at the offices of the Einaudi publishers in Turin. The letters for these years have only recently been published. I will refer to them by the date on which they were written.

55. Cortesi, *Turati Giovane*, p. 47.

56. See Santarelli, *La revisione del marxismo*, pp. 35–38. See Masini, *La scapigliatura*, pp. 22–23, 127–30; Cortesi, *Turati Giovane*, pp. 105–7.

57. See Croce, *Storia d'Italia*, pp. 174–75.

Chapter II

1. On the early period of the Italian Socialist movement, see Hostetter, *Italian Socialist Movement*; Aldo Romano, *Storia del movimento socialista in Italia*, 3 vols. (Bari: Laterza, 1966–67); and Franco della Peruta, "Il socialismo italiano dal 1875 al 1882," in Istituto Giangiacomo Feltrinelli, *Annali, 1958* (Milan: Feltrinelli, 1958), pp. 15–104.

2. Giorgio Candeloro, *Storia dell'Italia moderna*, vol. 6, *Lo sviluppo del capitalismo e del movimento operaio* (Milan: Feltrinelli, 1970), pp. 50–57.

3. Costa's letter is in *La plebe: Monitore quotidiano del presente per l'avvenire* (Lodi, later Milan), 3 August 1879. See also Roberto Michels, *Storia critica del movimento socialista italiano* (Florence: La voce, 1926), p. 75; and G. Bosio and F. della Peruta, "La 'svolta' di Andrea Costa, con documenti sul soggiorno in Francia," *Movimento operaio* 4 (1952): 237–313.

4. Candeloro, *Storia dell'Italia moderna*, 6:169–73.

5. See Gastone Manacorda, *Il movimento operaio italiano attraverso i suoi congressi (1853–1892)*, pp. 135–40, 145–48, 164–71, and especially 267–89. The program of Costa's Partito rivoluzionario is reprinted on pp. 340–48.

6. "Chi siamo e cosa vogliamo," *Fascio operaio*, 29 July 1883. On the origins of the POI, see Manacorda, *Il movimento operaio*, pp. 158–63.

7. "Gli operai e la scienza," *Fascio operaio*, 12 August 1883. See also Alfredo Angiolini, *Socialismo e socialisti in Italia* (Rome: Riuniti, 1966), pp. 146–93; and Manacorda, *Il movimento operaio*, pp. 199–210.

8. See Denis Mack Smith, *Italy* (Ann Arbor: University of Michigan Press, 1959), pp. 133–34.

9. Engels's letter is in *La plebe*, 26 February 1877. For a discussion of the relationship between the *La plebe* group and the German Socialists, see Ernesto Ragionieri, *Socialdemocrazia tedesca e socialisti italiani, 1875–1895*, pp. 45–78.
10. Candeloro, *Storia dell'Italia moderna*, 6: 57–58, 173–74, 165–69.
11. Ibid., pp. 176–78.
12. Ibid., pp. 175–76, 366.
13. See Manacorda, *Il movimento operaio*, pp. 220–22, 223–24; Liliana Dalle Nogare and Stefano Merli, eds., *L'Italia radicale: Carteggi di Felice Cavalotti, 1867–1898* (Milan: Feltrinelli, 1959), pp. 289–94, 357–58; Candeloro, *Storia dell'Italia moderna*, 6: 311; Schiavi, *Lettere di corrispondenti*, pp. 48–56; Salvatore Massino Ganci, ed., *Democrazia e socialismo in Italia: Carteggi di Napoleone Colajanni, 1878–1898* (Milan: Feltrinelli, 1959), pp. 225–26; and Catalano, *Turati*, pp. 60–65. The quarrel caused Turati to move definitively into the socialist camp.
14. *Fascio operaio*, 30–31 October 1886. See also Manacorda, *Il movimento operaio*, pp. 224–27.
15. Partito dei lavoratori italiani, *Rapporto al congresso internazionale di Zurigo (1893) sulla costituzione e sull'azione del partito dei lavoratori italiani* (Milan: Critica sociale, 1893), pp. 6–8.
16. See Filippo Turati, "La democrazia e gli operai," *Cuore e critica*, April 1887.
17. Cortesi, *Turati Giovane*, pp. 325–73.
18. Candeloro, *Storia dell'Italia moderna*, 6: 311.
19. Partito dei lavoratori italiani, *Rapporto*, p. 68.
20. "The redemption of labor / Will be the task of its children / Either we will live by our labor / Or fighting we will die!" The text is in *Fascio operaio*, 20–21 March 1886.
21. See Ghisleri's letter announcing the changeover in *Cuore e critica*, 24 December 1890.
22. Turati's declaration of policy is in ibid. See also Candeloro, *Storia dell'Italia moderna*, 6: 378–80, and Schiavi, *Lettere di corrispondenti*, pp. 78–80.
23. Croce, *Storia d'Italia*, p. 162.
24. Arturo Labriola is not to be confused with Antonio Labriola. See Schiavi, *Lettere di corrispondenti*, pp. 90–91, 96, and Antonio Labriola, *Lettere a Engels*, pp. 191–93.
25. Michels, *Storia critica*, p. 111.
26. Luigi Cortesi, *La costituzione del Partito socialista italiano*, pp. 32, 163–67.
27. See Manacorda, *Il movimento operaio*, pp. 297–301; and Ragionieri, *Socialdemocrazia tedesca*, pp. 177–84.
28. All the quotations are from the *Programma socialista discusso e approvato dalla Lega socialista milanese nelle adunanze del 28 febbraio, 11, 12 e 1° aprile 1891* (Milan: Tip. degli operai, 1891). See also Cortesi, *La costituzione*, pp. 164–67; and Candeloro, *Storia dell'Italia moderna*, 6: 381–82.
29. Archivio centrale dello stato, C.P.C., Ufficio riservato, busta 5241, doc. no. 16116.
30. See La critica sociale, "Una opinione sugli anarchici," *Critica sociale*, 31 May 1891.
31. La critica sociale, "I partiti politici e i socialisti," *Critica sociale*, 15 January 1891.
32. Noi, "Per i profani," *Critica sociale*, 1 November 1891.
33. La critica sociale, "La storia di due code di cavallo, e il programma socialista," *Critica sociale*, 10 July 1891.

34. La critica sociale, "Necessità di un programma pratico," *Critica sociale*, 1 August 1892.

35. Filippo Turati, "L'azione parlamentare dei socialisti in Italia," *Critica sociale*, 16 September 1892.

36. La critica sociale, "Il momento attuale socialista in Italia," *Critica sociale*, 16 September 1892.

37. La critica sociale, "Congresso operaio," *Critica sociale*, 16 August 1892.

38. *Congresso operaio italiano tenutosi in Milano nei giorni 2−3 agosto*, pp. 5−8. See also Cortesi, *La costituzione*, pp. 31−38.

39. *Congresso operaio italiano*, pp. 11−15. See also Cortesi, *La costituzione*, pp. 32−35; and Candeloro, *Storia dell'Italia moderna*, 6:382−83.

40. See Cortesi, *La costituzione*, pp. 34−37; Labriola, *Lettere a Engels*, pp. 67−68, 75−77; and *Lotta di classe*, 13−14 August 1892.

41. Cortesi, *La costituzione*, p. 33; Schiavi, *Lettere di corrispondenti*, p. 89; and Labriola, *Lettere a Engels*, pp. 13−14, 28, 31−35.

42. La critica sociale, "Il congresso operaio nazionale in Milano," *Critica sociale*, 20 August 1891.

43. On Prampolini, see Paolo Colliva, *Camillo Prampolini e i lavoratori reggiani*, and the chapter on Bissolati and Prampolini in *Figure del primo socialismo italiano* (n.p.: Edizioni radio italiani, 1951), pp. 37−44.

44. Cortesi, *La costituzione*, pp. 49−54.

45. Christopher Seton-Watson, *Italy from Liberalism to Fascism* (London: Methuen, 1967), pp. 157−58; also Lazzari, "Memorie," pp. 794−95; Shepard B. Clough, *The Economic History of Modern Italy*, pp. 152−53; and Felice Anzi, *Origini e funzioni delle camere del lavoro*. According to Antonio Labriola, Werner Sombart was enthusiastic about the Italian *camere*, especially the one in Milan; see Labriola, *Lettere a Engels*, p. 144. See also Candeloro, *Storia dell'Italia moderna*, 6:389−92.

46. A copy of this *numero unico*, apparently the only one extant, is in the library of Lelio Basso (Rome). He was kind enough to let me consult it.

47. "La lotta di classe moderna," *Lotta di classe: Numero unico*, 18 June 1892.

48. "Un nuovo contingente," ibid.

49. "Il voto degli esercenti," ibid.

50. "E le altre classi?" ibid.

51. See Lelio Basso, "Alle origini del partito socialista italiano," *Rivista storica del socialismo*, no. 10 (May−August 1960), pp. 471−77.

52. Candeloro, *Storia dell'Italia moderna*, 6:382−83. The 1887 program of the POI appeared in *Fascio operaio*, 1−2 October 1887; the Central Committee's draft appeared in *Lotta di classe*, 30−31 July 1892.

53. The invitations are conveniently reprinted in Cortesi, *La costituzione*, pp. 258−61.

54. La lotta di classe [Filippo Turati], "Il programma del partito," *Lotta di classe*, 13−14 August 1892.

55. La lotta di classe, "Lo statuto del partito," ibid. See also Cortesi, *La costituzione*, pp. 60−64.

56. Karl Marx, *Critique of the Gotha Programme* (New York: International Publishers, 1933). See also Labriola, *Lettere a Engels*, p. 9.

57. See Manacorda, *Il movimento operaio*, pp. 320−22; Ragionieri, *Socialdemocrazia tedesca*, pp. 307−20; and Schiavi, *Lettere di corrispondenti*, pp. 94−96.

58. See Arfé, *Storia del socialismo*, pp. 9−10, 12−15, 18, 21. Labriola later reversed his negative judgment; see Manacorda, *Il movimento operaio*, p. 329.

59. Cortesi, *La costituzione*, p. 168, n. 84.

60. Ibid., pp. 66–71; Candeloro, *Storia dell'Italia moderna*, 6:368–71; Gastone Manacorda, "Formazione e primo sviluppo del partito socialista in Italia: Il problemma storico e i più recenti orientamenti storiografici," *Studi storici* 1, no. 1 (1963): 23–50. See also Labriola, *Lettere a Engels*, pp. 42–44, 63, 65, 67–68, 70–71; and Schiavi, *Lettere di corrispondenti*, pp. 62–99. The Turati-Labriola and Turati-Engels correspondence has been lost.

61. See Cortesi, *La costituzione*, pp. 73–74.

62. Ibid., pp. 76–77, reprints the statement that was published in several newspapers on 11 and 12 August 1892.

63. Ibid., pp. 74–76.

64. Turati's letter is cited in ibid., pp. 77–78.

65. Ibid., p. 78.

66. Ibid., pp. 79–80.

67. Ibid., pp. 112–20.

68. Ibid., pp. 125–28.

69. The stenographic report of the Congress of Genoa is in *Lotta di classe*, 20–21 August 1892. Cortesi (*La costituzione*, pp. 128–40), and Manacorda (*Il movimento operaio*, pp. 312–31) give good accounts.

70. Cortesi, *La costituzione*, pp. 141–42.

71. Ibid., pp. 141–49. Cortesi gives a list of the organizations that adhered to the socialist congress and their representatives in his appendix. Andrea Costa and the Romagnol socialists were cut from all of these maneuvers; see Kuliscioff, *Lettere d'amore a Andrea Costa*, p. 323, and Manacorda, *Il movimento operaio*, pp. 326–29.

72. Cortesi summarizes the proceedings at the Sala Sivori, *La costituzione*, pp. 174–78; see also pp. 285–88.

73. Ibid., pp. 168–70.

74. *Lotta di classe*, 20–21 August 1892. Lazzari, Maffi, and other delegates wanted to keep the original wording of the draft proposal, which invited all workers' organizations, no matter what their methods, into the new party.

75. See Manacorda, *Il movimento operaio*, pp. 322–24. From this point, "Socialist," with a capital *S* will refer to a member of the Socialist party, and "Party," with a capital *P* will refer to the Italian Socialist party.

76. Ibid. See, besides Cortesi, Arfé, *Storia del socialismo*, pp. 9–21, and Candeloro, *Storia dell'Italia moderna*, 6:385–89.

77. The official name of the new organization was the Partito dei lavoratori italiani. In 1893 this was changed to the Partito socialista dei lavoratori italiani, and finally in 1895 to Partito socialista italiano (PSI), the name it was to keep.

78. See Cortesi, *La costituzione*, pp. 161–73, and Manacorda, *Il movimento operaio*, pp. 323–25.

79. Cortesi admits this, see *La costituzione*, p. 173. In comparing the program adopted at Genoa with that which the German Socialists adopted at Erfurt, Werner Sombart concluded that while Erfurt clearly expressed the Marxist interpretation of the evolution of society, the Genoa program was guided by ethical categories: the proletariat is unjustly exploited; therefore, the means of exploitation must be done away with. See Ragionieri, *Socialdemocrazia tedesca*, p. 320.

80. See Arfé, *Storia del socialismo*, pp. 22–23.

81. See article 6 of the Party constitution in *Lotta di classe*, 20–21 August 1892.

82. Ibid., article 10.

83. Ibid., article 11.

84. Ibid., articles 13–15.
85. Ibid., article 3.
86. Two hundred and ninety-four organizations with a total membership of 107,830 had joined the Socialist party by 1893. See Partito dei lavoratori italiani, *Rapporto*, p. 16. See also Partito socialista italiano, *Da Parma a Firenze*, p. 4.
87. See Arfé, *Storia del socialismo*, pp. 30–34.
88. Partito socialista dei lavoratori italiani, *Il congresso di Reggio Emilia*, p. 22.
89. The text of Turati's speech at the International Socialist Congress held in Zurich is in *Lotta di classe*, 2–3 September 1893, under the title, "Le alleanze coi partiti affini." See also the electoral manifesto of the Central Committee in *Lotta di classe*, 15–16 October 1892. On this problem, see also La lotta di classe, "La democrazia e il partito operaio socialista," *Lotta di classe*, 3–4 September 1892; and Filippo Turati, "L'eterna questione," *Critica sociale*, 30 March 1891. On these elections, see also Labriola, *Lettere a Engels*, pp. 86–90.
90. Filippo Turati, "I socialisti e le elezioni," *Cuore e critica*, 4 November 1890.
91. The question as to when and why Turati supported political alliances with "radical bourgeois" groups, and whether this represented a change (*svolta*) in his basic policy, has long been debated among historians. After examining the question, a recent article concludes, "sembra legittimo sostenere . . . che con essa [the decision to support alliances in 1894] il direttore della *Critica sociale* non rinegava nulla delle sue scelte di principio, né modificava il proprio modo di vedere compiti e funzioni del socialismo." I agree with this conclusion. See Lorenzo Strik Lievers, "Turati, la politica delle alleanze, e una celebre lettera di Engels," *Nuova rivista storica* 57 (January–April 1973): 159.
92. See "Contradizioni e fatiche," *Lotta di classe*, 8–9 July 1893.
93. Partito socialista, *Il congresso di Reggio Emilia*, pp. 25–29.
94. Ibid., p. 29.
95. The Italian Socialist deputies were generally cultured men who came from the bourgeoisie. Between 1892 and 1895, for example, out of ten deputies, nine came from the bourgeoisie. In 1900, twenty-seven out of thirty-two came from the bourgeois class, and only two were workers. In 1903, twenty-eight deputies had university degrees, three were petits bourgeois, and only two were workers. In Germany at the same time, thirteen had university degrees, fifteen were petits bourgeois, and fifty-three were workers. Roberto Michels, *Il proletariato e la borghesia nel movimento socialista italiano*, pp. 97–100. See, on this question, "Brigantaggio di classe," *Lotta di classe*, 28–29 January 1893.

Chapter III

1. Gastone Manacorda, "Il primo ministero Giolitti," pt. 1, *Studi storici* 2, no. 1 (January–March 1961): 88–90. See also Candeloro, *Storia dell'Italia moderna*, 6:410–11.
2. On these points, see Tommaso Palamenghi-Crispi, *Francesco Crispi: Politica interna. Diario e documenti raccolti e ordinati da T. Palamenghi-Crispi*, pp. 273–76; Tommaso Palamenghi-Crispi, *Giolitti: Saggio storico-biografico* (Rome: L'universelle, 1913), pp. 6–27, 29–40; Ivanoe Bonomi, *La politica italiana da Porta Pia a Vittorio Veneto*, pp. 85–88. For Giolitti's own account of his first ministry, see his *Memorie della mia vita*, pp. 62–82.
3. See Clough, *Economic History of Modern Italy*, pp. 124–32. For the effects of the scandal on the Giolitti "legend," see John Thayer, *Italy and the Great War*, pp. 56–68. Relevant accounts dating from the period are in Napoleone Colajanni, *Banche e parlamento*, 2d ed. (Milan: Treves, 1893), and Labriola, *Lettere a*

Engels, pp. 93, 96–97, 106–7, 179–82. See Palamenghi-Crispi, *Giolitti*, pp. 41–43, 51–108 (see also pp. 173–267). Giolitti's version of the story is in his *Memorie*, pp. 81–99. The most plausible explanation of the whole affair is Gastone Manacorda, "Il primo ministero Giolitti," pt. 2 *Studi storici* 3, no. 1 (January–March 1962): 88–103.

4.   Manacorda, "Il primo ministero Giolitti," pt. 2, pp. 103–5.

5.   See Palamenghi-Crispi, *Francesco Crispi*, pp. 284–94, and Giolitti, *Memorie*, pp. 74–78.

6.   Manacorda, "Il primo ministero Giolitti," pt. 2, pp. 106–20. On the *fasci* and Giolitti, see S. F. Romano, *Storia dei fasci siciliani* (Bari: Laterza, 1959), pp. 349–60; see pp. 262–346 for their origins and development. The entire issue of *Movimento operaio* 6, no. 6 (November–December 1954), is dedicated to the *fasci*. The most complete recent examination is Gastone Manacorda et al., *I fasci siciliani*. An important contemporary account of the activities of the *fasci* can be found in Napoleone Colajanni, *Gli avvenimenti in Sicilia e le loro cause*, pp. 157–261.

7.   Romano, *Storia dei fasci*, p. 429; and Colajanni, *Gli avvenimenti*, p. 191.

8.   See Palamenghi-Crispi, *Francesco Crispi*, pp. 294–97; Romano, *Storia dei fasci*, pp. 469–99; Giolitti, *Memorie*, p. 84; Colajanni, *Gli avvenimenti*, pp. 260–394; and Francesco de Stefano and Francesco Luigi Oddo, *Storia della Sicilia* (Bari: Laterza, 1963), pp. 271–341. Crispi believed that French and Russian agents anxious to detach Sicily from Italy were involved in the uprising; see Palamenghi-Crispi, *Francesco Crispi*, pp. 310–13; and Colajanni, *Gli avvenimenti*, pp. 361–63.

9.   Partito socialista, *Il congresso di Reggio Emilia*, p. 6. For the Sicilian "presence" at the congresses of Genoa and Reggio Emilia, see Luigi Cortesi, "Il Partito socialista e il movimento dei fasci (1892–1894)," *Movimento operaio* 6, no. 6 (November–December 1954): 1070–80. On the defense of the Socialists, see Giuseppe Giuffrida de Felice, *Commenti e note alla sentenza di condanna pronunciata dal tribunale militare di Palermo nel 30 maggio 1894 contro de Felice, Bosco, Barbato, Ferro, Montallo, Petrine e Benzi*, pp. 29–32; Stefano Merli, ed., *Autodifese di militanti operai e democratici italiani davanti ai tribunali* (Milan: Avanti!, 1958), pp. 65–72; Nicola Barbato, *Il socialismo difeso al tribunale di guerra*; and A. Rossi, *L'agitazione in Sicilia: A proposito delle ultime condanne* (Milan: Max Kantorwicz, 1894).

10. "Rivoluzione," *Lotta di classe*, 30–31 December 1893. See also De Stefano and Oddo, *Storia della Sicilia*, p. 313; and Romano, *Storia dei fasci*, pp. 528–46.

11. La critica sociale, "La Sicilia insorta," *Critica sociale*, 16 January 1894. See also De Stefano and Oddo, *Storia della Sicilia*, pp. 311–12.

12. See Cortesi, "Il Partito socialista e il movimento dei fasci," pp. 1081–111. See also Candeloro, *Storia dell'Italia moderna*, 6:432–33.

13. "I pieni poteri," *Lotta di classe*, 7–8 July 1894. See Palamenghi-Crispi, *Francesco Crispi*, pp. 321–22.

14. Candeloro, *Storia dell'Italia moderna*, 6:429–30; "Le leggi eccezionali," *Lotta di classe*, 7–8 July 1894. See also Palamenghi-Crispi, *Francesco Crispi*, pp. 307–10, 313–31.

15. La critica sociale, "Condannati," *Critica sociale*, 1 September 1894. Turati was able to benefit from a partial amnesty.

16. Filippo Turati, "Il fondamento dello stato borghese e l'obligazione del diritto di voto," *Critica sociale*, 16 April 1894; and La critica sociale, "Il governo nell'imbarazzo," *Critica sociale*, 16 June 1894.

17. La critica sociale, "Il trionfo dell'ordine," *Critica sociale*, 1 October 1894. In the same issue, see Filippo Turati, "Nel paese dei fasci."

18. Fausto Fonzi, *Crispi e lo "Stato di Milano*," pp. 228–32, dates the change in Turati's thinking from 22 October 1894, but I believe that the dissolution of the Socialist party provided the occasion for making his policy public and was not a sudden shift. See the letter from Turati to Engels, dated 24 October 1894, in Istituto Feltrinelli, "Corrispondenza Friedrich Engels–Filippo Turati, 1891–1895," in *Annali, 1958*, pp. 268–69.

19. Anna Kuliscioff's letter and a postscript by Turati is in Gianni Bosio, ed., *Karl Marx–Friedrich Engels: Scritti italiani*, pp. 164–66; and in Istituto Feltrinelli, *Annali, 1958*, pp. 251–52.

20. F. Engels, "La futura rivoluzione italiana e il partito socialista," *Critica sociale*, 1 February 1894. See also the comment by Noi in the same issue. Engels's letter to Turati can also be found in Bosio, *Marx–Engels*, pp. 170–71, and Istituto Feltrinelli, *Annali, 1958*, pp. 253–58.

21. See the commentary to Engels's letter in *Critica sociale*, 1 February 1894. Strik Lievers, in "Turati," argues that Turati and Kuliscioff were disappointed in Engels's answer precisely because he did emphasize the limited nature of political alliances, but they nevertheless skillfully used the letter to bolster their own point of view. See *Nuova rivista storica* 57, nos. 1–2 (January–April 1973): 146–50.

22. La critica sociale, "Intransigenza nel programma, transigenza nei metodi: È questa la nostra strada?" *Critica sociale*, 16 February 1894.

23. La critica sociale, "Le leggi eccezionali e il nostro partito," *Critica sociale*, 16 July 1894. Candeloro, *Storia dell'Italia moderna*, 6:437. See also Labriola, *Lettere a Engels*, pp. 170–71; Palamenghi-Crispi, *Francesco Crispi*, pp. 330–31; and especially Fonzi, *Crispi*, pp. 219–56.

24. "Nessun equivoco!" *Lotta di classe*, 3–4 November 1894.

25. "Crispi voleva le barricate," *Lotta di classe*, 3–4 November 1894. See also "La vendetta dei socialisti," *Lotta di classe*, 17–18 November 1894.

26. La critica sociale, "Per la conquista della libertà," *Critica sociale*, 1 November 1894. See also Labriola's pessimistic letter to Engels on what was happening in Italy in general and to the Socialists in particular, *Lettere a Engels*, pp. 162–64. For the feud between Crispi and Cavallotti, see Palamenghi-Crispi, *Francesco Crispi*, pp. 333–36, 339–40.

27. See Turati's letter in *Lotta di classe*, 10–11 November 1894.

28. See Strik Lievers, "Turati," pp. 150–54.

29. Noi, "Le future elezioni amministrative," *Critica sociale*, 16 December 1894. See also Fonzi, *Crispi*, pp. 232–36.

30. Federico Engels, "Il socialismo internazionale e il socialismo italiano," *Critica sociale*, 1 November 1894. The letter is reprinted in Bosio, *Marx–Engels*, pp. 176–78.

31. "Parlamentarismo," *Lotta di classe*, 29–30 December 1894.

32. See Labriola, *Lettere a Engels*, p. 164. The letter is dated 24 September 1894.

33. Arturo Labriola, "Le future elezioni e la tattica del partito socialista," *Critica sociale*, 1 January 1895. See also Fonzi, *Crispi*, pp. 236–37.

34. "Le future battaglie elettorali e il nostro partito," *Lotta di classe*, 5–6 January 1895.

35. Lazzari, "Memorie," pp. 805–6.

36. La critica sociale, "Tattica elettorale: Il nostro parere," *Critica sociale*, 16 January 1895.

37. "Elezioni amministrative di Milano," *Lotta di classe*, 9–10 February 1895. Antonio Labriola expressed his usual negative judgment on these elections; see *Lettere a Engels*, p. 190. For a detailed analysis of these elections, see Fonzi, *Crispi*, pp. 305–84.

38. See G. D'Angelo and Filippo Turati, "Il materialismo economico e la tattica socialista," *Critica sociale*, 1 April 1895. See also Labriola, *Lettere a Engels*, p. 187, for a comment on the tactics of the Milanese.

39. La critica sociale, "Alla conquista del comune," *Critica sociale*, 16 February 1895.

40. See Fonzi, *Crispi*, pp. xii–xv.

41. "Le future battaglie elettorali e il nostro partito," *Lotta di classe*; and "Congresso socialista di Parma," *Lotta di classe*, 19–20 January 1895. Milan was still the center of Italian socialism. See Labriola, *Lettere a Engels*, p. 170.

42. See Fonzi, *Crispi*, pp. 238–40.

43. Stenographic reports and comments on the Parma congress are in *Lotta di classe*, 19–20 January 1895, and in *Critica sociale*, 16 January 1895. See also Angiolo Cabrini, "Per riogranizzare il partito," *Critica sociale*, 1 December 1894; and Candeloro, *Storia dell'Italia moderna*, 6:437–38.

44. Arfé, *Storia del socialismo*, p. 34.

45. See the stenographic reports cited above. The constitution of the Party as it stood after the modifications made at Parma is reprinted in Franco Pedone, *Il Partito socialista italiano nei suoi congressi*, 1:56–60.

46. The Minimum Program is in *Critica sociale*, 16 April 1895. See also Partito socialista italiano, *Relazione per la riforma del programma minimo politico e amministrativo al congresso nazionale del partito socialista italiano, 20 settembre 1897*.

47. See Pedone, *Il Partito socialista*, 1:60.

48. See Partito socialista italiano, *Rapport du Parti socialiste italien au Congrès ouvrier-socialiste international* (Londres, 1896), pp. 14–15, and Fonzi, *Crispi*, pp. 363, 451–504. *Lotta di classe* claimed such a great victory, which it attributed to the new tactics, that Turati felt obliged to inject a word of caution. See especially the 1–2 June issue; Turati's letter of 19 June 1895 to Engels, in "Corrispondenza Friedrich Engels–Filippo Turati," in Istituto Feltrinelli, *Annali, 1958*, pp. 273–74; and La critica sociale, "Dopo i ballotaggi," *Critica sociale*, 16 June 1895.

49. On Crispi's and Italy's involvement in East Africa during this period, see Giolitti, *Memorie*, pp. 100–101; Roberto Battaglia, *La prima guerra di Africa* (Turin: Einaudi, 1958), pp. 15–138, 170–207, 230–64.

50. See Battaglia, *La prima guerra*, pp. 267–559. See also *Francesco Crispi: La prima guerra d'Africa. Storia diplomatica della colonia Eritrea dalle origini al 1896 sopra documenti dell'Archivio Crispi ordinati da T. Palamenghi-Crispi* (Milan: Treves, 1914), pp. 222–25, 248–54.

51. Battaglia, *La prima guerra*, pp. 563–611; and Giolitti, *Memorie*, pp. 101–2.

52. See Luciano Cafagna, "La formazione di una 'base industriale' fra il 1896 e il 1914," in Alberto Caracciolo, *La formazione dell'Italia industriale* (Bari: Laterza, 1963), pp. 137–64.

53. Candeloro, *Storia dell'Italia moderna*, 6:464–65, writes that "è certo che la caduta di Crispi fu un sucesso dell'ala più progredita e più intraprendente della borghesia italiana e al tempo stesso fu un sucesso delle forze popolari."

54. On the tariff of 1887, see Epicarmo Corbino, *L'economia italiana dal 1860 al 1960* (Bologna: Zanichelli, 1962), pp. 60–62; Rodolfo Morandi, *Storia della grande industria in Italia* (Turin: Einaudi, 1966), pp. 130–31; and Rosario Ro-

meo, *Breve storia della grande industria in Italia* (Bologna: Cappelli, 1972), pp. 58–60. On the Milanese attitude toward Crispi, see Fonzi, *Crispi*, pp. xvi–xxvii, 3–12, 17–24, and Turati's letter to Engels in Istituto Feltrinelli, *Annali*, *1958*, p. 260.

55. Fonzi, *Crispi*, pp. 505–17.

56. Filippo Turati, "Becchi e bastonati: L'impresa d'Africa e la borghesia italiana," *Critica sociale*, 16 January 1896. See also Battaglia, *La prima guerra*, pp. 705–707.

57. On the Battle of Adowa, see Battaglia, *La prima guerra*, pp. 611–789. For the international implications of Italian actions in Africa, see Arthur Marsden, "Salisbury and the Italians in 1896," *Journal of Modern History* 40, no. 1 (March 1968): 91–117.

58. See Battaglia, *La prima guerra*, pp. 793–809.

59. See Fonzi, *Crispi*, pp. 517–40.

60. Mario Belardinelli, *Un esperimento liberal-conservatore: I governi di Di Rudinì (1896–1898)*, pp. 71–73.

61. King Umberto I had given the mandate to form a government to Gen. Cesare Ricotti because of the troubled situation following the defeat at Adowa. Ricotti, in turn, secured the acceptance of Rudinì. Ricotti was a well-known adversary of the king's military plans, but the troubled situation after Adowa forced Umberto to turn to him. For an explanation of the political situation, see Gastone Manacorda's introduction to Luigi Pelloux, *Quelques souvenirs de ma vie*, pp. xxxiii–xxxviii. For more on the formation of Rudinì's cabinet, and interesting insights on what it meant, see Lucio Villari, "I fatti di Milano del 1898: La testimonianza di Eugenio Torelli Viollier," *Studi storici*, no. 3 (1967); and Anna Ginsberg Rossi-Doria, "A proposito del secondo ministero di Rudinì," *Studi storici* 9, no. 2 (1968). See also Giolitti, *Memorie*, pp. 102–3.

62. Giolitti, *Memorie*, p. 103, criticizes Rudinì for pulling back too far in Africa. For the partial amnesty, see Bonomi, *La politica italiana*, pp. 121–22.

63. See dalle Nogare and Merli, *L'Italia radicale*, pp. 376–78, and especially pp. 214–24. See also Pelloux, *Quelques souvenirs*, p. 176; Saverio Cilibrizzi, *Storia parlamentare politica e diplomatica d'Italia da Novara a Vittorio Veneto*, 3 : 83–84; and Seton-Watson, *Italy*, p. 183.

64. Seton-Watson, *Italy*, p. 186.

65. La critica sociale, "Per un voto di disperazione," *Critica sociale*, 16 June 1896.

66. See Turati's letter to Cavallotti, dated 4 April 1896, in dalle Nogare and Merli, *L'Italia radicale*, pp. 360–61.

67. See *Lotta di classe*, 20–21 June 1896.

68. See La critica sociale, "Le tre giornate di Firenze," *Critica sociale*, 16 June 1896.

69. The original motion in Turati's handwriting, with comments by Bissolati, is preserved in Prof. Pier Carlo Masini's "Biblioteca Max Nettau," in Palazzago (Bergamo). I thank him for making the document available to me.

70. La critica sociale, "Il catenaccio al partito (Echi del congresso regionale di Brescia)," *Critica sociale*, 1 May 1896.

71. See Ivanoe Bonomi, *Le vie nuove del socialismo* (Palermo: Sandron, 1907). Bonomi dedicated his book to Anna Kuliscioff.

72. Partito socialista italiano, *Congresso socialista: Rapporti della direzione del partito, relazioni sull'organizzazione, sulla tattica, sulla stampa, sulla propaganda. Verbali delle discussioni (Firenze 11–12–13 luglio 1896)*, p. 59.

73. Ibid.

74. See ibid., pp. 60–68.

75. Ibid., p. 29.

76. Ibid., p. 41. Labriola's conclusions on the Minimum Program are in *Lotta di classe*, 4–5 July 1896.

77. The discussion of this issue is in PSI, *Congresso socialista*, pp. 68–78.

78. Gaetano Arfé, *Storia dell'Avanti!*, 1 : 5–11, and *Storia del socialismo*, pp. 35–41.

79. Arfé, *Storia dell'Avanti!*, 1 : 10.

80. Arfé, *Storia del socialismo*, p. 42.

81. *Avanti!*, 25 December 1896.

82. Arfé, *Storia del socialismo*, pp. 42–46, and *Storia dell'Avanti!*, 1 : 12–13.

83. See Villari, "I fatti di Milano," pp. 536–37.

84. Belardinelli, *Un esperimento liberal-conservatore*, pp. 121–35. See also Seton-Watson, *Italy*, pp. 188–90.

85. *Avanti!*, 6 and 13 March 1897. See also Arfé, *Storia dell'Avanti!*, 1 : 11.

86. La critica sociale, "Serriamo le file," *Critica sociale*, 1 August 1896. See also Bonomi, *Le vie nuove*, p. 123.

87. Filippo Turati, "La commedia della reazione," *Critica sociale*, 16 January 1897; La critica sociale, "La censura restituita: A difesa del giornale del partito," *Critica sociale*, 1 August 1897.

88. See "Il domicilio coatto: L'appello del comitato milanese," *Critica sociale*, 1 August 1897.

89. The electoral manifesto is in *Avanti!*, 13 March 1897.

90. For the results as interpreted by the Socialists, see *Avanti!*, 22 and 31 March and 4 April 1897.

91. "Socialisti e governi," *Avanti!*, 23 March 1897.

92. Belardinelli, *Un esperimento liberal-conservatore*, pp. 141–70.

93. The stenographic report of the Congress of Bologna was published in *Avanti!*, 20, 21, and 22 September 1897. See also the interesting reports written for this congress: Partito socialista italiano, *Bilancio e relazione finanziaria del partito e bilanci della "Lotta di classe" e della libreria al congresso nazionale del Partito socialista italiano*, and *Rapporto sull'azione del gruppo parlamentare al congresso nazionale* (Bologna, 18–19–20 September 1897).

94. *Avanti!*, 21 September 1897.

95. Ibid.

Chapter IV

1. Napoleone Colajanni, *L'Italia nel 1898*, pp. 21–24; and Angiolini, *Socialismo e socialisti*, pp. 311–12.

2. Clough, *The Economic History of Italy*, pp. 123–24; and Colajanni, *L'Italia nel 1898*, p. 25.

3. See Ente per la storia del socialismo e del movimento operaio italiano (hereafter referred to as E.S.M.O.I.), *Attività parlamentare dei socialisti italiani, 1882–1900*, p. 382.

4. Angiolini, *Socialismo e socialisti*, p. 312; and Colajanni, *L'Italia nel 1898*, p. 119.

5. See Filippo Turati, "Pane e libertà," *Critica sociale*, 10 February 1898, and "Ci buffuniano," *Critica sociale*, 10 March 1898; E.S.M.O.I., *Attività parlamentare*, 1 : 381–85; Raffaele Colapietra, *Il novantotto*, pp. 65–67; and Angiolini, *Socialismo e socialisti*, p. 314.

6. Belardinelli, *Un esperimento liberal-conservatore*, pp. 245–55. See also Colajanni, *L'Italia nel 1898*, pp. 125–26, 137–39; and Pelloux, *Quelques souvenirs*, pp. xii–xxvi.

7. See Angiolini, *Socialismo e socialisti*, pp. 312–14; Colapietra, *Il novantotto*, p. 77; and Colajanni, *L'Italia nel 1898*, pp. 119–31.

8. See Cilibrizzi, *Storia parlamentare*, p. 72.

9. See E.S.M.O.I., *Attività parlamentare*, 1:340, 341. Turati's speech, giving the Socialist group's version, is in Filippo Turati, *Discorsi parlamentari*, 1:52–54.

10. Angiolini, *Socialismo e socialisti*, pp. 310–11.

11. See Cilibrizzi, *Storia parlamentare*, pp. 67–72; and Bonomi, *La politica italiana*, p. 125.

12. Angiolini, *Socialismo e socialisti*, p. 311.

13. Belardinelli, *Un esperimento liberal-conservatore*, pp. 121–34, 215–41.

14. Turati's speech to the Chamber on behalf of the Socialist deputies is in his *Discorsi parlamentari*, 1:55–60.

15. Colajanni, *L'Italia nel 1898*, pp. 24–25; and Colapietra, *Il novantotto*, p. 77.

16. See Colajanni, *L'Italia nel 1898*, pp. 25–28.

17. The leaflet is reprinted in Colapietra, *Il novantotto*, pp. 214–16. The document is signed "The Milanese Socialists" and was attributed to Turati. This attribution has not been proved and, in my opinion, the style is not Turati's.

18. Colajanni, *L'Italia nel 1898*, pp. 31, 33–34; and Angiolini, *Socialismo e socialisti*, pp. 322–23.

19. The map had been printed by the city. The letter *f* stood for tram stops and *b* for *bocche d'incendio*.

20. Apparently there was a plan by some army officers to kill Turati. See the letter of Dr. Ercole in Filippo Turati and Anna Kuliscioff, *Carteggio, vol. 1, Maggio 1898–giugno 1899*, pp. 517–18. See also Colajanni, *L'Italia nel 1898*, p. 42; and Angiolini, *Socialismo e socialisti*, p. 336.

21. See Colajanni, *L'Italia nel 1898*, pp. 29–45; Angiolini, *Socialismo e socialisti*, pp. 323–27; Colapietra, *Il novantotto*, pp. 81–84; Turati and Kuliscioff, *Carteggio*, 1:xxiii–xxxiii; Bonomi, *La politica italiana*, pp. 127–32; Villari, "I fatti di Milano," pp. 534–49; and Umberto Levra, *Il colpo di stato della borghesia*, p. 115.

22. See Luigi Albertini, *Venti anni di vita politica*, vol. 1, *L'esperienza democratica italiana dal 1898 al 1914*, p. 14.

23. On these "Swiss bands," see Colajanni, *L'Italia nel 1898*, pp. 53–54. See also Belardinelli, *Un esperimento liberal-conservatore*, pp. 353–56. The testimony is in *I Tribunali* (Milan), supplement to no. 83 (28–29 July 1898).

24. Albertini, *Venti anni*, 1:7–10.

25. The work cited is Levra, *Il colpo di stato*. It adopts the views of Arturo Labriola's *Storia di dieci anni* (1910), a polemical antireformist work that misrepresents the interpretation of the reformists regarding the 1898 disturbances; see pp. 121–23.

26. Turati and Kuliscioff, *Carteggio*, 1:346–49. G. Battista Pirelli testified during Turati's trial that a delegation consisting of Turati, Bissolati, and several workers asked Pirelli to keep his factory opened and that Pirelli himself believed he should do so. He testified that the day before he had received permission from the authorities to remain open, but "mi telefonarono dal Comando, dimostrandomi l'opportunità di tener chiuso anche il lunedì," *I Tribunali*, supplement to no. 83 (29–30 July 1898).

27. Albertini, *Venti anni*, 1:5–6; and Morandi, *Storia della grande industria*, pp. 149–56. For a description of the worsening conditions in Milan, see Levra, *Il colpo di stato*, pp. 101–16, and especially Volker Hunecke, "Comune e classe operaia a Milano," *Studi storici* 18, no. 3 (July-September 1976):63–96.

28. See Angiolini, *Socialismo e socialisti*, pp. 317–28; Colajanni, *L'Italia nel 1898*,

pp. 63–67, 73–74; Croce, *Storia d'Italia*, p. 225; E. S. M.O.I., *Attività parlamentare*, 1:412; and Rossi-Doria, "A proposito del secondo ministero Di Rudinì," pp. 404–16. See also *Avanti!*, 28 April, 3, 4, 5, 8, 9, 10, 11, 13, 14, 15, 17 May 1898; and Turati and Kuliscioff, *Carteggio*, 1:334, 349.

29. Levra, *Il colpo di stato*, pp. 81–92, 115–21.

30. Belardinelli, *Un esperimento liberal-conservatore*, pp. 343–49.

31. Ibid., pp. 355–66. Sonnino's speech is in *Atti parlamentari (Camera dei deputati), XX Leg., 1ª sess., discussioni*, 16 June 1898, pp. 6267–71.

32. See Levra, *Il colpo di stato*, pp. 20–21.

33. See Schiavi's introduction to Turati and Kuliscioff, *Carteggio*, 1:xxviii.

34. See Albertini, *Venti anni*, 1:9; and Colajanni, *L'Italia nel 1898*, pp. 95–104.

35. Turati and Kuliscioff, *Carteggio*, 1:437–39.

36. The debate is in *Atti parlamentari (Camera), XX Leg., 1ª sess. discussioni*, 9 July 1898, pp. 6656–92. Turati wrote that he was "indignant"; see Turati and Kuliscioff, *Carteggio*, 1:31.

37. The court proceedings of the trial are in *I Tribunali*, supplement to no. 83 (27–28, 28–29, 30–31 July, and 1–2 August 1898); the sentences are in the 22–23 August 1898 supplement to no. 84. Turati's appeal is in the supplement to no. 87. For accounts of the trial, see Colajanni, *L'Italia nel 1898*, pp. 93–98, 105–17; Turati and Kuliscioff, *Carteggio*, 1:31, 38–39, 40–42, 44–45, 506–9, 511–13, and Schiavi's introduction, pp. xxxi–xxxii; part of Turati's speech is in *Autodifese di militanti operai e democratici italiani davanti ai tribunali*, pp. 75–92, and in *Avanti!*, 22, 24 June, 11, 27–28, 29, 30 July, 1, 2, 4 August 1898. I might note here that there was a serious question as to whether military tribunals were constitutional or not. See Colajanni, *L'Italia nel 1898*, p. 87; "I tribunali e lo stato," in *Avanti!*, 5 June 1898; and especially G. A. Ruiz, *The Amendments to the Italian Constitution* (Philadelphia: American Academy of Political and Social Science, 1895), pp. 52–53.

38. See Pelloux, *Quelques souvenirs*, pp. xliv–lvi, lxii–lxiv, 156–64, 176–77; Giolitti, *Memorie*, p. 106; Colapietra, *Il novantotto*, p. 76; Levra, *Il colpo di stato*, p. 184; Belardinelli, *Un esperimento liberal-conservatore*, pp. 378–79; Albertini, *Venti anni*, 1:15–16; and Cilibrizzi, *Storia parlamentare*, pp. 88–89.

39. See Bonomi, *La politica italiana*, pp. 137–39; and Cilibrizzi, *Storia parlamentare*, pp. 104–5, 109–10.

40. Giolitti, *Memorie*, p. 106.

41. "I disegni della reazione," *Avanti!*, 31 June 1899.

42. See "Le leggi contro lo statuto," *Avanti!*, 9 February 1899, and "A difesa dello statuto," *Avanti!*, 12 February 1899. Some Socialists, including Gaetano Salvemini, argued that the Constitution did not guarantee the basic liberties and that for fifty years the "popular parties" had been defending an instrument that was meant to thwart revolution. See Tre stelle [Gaetano Salvemini], "Perchè difendiamo lo statuto," *Avanti!*, 21 February 1899, and the articles signed by Ciccotti and Il pessimista [Salvemini] in *Avanti!* in February, March, and April. The discussion can be followed with greater ease in Gaetano Salvemini, *Movimento socialista e questione meridionale*, in *Opere IV*, 2 vols. (Milan: Feltrinelli, 1963), 2:102–21.

43. See Giolitti, *Memorie*, pp. 106–7; Pelloux, *Quelques souvenirs*, pp. lxvii, 194; and *Dalle carte di Giovanni Giolitti: Quarant'anni di politica italiana*, 1:355.

44. See Levra, *Il colpo di stato*, pp. 312–43; and Giolitti, *Quarant'anni*, 1:356. See also *Avanti!*, 8 and 16 March 1899.

45. See Un deputato [Sidney Sonnino], "Torniamo allo Statuto," *Nuova antologia* (Rome) 67 (1 January 1897). See also Pelloux, *Quelques souvenirs*, pp. lxviii–

lxxi; Thayer, *Italy and the Great War*, pp. 126–32; Giampiero Carocci, *Il parlamento nella storia d'Italia* (Bari: Laterza, 1964), p. 306; and Sonnino's speech in the Chamber of Deputies in which he restates his principles, *Atti parlamentari (Camera), discussioni*, Leg. XX, 1ª sess. 16 June 1898, pp. 6267–71.

46. See Carocci *Il parlamento nella storia d'Italia*, p. 306; and Angiolini, *Socialismo e socialisti*, p. 345. For some of the discussion between the Socialists and other factions of the Extreme Left, see the article by Gaetano Salvemini, "Radicali repubblicani e socialisti," originally published in Colajanni's *Rivista popolare di politica, lettere, e scienze sociali* and reprinted in Gaetano Salvemini, *Movimento socialista*, pp. 64–67.

47. Turati and Kuliscioff, *Carteggio*, 1:285–86. See also Turati's article in *Avanti!*, 11 June 1899.

48. See Cilibrizzi, *Storia parlamentare*, pp. 110–13; and Pelloux, *Quelques souvenirs*, pp. 195–96. E.S.M.O.I., *Attività parlamentare*, 1:493–529, is an excellent guide to the parliamentary discussions.

49. *Atti parlamentari (Camera), Leg. XX., 2ª sess. discussioni*, 21 June 1899, p. 4688. See also Albertini, *Venti anni*, 1:18.

50. Sonnino's proposals came from the usage in the English House of Commons. See Cilibrizzi, *Storia parlamentare*, p. 115.

51. E.S.M.O.I., *Attività parlamentare*, 1:529–34.

52. See Bonomi, *La politica italiana*, p. 142; and Pelloux, *Quelques souvenirs*, pp. 197–98. For the denunciation of this technique by the Socialists, see "Pellougnac," *Avanti!*, 25 June 1899. *Avanti!* had reported as early as 13 June that Pelloux would use this technique.

53. See *Atti parlamentari (Camera), Leg. XX, 2ª sess. discussioni*, 28 June 1899; E.S.M.O.I., *Attività parlamentare*, 1:534–36; Pelloux, *Quelques souvenirs*, pp. 197–98; and Cilibrizzi, *Storia parlamentare*, pp. 115–17.

54. See *Atti parlamentari (Camera), Leg. XX, 2ª sess. discussioni*, 30 June 1899, pp. 4875–81; and *Avanti!*, 1 and 2 July 1899.

55. See Bonomi, *La politica italiana*, pp. 144–45; and Croce, *Storia d'Italia*, pp. 228–29.

56. See *Atti parlamentari (Camera), Leg. XX, 2ª sess. discussioni*, 25 and 28 November 1898, pp. 166–68, 260–63; and Turati and Kuliscioff, *Carteggio*, 1:313, 372, 389–90, 392–93, 490, 494.

57. See Turati and Kuliscioff, *Carteggio*, 1:311, 370–74, 380–81, 393–94; and Claudio Treves, *Un socialista*, p. 12.

58. Angiolini, *Socialismo e socialisti*, pp. 347–48, 357; Turati and Kuliscioff, *Carteggio*, 1:334.

59. Civilian juries acquitted several persons previously condemned by military tribunals, including the popular Socialist deputy Giuseppe Pescetti. Pelloux's minister of war, Gen. G. Mirri, had to resign when documents linked him with criminal elements in Sicily in an attempt to influence the elections there. In addition, the Socialists made a cause célèbre of an anarchist who had been condemned for throwing a bomb in 1878 and was still in jail almost twenty years after proof of his innocence had come to light. Nominated as a protest candidate by the Socialists, he was elected to the Chamber and eventually pardoned. Accounts of these activities can be found in Angiolini, *Socialismo e socialisti*, pp. 347–49, 357–58; Turati and Kuliscioff, *Carteggio*, 1:306, 414–15, 419; Pelloux, *Quelques souvenirs*, pp. 201–2. See also *Avanti!*, 15 December 1899; and E.S.M.O.I., *Attività parlamentare*, 1:180, 502, 552, 558–59, 563, 570, 575.

60. Angiolini, *Socialismo e socialisti*, pp. 349–56, provides a good inventory of Party resources in 1899.

61. La critica sociale, "Ripigliando," *Critica sociale*, 1 July 1899. While in jail, Turati had thought of the possibility of permanently discontinuing the *Critica*, but the demand for this journal was so overwhelming that publication was resumed immediately upon his release. On this point, see Turati and Kuliscioff, *Carteggio*, 1:465, 471, 516–17.

62. The interview is in *Avanti!*, 11 June 1899.

63. [T.]-k, "L'alleanza dei partiti popolari," *Critica sociale*, 1 December 1899.

64. See ibid.

65. Filippo Turati, "Le voci delle opposizzioni," *Critica sociale*, 1 November 1899.

66. Pelloux, *Quelques souvenirs*, p. lxxiv. See also Bonomi, *La politica italiana*, p. 143; and *Avanti!*, 9 and 21 February 1900.

67. For the action of the Socialist deputies, see E.S.M.O.I., *Attività parlamentare*, 1:576–600.

68. Albertini, *Venti anni*, 1:22.

69. *Atti parlamentari (Camera), Leg. XX, 3ª sess. discussioni*, 21 March 1900, p. 2859; and E.S.M.O.I., *Attività parlamentare*, 1:601, 604–10.

70. See *Atti parlamentari (Camera), Leg. XX, 3ª sess. discussioni*, 29 and 30 March 1900, pp. 3121–23, 3125. E.S.M.O.I., *Attività parlamentare*, 1:611–12; Pelloux, *Quelques souvenirs*, p. 199.

71. Giolitti, *Memorie*, p. 110.

72. See Giolitti's speech in his *Discorsi parlamentari*, 3:622–25.

73. On these points, see *Atti parlamentari (Camera), Leg. XX, 3ª sess. discussioni*, 3 April 1900, pp. 3139–41, and 15 May 1900, pp. 3143–57. See also Pelloux, *Quelques souvenirs*, pp. 199–200.

74. Pelloux, *Quelques souvenirs*, pp. 207–8.

75. See Angiolini, *Socialismo e socialisti*, pp. 361–62.

76. See *Avanti!*, 28 May 1900, and "Le candidature dei partiti popolari," 23 June 1900.

77. A total of 649,485 votes were cast for all the opposition factions, while government supporters received 611,425 votes. The popular vote for the Socialists went from 121,000 to 215,841. See "Il trionfo dell'estrema sinistra," *Avanti!*, 5 June 1900, and "La seconda vittoria," 12 June 1900; Angiolini, *Socialismo e socialisti*, pp. 362–66.

78. Pelloux, *Quelques souvenirs*, pp. 208–9.

79. Labriola, *Storia di dieci anni*, pp. 25–27, 40.

80. Levra, *Il colpo di stato*, pp. 124–84; and Belardinelli, *Un esperimento liberal-conservatore*, pp. 349–52. See also the review of Belardinelli's book in *Storia contemporanea* (Rome) 7, no. 2 (April–June 1977): 369–74.

81. See Levra, *Il colpo di stato*, pp. 227–30.

82. Labriola, *Ministero e socialismo*, p. 3.

83. See Bonomi, *La politica italiana*, pp. 144–45; and Albertini, *Venti anni*, 1:23.

84. Manacorda repeatedly makes this point in his introduction to Pelloux's memoirs; see, for example, *Quelques souvenirs*, p. lxxi.

85. Croce, *Storia d'Italia*, pp. 225–26. See also Papafava, *Dieci anni, di vita italiana*, 2 vols. (Bari: Laterza, 1913), 1:2–3.

86. E.S.M.O.I., *Attività parlamentare*, 1:595.

87. Turati, *Discorsi parlamentari*, 1:96–98. "[Q]uando il nostro braccio pesasse davvero sulla bilancia dei pubblici negozi, non potremmo, anche se volessimo, tradire mai quei principii di libertà che abbiamo oggi rivendicati." Albertini's argument that the obstructionism of this period led to a policy of compliance on the part of later governments toward the extreme parties "which led us to fascism" (Albertini, *Venti anni*, 1:26–27) is far-fetched. The rules of the Chamber

were in fact changed with the cooperation of the Socialists so that obstructionism became very difficult (see E.S.M.O.I., *Attività parlamentare*, 2:142–44).
Mack Smith argues that a coalition similar to the one that formed in 1899 might
have been able to stop Mussolini after World War I (*Italy*, p. 196).

88. Croce, *Storia d'Italia*, p. 225.

Chapter V

1. On the background, see Pelloux, *Quelques souvenirs*, pp. 210–11.
2. E. Scarfoglio, cited by Cilibrizzi, *Storia parlamentare*, p. 160.
3. Ibid., pp. 129–30; and Albertini, *Venti anni*, 1:26.
4. *Avanti!*, 25 June 1900; and Turati, *Discorsi parlamentari*, 1:124–32. See also
    E.S.M.O.I., *Attività parlamentare*, 2:3–4.
5. See Colajanni, *L'Italia nel 1898*, pp. 69–70; and *Atti parlamentari (Camera)*,
    Leg. XX, 1ª sess. discussioni, 24 June 1898, p. 6329. On the assassination itself,
    see Labriola, *Storia di dieci anni*, pp. 74–75; Domenico Bartoli, *Vittorio
    Emanuele III* (Milan: Mondadori, 1946), pp. 59–69; and Pelloux, *Quelques sou-
    venirs*, pp. 212–14. On Bresci, see Arrigo Petacco, *L'anarchico che venne dal-
    l'America*, 2d ed. (Milan: Mondadori, 1974).
6. Labriola, *Storia di dieci anni*, pp. 77–79.
7. *Avanti!*, 30 July 1900; E.S.M.O.I., *Attività parlamentare*, 2:8–9. Turati's speech
    is in his *Discorsi parlamentari*, 1:133–34.
8. Turati was tempted to take the case because he felt Bresci would not be able to
    get anyone else to defend him and probably would not get a fair trial, but Turati
    had not practiced in court for ten years. He expressed the opinion that the police
    may have prompted Bresci to ask for him in order to embarrass the Socialists.
    See Filippo Turati to Anna Kuliscioff, 18 August 1900. The man who eventually
    defended Bresci was the ex-anarchist Francesco Saverio Merlino. Bresci was sen-
    tenced to life imprisonment but was later found hanged in his cell under
    mysterious circumstances. The official ruling was suicide.
9. Gioacchino Volpe, *Vittorio Emanuele III* (Milan: Istituto per gli studi di politica
    internazionale, 1939), pp. 155–60. On the new king at this particular juncture,
    see ibid., pp. 9–44; Pelloux, *Quelques Souvenirs*, pp. lxxvi–lxxx; and Labriola,
    Storia di dieci anni, pp. 83–84. A cartoon showed Vittorio swearing to uphold
    the Constitution while a woman symbolizing Italy answers: "And I bless you, o
    my king, son and grandson of kings who have never lied." See GEC [Enrico
    Gianieri], *Il piccolo re Vittorio Emanuele nella caricatura* (Turin: Fiorini, 1945),
    p. 33.
10. [T]-k, "Dichiarazioni necessarie: Rivoluzionari od opportunisti?" *Critica
    sociale*, 1 January 1900.
11. Un travet [G. Salvemini], "Commenti forse inutili alle 'dichiarazioni neces-
    sarie,'" *Critica sociale*, 16 February 1900; also in Salvemini, *Movimento so-
    cialista*, pp. 138–48.
12. Filippo Turati, "In vista del congresso," *Critica sociale*, 1 September 1900.
13. Partito socialista italiano, *Rendiconto del VI congresso nazionale* (Rome, 8–11
    September 1900), pp. 73–77. Other orators representing the same point of view
    were Frilli and Bertelli, in ibid., pp. 71–73. See also the report on tactics made by
    Alfredo Zerboglio, *La tattica*.
14. PSI, *Rendiconto del VI congresso*, pp. 77–80.
15. Ibid., pp. 82–83.
16. Ibid., p. 86.
17. Ibid., p. 80.

18. Ibid., pp. 55–64, 67–69. The motion was presented by Ivanoe Bonomi. For further information, see Bonomi's report to the congress, *Sull'azione del partito nelle amministrazioni locali.*

19. PSI, *Rendiconto del VI congresso*, pp. 10–17.

20. Ibid., pp. 17–22; see also pp. 22–25, 53–55.

21. Ibid., pp. 27–52. See also Bissolati's report to the Congress, *Relazione sull'Avanti!.*

22. PSI, *Rendiconto del VI congresso*, pp. 121–26; and also the report on the Minimum Program, *Il Programma minimo socialista* (n.p., 1900), signed by Turati, Treves, and Carlo Sambucco.

23. See "Per la riforma del Programma minimo," *Critica sociale*, reprinted in Salvemini, *Movimento socialista*, pp. 148–54.

24. See Giuseppe Mammarella, *Riformisti e rivoluzionari nel Partito socialista italiano*, pp. 68–74.

25. PSI, *Rendiconto del VI congresso*, pp. 105–16.

26. See Filippo Turati, "In vista del congresso," *Critica sociale*, 1 September 1900.

27. PSI, *Rendiconto del VI congresso*, pp. 91–101. The congress rejected an unwieldly proposal by the historian Ettore Ciccotti. See his report to the Congress, *Sull'organizzazione politica ed economica del Partito socialista italiano* (Modena: Tip. degli operai, 1900).

28. [T]-k, "La sintesi del congresso di Roma," *Critica sociale*, 1 October 1900.

29. See Rinaldo Rigola, *Storia del movimento operaio italiano* (Milan: Ed. Domus S.A., 1946), pp. 192–99.

30. Angiolini, *Socialismo e socialisti*, pp. 378–86.

31. *Atti parlamentari (Camera), XXI Leg., 1ª sess., discussioni*, 6 February 1901, pp. 2224–27. See also E.S.M.O.I., *Attività parlamentare*, 2 : 41–48; and Cilibrizzi, *Storia parlamentare*, pp. 154–60.

32. For the relevant debate, motions, and votes, see *Atti parlamentari (Camera), XXI Leg., 1ª sess., discussioni*, 4 February 1901, pp. 2128–55; 5 February, pp. 2164–88; and 6 February, pp. 2194–227. Giolitti gives the background in his *Memorie*, pp. 122–23. See also Angiolini, *Socialismo e socialisti*, pp. 386–87; and Papafava, *Dieci anni*, 1 : 146–48.

33. See Emilio Ondei, *Giuseppe Zanardelli e un trentennio di storia italiana* (Brescia: Tip. Pavoniana, 1954), p. 142.

34. See Papafava, *Dieci anni*, 1 : 148–51.

35. Giolitti, *Memorie*, p. 121.

36. See Ferri's speech in *Atti parlamentari (Camera), XXI Leg., 1ª sess.*, 7 March 1901, 3 : 2238–44.

37. See the interview with Marcora in *Il tempo*, 17 February 1901.

38. Turati to Kuliscioff, 2 February 1901.

39. Turati to Kuliscioff, 4 February 1901.

40. See *Il tempo*, 14 and 15 February 1901: Actually total expenses related to the army were about 40 million more. These figures do not include sums for the navy.

41. Turati to Kuliscioff, 7 March 1901.

42. Kuliscioff to Turati, 1 April 1901.

43. Partito socialista italiano, *Relazione della direzione del partito* (Imola, 6–7–8 September 1902), pp. 16–21.

44. Filippo Turati, "Il caso per caso e i 'casi' di Milano," *Avanti!*, 24 August 1901.

45. The story of this meeting is in Turati to Kuliscioff, 14 June 1901.

46. Giovanni Giolitti, *Discorsi extraparlamentari*, pp. 211–32, 237–46.

47. See Giolitti, *Memorie*, pp. 121–23.

48. Giolitti, *Discorsi parlamentari*, 2:626–33; and Giolitti, *Memorie*, pp. 119–21.

49. Ministero di agricultura, industria, e commercio, Direzione generale della statistica, *Annuario statistico italiano, 1904* (Rome: Tip. nazionale di G. Bertero E.C., 1904), p. 367.

50. *Atti parlamentari (Senato del regno), XXI Leg., 1ª sess., discussioni*, 22 April 1901, p. 1320, 29 April, pp. 1334–37, 30 April, pp. 1350–77. Giolitti's response is in his *Discorsi parlamentari*, 2:636–43.

51. Sonnino's speech is in *Discorsi parlamentari di Sidney Sonnino*, 3 vols. (Rome: Tip. della Camera dei deputati, 1925), 3:34–51.

52. Giolitti's complete speech is in his *Discorsi parlamentari*, 2:652–74.

53. See *Atti parlamentari (Camera), XXI Leg., 1ª sess., discussioni*, 19 June 1901, 6:5398.

54. Ferri made the announcement; see *Atti parlamentari (Camera), XXI Leg., 1ª sess., discussioni*, 22 June 1901, 6:5577–85. For the activities of the Socialist deputies during this period, see E.S.M.O.I., *Attività parlamentare*, 2:108–18.

55. *Atti parlamentari (Camera), XXI Leg., 1ª sess., discussioni*, 22 June 1901, 6:5601–602.

56. See *Avanti!*, 23 and 24 June 1901.

57. *Avanti!*, 20 June 1901. See Papafava, *Dieci anni*, 1:182; and E.S.M.O.I., *Attività parlamentare*, 2:120.

58. For this backlash, which was especially strong in Turin, Florence, Naples, and Milan, see Mammarella, *Riformisti e rivoluzionari*, p. 113.

59. Giolitti's speech is in *Atti parlamentari (Camera), XXI Leg., 1ª sess.*, 29 June 1901, 6:6124–26.

60. Ibid., pp. 6126–29.

61. The article was reprinted in *Avanti!* and other newspapers and also went into several editions as an independent work. For convenience, I will refer to the first of these editions below.

62. Filippo Turati, *Il Partito socialista e l'attuale momento politico*, pp. 3–5.

63. Ibid., p. 6.

64. Ibid., pp. 7–9, 21–22.

65. Ibid., pp. 11–23.

66. On economic developments during this period, see Caracciolo, *La formazione dell'Italia industriale*, especially the essay by Rosario Romeo; Morandi, *Storia della grande industria*, pp. 65–114; Epicarmo Corbino, *Annali dell'economia italiana*, 6 vols. (Città di Castello: Tip. Leonardo da Vinci, 1938), vol. 5, chap. 3; Clough, *Economic History of Italy*, chap. 3; Gianni Toniolo, ed., *Lo sviluppo economico italiano* (Bari: Laterza, 1973), pp. 18–30, 132–40; and Candeloro, *Storia dell'Italia moderna*, 7:94–122.

67. Giolitti, *Discorsi parlamentari*, 2:658–59.

68. Arturo Labriola, *Ministero e socialismo*, pp. 3–10, 17, 22–23.

69. Ibid., pp. 11, 18–19, 28–30.

70. Kuliscioff to Turati, 8 August 1901.

71. Kuliscioff to Turati, 14 August 1901.

72. See Francesco Saverio Merlino, *Colletivismo, lotta di classe, e . . . ministero!*

73. Filippo Turati, "Risposta ai contradittori," *Critica sociale*, 1 and 16 September 1901, and "Le confessioni di Saverio Merlino," 1 October 1901.

74. See Mammarella, *Riformisti e rivoluzionari*, pp. 113–14.

75. Spencer Di Scala, "Filippo Turati e la scissione del Partito socialista milanese del 1901," *Rassegna di politica e di storia* 16, no. 183 (January–March 1970): 1–6.

76. Zanardelli's speech is in *Atti parlamentari (Camera), XXI Leg., 1ª sess.*, 7 March 1901, 3:2233–37.

77. Ibid., pp. 2238–44.

78. See Pelloux, *Quelques souvenirs*, p. xxi.

79. Toniolo, *Lo sviluppo economico*, pp. 28–29. On the tariff, see also Alexander Gerschenkron, "Notes on the Rate of Industrial Growth in Italy, 1881–1913," *Journal of Economic History* 15, no. 4 (December 1955): 367–70.

80. See Labriola, *Storia di dieci anni*, pp. 173–74. Ferri stated: "e la chiamata di Giuseppe Zanardelli al ministero ha avuto il diretto contracolpo parlamentare, che le spese straordinarie militari sono passate più liscie che sotto qualsiasi altro ministero" (*Atti parlamentari, XXI Leg., 1ª sess.*, 6:5584).

81. See Mammarella, *Riformisti e rivoluzionari*, p. 93. See also Zanardelli's cogent speech of 30 March 1901, in his *Discorsi parlamentari*, 3 vols. (Rome: Tip. della Camera, 1905), 3:456–66. There was widespread agreement even on the right that Italy could not afford to go on spending so much money for arms, under pain of ruining her finances; see, for example, Sonnino, *Discorsi parlamentari*, 3:13–24.

82. See the proposals by Ettore Ciccotti and other Socialist deputies, including Turati, in *Atti parlamentari (Camera), XXI Leg., 2ª sess.*, 4 December 1902, 5:4284–90; and 20 February 1903, 6:5393–401, and Corbino, *Annali*, 5:336–38, 350–52.

83. See Mammarella, *Riformisti e rivoluzionari*, p. 94.

84. See Rigola, *Storia del movimento operaio*, pp. 231–33; and Maurice Neufeld, *Italy*, pp. 328–29.

85. For a detailed examination of the structure, policies, and problems of the agricultural leagues, see Giuliano Procacci, "Geografia e struttura del movimento contadino della valle padana nel suo periodo formativo (1901–1906)," *Studi storici* 5:no. 1 (January–March 1964):41–120.

86. Gioacchino Volpe, "Partiti politici e contrasti sociali in Italia all'inizio del nuovo secolo," *Nuova antologia* 441, no. 1764 (December 1947):338.

87. See *La posta*, 1 and 24 January, 1 and 15 February 1902. Turati's letter of acceptance of the presidency is in the 15 February 1902 issue. For the organization of the cooperative, see *L'Unione postale telegrafica telefonica*, 1 May 1906. See also Turati's introduction to Demetrio Alati, *Gli agenti dello stato al bivio* (Milan, 1902).

88. See Rigola, *Storia del movimento operaio*, pp. 219–22, 226–31, 244–49; and Neufeld, *Italy*, pp. 326–32.

89. See Enrico Foselli, *Cento anni di legislazione sociale, 1848–1950*, 2 vols. (Milan: Bernabò, 1951), 1:191–99, and 2:113–16; Angiolo Cabrini, *La legislazione sociale*, pp. 70–89; and Neufeld, *Italy*, pp. 332–33.

90. Labriola tells the story himself in his *Storia di dieci anni*, pp. 177–88. On the same question, see also Zanardelli's *Discorsi parlamentari*, 3:517–48.

91. See Zanardelli, *Discorsi parlamentari*, 3:552–66. See also Sonnino's speech on the South delivered in the wake of Zanardelli's visit, in Sonnino's *Discorsi parlamentari*, 3:84–92. Some Socialists suspected Zanardelli's motives; see Candeloro, *Storia dell'Italia moderna*, 7:148.

92. See Ondei, *Zanardelli*, pp. 159–66; and Cilibrizzi, *Storia parlamentare*, 3:185–203.

93. See Labriola, *Storia di dieci anni*, pp. 188–99; and Mammarella, *Riformisti e rivoluzionari*, pp. 95–96.

94. See *Atti parlamentari (Camera), XXI Leg., 1ª sess.*, 7 March 1901, 3:2237. For a detailed explanation of Wollemborg's proposals, see Corbino, *Annali*, 5:333–34.

95. See Corbino, *Annali*, 5:334–36; and *Un vecchio parlamentare, Il ministero Zanardelli* (Rome: Società Ed. Romana, 1901), pp. 89–90, 157–58.
96. See Mammarella, *Riformisti e rivoluzionari*, pp. 96–98.
97. For more on the proposals eventually passed, see Corbino, *Annali*, 5: 338–41; and Sonnino, *Discorsi parlamentari*, 3 : 182–83.

Chapter VI

1. Giovanni Lerda, *Sull'organizzazione politica del partito socialista italiano*, pp. 10–11.
2. Partito socialista italiano, *Rendiconto del VII congresso nazionale* (Imola, 1902), pp. 10–45.
3. Turati's speech is in ibid., pp. 45–55.
4. On the early period of Labriola's life, see his *Spiegazioni a me stesso*, pp. 13–100; and Dora Marucco, *Arturo Labriola e il sindicalismo rivoluzionario in Italia*, pp. 17–103.
5. Labriola's speech is in PSI, *Rendiconto del VII congresso*, pp. 39–44. See also Marucco, *Labriola*, p. 147.
6. F. Bonavita, *Questioni al congresso*, pp. 4–13.
7. Ferri's speech is in PSI, *Rendiconto del VII congresso*, pp. 56–64.
8. Ibid., pp. 65–68, 71–72; and Pedone, *Il Partito socialista*, 1 : 166–69. See also the written reports in favor of the opposing motions. For the reformists, see Ivanoe Bonomi, *L'azione politica del Partito socialista e i suoi rapporti con l'azione parlamentare*; and for the revolutionaries, see Romeo Soldi, *L'azione politica del proletariato e i suoi rapporti coll'azione parlamentare*.
9. For the relevant debate, see PSI, *Rendiconto del VII congresso*, pp. 77–84.
10. On *Avanti!*, see ibid., pp. 85–90, and *L'Avanti!, Resoconto della direzione del giornale al VII congresso nazionale*.
11. Mammarella, *Riformisti e rivoluzionari*, pp. 142–48.
12. See Giampiero Carocci, *Giolitti e l'età giolittiana*, pp. 66–68; and G. Natale, *Giolitti e gli italiani*, pp. 428–41. And see Giolitti's speech in the Chamber on 21 June 1901, *Discorsi parlamentari*, 2 : 665.
13. Mammarella, *Riformisti e rivoluzionari*, pp. 149–51; and Filippo Turati, "Il sanque," *Critica sociale*, 16 October 1902. For Giolitti's explanation, see his *Discorsi parlamentari*, 2 : 739–52.
14. See Carocci, *Giolitti*, p. 69. The telegram informing the prefects of the cabinet's decision is in Giolitti, *Quarant'anni*, 2 : 173–74.
15. On the railway strike and its ramifications, see Carocci, *Giolitti*, pp. 68–69; Natale, *Giolitti*, pp. 493–98; and Giolitti, *Quarant'anni*, 2 : 146, 150, 158–61, 173–74, 176–90, 217–18.
16. See Natale, *Giolitti*, pp. 499–502; and Giolitti, *Quarant'anni*, 2 : 153, 168, 171–72, 191–96, and 146, 148–52, 153; see also Giolitti, *Discorsi parlamentari*, 2 : 690–93.
17. Giolitti, *Quarant'anni*, 2 : 160–61, 185–86, 217–18.
18. Carocci, *Giolitti*, p. 69.
19. [F.]t., "Scioperi vani," *Lotta di classe*, 24 August 1901. For other articles expressing the same theme, see "Contro lo sciopero . . . del senso comune," 31 August 1901; f.t., "Novità con tanto di barba: Ancora contro gli scioperi sconclusionati," 7 September 1901; "Tutti d'accordo!" 14 September 1901; and "In tema di scioperi, tutti d'accordo!" 21 September 1901. See also Filippo Turati, "I 'socialisti rivoluzionari' alla prova," *Critica sociale*, 1–16 April 1903.

20. See Papafava, *Dieci anni*, 1:235–37; and Andrea Costa, *Il gruppo parlamentare socialista* (Imola: Coop. tip. ed., 1902), pp. 8–10. See also Labriola, *Storia di dieci anni*, pp. 201–19. Ferri's campaign in *Avanti!* to ensure that the czar would be jeered wherever he went in Italy was the ostensible reason why the visit was postponed. See Gastone Manacorda, "L'eco italiano della prima rivoluzione russa," in *Storiografia e socialismo*, pp. 125–29. Turati denounced *Avanti!*'s campaign. See La critica sociale and Ivanoe Bonomi, "La politica del fischio," *Critica sociale*, 16 September–1 October 1903.

21. Kuliscioff to Turati, 15, 24, 20, 21, 22, 23 March 1903.

22. Kuliscioff to Turati, 24, 25 March 1903.

23. *Avanti!*, 26 March 1903.

24. See Mammarella, *Riformisti e rivoluzionari*, pp. 151–53. Turati's speech is in his *Discorsi parlamentari*, 1:244–58.

25. For Giolitti's ideas on these points, see his *Discorsi parlamentari*, 2:690–91, 693–714, 725–27, 753–57.

26. Kuliscioff to Turati, 2 April 1903. The letters of 27, 29, 31 March and 1 April 1903 express the same sentiments.

27. Giolitti, *Quarant'anni*, 2:303–5.

28. See, for example, the laudatory letter of Oddino Morgari, in ibid., p. 309.

29. Labriola, *Spiegazioni*, pp. 116–18; and Marucco, *Labriola*, pp. 149–50.

30. *Avanguardia* was an extremely agressive newspaper, which had the collaboration of some of the best-known revolutionaries of the period, including Tomaso Monicelli, Vittorio Friederichsen, Romeo Soldi, Giovanni Allievi, and Guido and Cesare Marangoni. Benito Mussolini was the Swiss correspondent. *Il tempo* was edited by Claudio Treves, and for a time Ivanoe Bonomi was second in command. According to Labriola, *Il tempo* was financed by Jewish bankers. See Labriola, *Spiegazioni*, pp. 118–20, 131–32. Mocchi apparently financed *Avanguardia*.

31. See Enzo Santarelli, "Sorel e il sorelismo in Italia," *Rivista storica del socialismo* 3, no. 10 (May–August 1960): 295–303. In Italy theoreticians of revolutionary syndicalism, besides Labriola, included Paolo Orano, Enrico Leone, and A. O. Olivetti; see Labriola, *Spiegazioni*, pp. 120–22.

32. Arturo Labriola, *Riforme e rivoluzione sociale*, 2 ed., pp. 5–10. At first Labriola believed that Socialist parliamentary action should be aimed at undermining Parliament from within and that reforms could be extracted during this process, but he dropped this idea after 1903 and reached the conclusion that has been cited. See Marucco, *Labriola*, pp. 150–51.

33. A. O. Olivetti, *Questioni contemporanee*, pp. 170–76. (This is the second edition of Olivetti's *Problemi del socialismo contemporanee*.)

34. Labriola, *Riforme e rivoluzione sociale*, pp. 97, 199–201.

35. See Benito Mussolini, "Democrazia parlamentare," *Avanguardia socialista*, 3 July 1904, A. O. Olivetti, "La reazione sindacalista," *Lotta di classe*, 2 March 1907, and Paolo Orano, "Lo sfacelo parlamentare," 12 January 1907. See also Labriola, *Riforme e rivoluzione sociale*, pp. 109–17.

36. Labriola, *Riforme e rivoluzione sociale*, pp. 18–38, 98–103, 135–64, 206–7; and Olivetti, *Questioni*, pp. 154–65, 170–72.

37. Labriola, *Riforme e rivoluzione sociale*, pp. 207–9, 217–22. See also Mussolini, "Democrazia parlamentare," and Paolo Mantica, "Sindacalismo e Partito socialista," *Lotta di classe*, 5 January 1907.

38. Labriola, *Riforme e rivoluzione sociale*, pp. 203–6, 208–12; A. O. Olivetti, "Socialismo e movimento operaio," pts. 1 and 2, *Lotta di classe*, 9 and 16 February 1907; Olivetti, *Questioni*, pp. 213–24; A. O. Olivetti, "Le difficoltà della lotta

proletaria," and Paolo Mantica, "Il compito del sindacato," *Lotta di classe*, 11 May 1907, and Olivetti, "Il socialismo e lo stato," 23 March 1907. See also Marucco, *Labriola*, pp. 153–58.

39. On "direct action," see Olivetti, *Questioni*, pp. 189–203; and Labriola, *Riforme e rivoluzione sociale*, p. 203. On the concept of the general strike, see Olivetti, "Socialismo e movimento operaio," pt. 2; and Labriola, *Riforme e rivoluzione sociale*, p. 211. See also Enrico Leone, "Lo sciopero generale," *Lotta di classe*, 13 April 1907.

40. Labriola, *Spiegazioni*, pp. 127–31; see also Marucco, *Labriola*, pp. 189–90.

41. See Unbroken, "La patria del riformismo," *Avanguardia socialista*, 4 January 1903.

42. Kuliscioff to Turati, 16 February 1903.

43. For the details, see *Il tempo*, 25, 26, 27, 28 June, 9, 10, 12 July 1902.

44. See *Il tempo*, 11, 12, 21 July 1902; 23 February, 5 March, 9 April, 14, 16, 17, 24 June, 25, 28, 29, 30 July, 6, 9 August 1903; and *Avanguardia socialista*, 22 February, 1, 8 March, 17 May, 21 June, 5, 19, 26 July, 2 August 1903. For the actual foundation of the reformist Gruppi socialisti milanesi (GSM), see *Il tempo*, 28 October 1903.

45. *Avanguardia socialista*, 11 July and 3 August 1903.

46. See *Avanguardia socialista*, 31 May 1903, Walter Mocchi, "Osate," 6 December 1903, W. M., "Preparando il congresso," 27 December 1903, and Costantino Lazzari, "Come deve avvenire la separazione," 22 November 1903.

47. See a.l., "Fallimento," *Avanguardia socialista*, 13 September 1903; Luigi Codevilla, "La politica nelle camera del lavoro," 18 October 1903; Cesare Marangoni, "Mentre si muta rotta . . . ," 8 November 1903. See also Neufeld, *Italy*, p. 336.

48. "Milano: Comitato d'azione socialista-economico," *Avanguardia socialista*, 6 September 1903.

49. On the strike, see especially *Avanguardia socialista*, 27 September, 4, 11, 18 October 1903, and "Alla camera del lavoro: Ancora lo sciopero della Nord," 11 October 1903. On the elections for 1903, see "Milano: Camera del lavoro. Alle urne!" 22 November 1903, and "Milano: Per le elezioni della camera del lavoro. Fecondità," 29 November 1903. For 1904, see "Milano socialista e proletaria: Le elezioni alla camera del lavoro. La fine dei dittatori," 8 May 1904, and gs., "La vittoria rivoluzionaria alla camera del lavoro," 15 May 1904. See also Labriola, *Spiegazioni*, p. 132.

50. See Romeo Soldi, "Per l'*Avanti*," *Avanguardia socialista*, 15 March 1903, as well as the 22 March issue; a.l., "Dello sciopero generale di Filippo Turati," 26 April 1903; A. de Mayo, "Dopo il Congresso d'Imola," 16 August 1903; *Il tempo*, 19 March 1903; Arfé, *Storia dell'Avanti*, 1:52–55; and Labriola, *Storia di dieci anni*, pp. 206–7. See also Marucco, *Labriola*, p. 148.

51. See a.l., "All'opposizione," *Avanguardia socialista*, 29 March 1903, and by the same author, "Per l'avvenire," 5 April 1903.

52. See Giolitti, *Quarant'anni*, 2:315–19.

53. See Kuliscioff to Turati, 25 June 1903; and Giolitti, *Quarant'anni*, 2:320–21.

54. Turati's letter is in Giolitti, *Quarant'anni*, 2:324–25.

55. Giolitti, *Memorie*, pp. 191–93.

56. Giolitti, *Quarant'anni*, 2:326.

57. Giolitti, *Discorsi parlamentari*, 2:762–63.

58. See "Il direttore del *Secolo*, Romussi, a Giolitti, a Roma" and "Giolitti a Vittorio Emanuele III, a San Rossore," in Giolitti, *Quarant'anni*, 2:327–29, 332–33; see also Carocci, *Giolitti*, pp. 89–90.

59. La critica sociale, "La causa profonda," *Critica sociale*, 1 November 1903.

60. See L'avanguardia, "La ripresa del ministerialismo socialista," *Avanguardia socialista*, 1 November 1903; a.l., "Intermezzo imprevisto," and C. L., "Le fasi della illusione e l'illusione delle fasi," 8 November 1903.
61. Carocci, *Giolitti*, p. 90.
62. See "Il deputato Bissolati a Giolitti, a Roma," in Giolitti, *Quarant'anni*, 2:333; and Turati, "La causa profonda." See also Candeloro, *Storia dell'Italia moderna*, 7:154–55.
63. *Avanti!*, 3, 30 November, 1 December 1903.
64. See Turati to Kuliscioff, 2 December 1903.
65. For more on this cabinet, see Giolitti, *Quarant'anni*, 2:330–32, 337–40; Candeloro, *Storia dell'Italia moderna*, 7:156–58; and Labriola, *Storia di dieci anni*, pp. 219–43.
66. Giolitti, *Discorsi parlamentari*, 2:758–68.
67. [L']homme qui rit, "L'ora gioconda," *Avanguardia socialista*, 22 November 1903.
68. L'avanguardia, "Per il congresso nazionale: Ai nostri amici," *Avanguardia socialista*, 31 May 1903, and "Per l'avvenire," 15 November 1903; Costantino Lazzari, "Come deve avvenire la seperazione," 22 November 1903; Walter Mocchi, "Osate!" 6 December 1903.
69. See Walter Mocchi, "Preparando il congresso," *Avanguardia socialista*, 20 December 1903; and by the same author, "Preparando il congresso: Chi vuole la scissione. Dedicato ad Enrico Ferri," 27 December 1903, and "Unità formale e secessione sostanziale," 17 January 1904.
70. "Pel congresso regionale lombardo," *Avanguardia socialista*, 20 December 1903.
71. For the preliminary maneuvering for position, see the "Milano" column in *Avanguardia socialista*, 17, 24 January and 7 February 1904; and "Pel congresso regionale lombardo," L'homme qui rit, "Da Cremona a Brescia," and Stop., "Le auto-smentite del 'Tempo'," all in the 14 February 1904 issue.
72. See Walter Mocchi, "Il nostro ordine del giorno al congresso lombardo di Brescia," *Avanguardia socialista*, 21 February 1904, and, in the same issue, "Il congresso regionale lombardo: Le vittorie dei rivoluzionari—i discorsi—le deliberazioni," "Le strida del *Tempo* . . . cattivo." See also "Il congresso regionale lombardo: Gli ultimi discorsi—i rivoluzionari in prevalenza—la chiusura," 28 February 1904.
73. *Il tempo*, 16 and 24 February 1904.
74. The regional congress did influence other local congresses to follow its lead. See "L'ordine del giorno di Rigola a Biella," *Avanguardia socialista*, 13 March 1904; Cesare Marangoni, "Prima del congresso Veneto," 20 March 1904, and, by the same author, "Il congresso regionale Veneto," 27 March 1904.
75. See Walter Mocchi, "Dopo il congresso di Brescia: Le dichiarazioni di Ferri," *Avanguardia socialista*, 6 March 1904; and L'avanguardia, "Ci Odiano," 13 March 1904. The interview with Labriola is in the 13 March issue. See also Marucco, *Labriola*, p. 159.
76. Walter Mocchi, "Unità formale e scissione sostanziale," and "Per la verità," *Avanguardia socialista*, 17 January 1904; Alfredo Polledro, "Preparando il congresso nazionale: L'unità," 13 March 1904; and Walter Mocchi, "Monarchici . . . finalmente!!," 28 February 1904. Rigola led the Right Center during the Congress of Bologna.
77. On these points, see the following articles in *Avanguardia socialista*: Mocchi, "Monarchici . . . finalmente!!"; "La solidarietà dei monarchici cogli ordini del giorno Turati-Treves," 28 February 1904; Paul Lafargue, "Siamo noi anar-

chici? . . . e che cosa sono . . . i possibilisti?," "Appunti parlamentari," 13 March 1904; "Siamo noi anarchici? Una lettera di Carlo Kautsky," l'h.q.r., "Appunti parlamentari: Il trionfo del Parlamento," "Domanda indiscreta al 'compagno' Filippo Turati," 20 March 1904; L'avanguardia, "Una vittoria," "Siamo noi anarchici?" 27 March 1904; Sergio Panunzio, "Preparando il congresso nazionale," 27 March 1904; l'h.q.r., "In articulo mortis," 3 April 1904; Scotino, "Il dilemma di Bologna," 20 March 1904; and Walter Mocchi, "Il centro: L'unità degli stipendi e delle schede elettorali," 3 April 1904.

78. See the editorial in *Avanguardia socialista*, 21 February 1904; and "Il nostro progetto per la Direzione del partito," 20 March 1904.

79. La critica sociale, "La fine delle tendenze: Il *non-expedit* dei 'socialisti rivoluzionari' e le organizzazioni economiche," *Critica sociale*, 16 February 1904. See also "Gli ordini del giorno del Congresso di Brescia," in the same issue.

80. Leonida Bissolati, *Socialismo e governi*, pp. 3–9.

81. See Kuliscioff to Turati, 16 March 1904.

82. "Un intervista della *Stampa* con Arturo Labriola," *Avanguardia socialista*, 3 April 1904.

83. Partito socialista italiano, *Rendiconto del VIII congresso nazionale* (Bologna, 1904), pp. 135–47; Labriola's motion is on p. 160. See also Arturo Labriola, *La politica del proletariato*, p. 10.

84. PSI, *Rendiconto del VIII congresso*, pp. 105–23. See Marucco, *Labriola*, pp. 161–66.

85. Marucco, *Labriola*, p. 160. For a later criticism of Turati on this same point, see Carlo Rosselli, *Vita e opera di Filippo Turati*.

86. For Turati's early ideas, see Filippo Turati, "Lo stato libero futuro e l'azione socialista presente: Polemica con E. de Marinis," *Critica sociale*, 10 March 1891; La critica sociale, "La storia di due code di cavallo, e il programma socialista," *Critica sociale*, 10 July 1891; and Filippo Turati, "La repubblica," *Critica sociale*, 16 November 1893. See also Turati, *Il partito socialista*, p. 7.

87. See Turati's speech in PSI, *Rendiconto del VIII congresso*, pp. 105–23.

88. "Analisi della crisi: Intervista con Walter Mocchi," *Avanguardia socialista*, 17 March 1906.

89. PSI, *Rendiconto del VIII congresso*, pp. 160–61. A new method of counting the vote was begun at this congress. The total number of Party members *represented* by the delegates was counted, not just the delegates themselves.

90. La critica sociale, "I due partiti (Echi del congresso)," *Critica sociale*, 16 April 1904; L'avanguardia, "Vita nuova," *Avanguardia socialista*, 24 April 1904.

91. L'avanguardia, "Vita nuova," *Avanguardia socialista*, 24 April 1904.

92. See Arfé, *Storia del socialismo*, p. 113. For Labriola's true assessment of Ferri, see Marucco, *Labriola*, pp. 152–53.

93. For the results of the referendum and the Directorate's action, see *Bollettino della Direzione del Partito socialista italiano*, 1 July 1904. A moderate proposal of Ferri's, which would have made an exception for Milan and would have allowed two sections to exist there, was defeated by an intransigent proposal by Guido Marangoni, who was deeply involved in the Milanese movement on the left. For the reaction of the several parties in Milan, see *Il tempo*, 27 May 1904, and the article "Cacciati" on 21 June 1904. For the comments of the left wing, see L'avanguardia, "L'esito del referendum," and Walter Mocchi, "Dopo il referendum," *Avanguardia socialista*, 26 June 1904. On the issue of Party discipline, see C. L., "La virtù della disciplina," and L'avanguardia, "Il proclama . . . alle turbe," *Avanguardia socialista*, 15 May 1904; F. Lagazzi and L'avanguardia, "Disciplina per tutti," 22 May 1904, and "Autonomia, Gruppo, Parla-

mento, e Direzione," 29 May 1904. See also Kuliscioff to Turati, 5 May 1904, in which Kuliscioff accuses the Directorate of trying to "dictate" to the deputies; and *Il tempo*, 17 October 1904, for the deputies' statement.

94. See *L'avanguardia*, "E sempre sangue!" *Avanguardia socialista*, 22 May 1904; "La protesta proletaria contro l'eccidio di Cerignola," 29 May 1904; and "Dopo Cerignola," 9 July 1904. See also Arturo Labriola, "Dalle sconfitte elettorali allo sciopero generale," *Avanguardia socialista*, 13 August 1904. The Sixth Congress of the International at Amsterdam was in the process of debating the general strike and of taking positions that pleased the revolutionary syndicalists.

95. See [G]s., "La vittoria rivoluzionaria alla camera del lavoro," *Avanguardia socialista*, 15 May 1904; Rigola, *Storia del movimento operaio*, p. 269; Giuliano Procacci, "Lo sciopero generale del 1904," *Rivista storica del socialismo* 5, no. 17 (September–December 1962): 405–6.

96. *Bollettino della Direzione*, 1 October 1904. Not all the members of the Directorate were present, given the short notice for the meeting.

97. Procacci, "Lo sciopero generale," pp. 408–11.

98. See ibid., pp. 411–31.

99. See "La proclamazione dello sciopero generale," *Il tempo*, 12 September 1904. Turati's speech is reported in *Il tempo*, 21 September 1904.

100. Procacci, "Lo sciopero generale," pp. 415, 417, 420; and Labriola, *Storia di dieci anni*, pp. 252–53.

101. *Avanti!*, 22 September 1904.

102. Giolitti, *Memorie*, pp. 145–47.

103. Procacci, "Lo sciopero generale," pp. 437–38.

104. Candeloro, *Storia dell'Italia moderna*, 7:184; see also Rigola, *Storia del movimento operaio*, pp. 269–70.

105. Enrico Leone, "Gli effetti politici," *Avanti!*, 22 September 1904.

106. "Tirando le somme," *Avanguardia socialista*, 24 September 1904; Procacci, "Lo sciopero generale," p. 433; and Marucco, *Labriola*, pp. 173–74.

107. La critica sociale, "L'ora delle responsabilità," *Critica sociale*, 16 September–1 October 1904.

108. See Mammarella, *Riformisti e rivoluzionari*, p. 170.

109. See Candeloro, *Storia dell'Italia moderna*, 7:184–85; Procacci, "Lo sciopero generale," pp. 433–34.

Chapter VII

1. See Arturo Carlo Jemolo, *Chiesa e stato in Italia* (Turin: Einaudi, 1965), pp. 59–60. For a more extensive discussion of the Catholic organizations, see Giovanni Spadolini, *L'opposizione cattolica da Porta Pia al '98*, pp. 243–370. See also Giorgio Candeloro, *Il movimento cattolico in Italia*, pp. 262–63; and Spadolini, *L'opposizione cattolica*, pp. 463–70.

2. Giovanni Spadolini, *Giolitti e i cattolici*, pp. 60–66.

3. G. Suardi, "Quando e come i cattolici poterono partecipare alle elezioni politiche," *Nuova antologia* 306 (November–December 1927): pp. 118–20. Pius was reported to have said that he would have the courage to abolish the *non expedit* should he become pope. See Jemolo, *Chiesa e stato*, pp. 110–14; and Giolitti, *Discorsi parlamentari*, 2:819–20.

4. Suardi, "Quando e come," pp. 121–22.

5. See Spadolini, *Giolitti e i cattolici*, pp. 68–77, 83–87; Giolitti, *Quarant'anni*, 2:362.

6.   Had there been proportional representation, the government would have had 259 solid supporters (out of 508) instead of 339 (using a standard formula). Each Socialist deputy represented 11,241 voters as compared to 2,488 for a *ministeriale*. In the South the government received 64 percent of the popular vote as compared to 45 percent in the North. The Socialists won 27.8 percent of the vote in the North but only 7.5 percent in the South. For these statistics, see *Compendio delle statistiche elettorali italiane dal 1848 al 1934* (Rome: F. Failli, 1946), 2:111–12, 124–27. See also *Avanti!*, 8, 9, 10, 15, 16 November 1904.

7.   La critica sociale, "Camera nuova e politica vecchia," *Critica sociale*, 1–16 November 1904.

8.   Giolitti, *Memorie*, p. 148; and Cilibrizzi, *Storia parlamentare*, 3:292–93.

9.   Kuliscioff to Turati, 2 December 1904; La critica sociale, "Atto di contrizione, e proponimento," *Critica sociale*, 16 December 1904. For the specific social reforms requested by the Socialists, see "La piattaforma," *Critica sociale*, and "Il Partito socialista di fronte alle elezioni," *Avanti!*, 18 October 1904. The document was written by Turati.

10. See *Il tempo*, 7 and 8 November 1904. Labriola received 714 votes to Turati's 4,572.

11. Mammarella, *Riformisti e rivoluzionari*, p. 174.

12. See *Avanti!*, 28 February to 2 March 1905; Labriola, *Storia di dieci anni*, pp. 270–81; Rigola, *Storia del movimento operaio*, pp. 292–93; and Cilibrizzi, *Storia parlamentare*, 3:296–97.

13. Giolitti, *Memorie*, pp. 154–55.

14. *Avanti!*, 5 March 1905.

15. Kuliscioff to Turati, 2 March 1905, and Turati to Kuliscioff, 4 March 1905. In an attempt to save appearances, the strike formally ended when Giolitti resigned.

16. See Cilibrizzi, *Storia parlamentare*, 3:306–9.

17. *Avanti!*, 17 April 1905; Rigola, *Storia del movimento operaio*, p. 294.

18. See La critica sociale, "Mentre si è in tempo ancora," *Critica sociale*, 16 April 1905; and "Ripresa d'armi," 16 August 1905. See also Turati's letters to Anna Kuliscioff dated 2 February, 1, 2, 3, 4 March 1905, and Kuliscioff to Turati, 25 and 27 February 1905. See also Turati's letter of 26 February.

19. See Rigola, *Storia del movimento operaio*, pp. 244–49; Giuliano Procacci, "La classe operaia," pp. 58–67, and the introductory essay by Franco Catalano in Luciana Marchetti, ed., *La confederazione generale del lavoro*, pp. xiv–xvi. See also Carlo Cartiglia, *Rinaldo Rigola e il sindacalismo riformista in Italia*, p. 52; and *Il tempo*, 8 May 1905.

20. Only 2,500 workers participated in strikes in Milan during 1904, compared to 30,755 in 1902. In 1904, only one new workers' organization was formed in the city, compared to twenty-one in 1902. The figures for both activities increased when reformist influence increased in later years. See Società umanitaria, *Le condizioni generali della classe operaia in Milano*, pp. ix, lv.

21. See, for example, *L'Unione postale telegrafica telefonica*, 1 and 12 November 1904. A perusal of Turati's *Discorsi parlamentari* will reveal the enormous effort he put into helping the *postelegrafonici*; during this period, for example, see 1:336–55.

22. On the struggle for the Umanitaria, see *Il tempo*, 2 and 5 February 1906; and *Avanguardia socialista*, 3 February 1906. See also Società umanitaria, *Un esperimento di avvocatura per i poveri* (Milan: Tip. degli operai, 1907).

23. See Ettore Fabietti, *Le biblioteche del popolo* (Milan: Consorzio delle biblioteche popolari, 1905), especially Turati's preface.

24. See Turati's speech to the second congress of the *Unione*, in *Atti del II congresso nazionale delle opere di educazione popolare* (Milan: Unione italiana dell'educazione popolare, 1913), pp. 202–8; for the organization's constitution, see *L'Unione italiana dell'educazione popolare* (Milan, n.d.); for an indication of Turati's predominant role in the organization, see Turati to Kuliscioff, 20 February 1913.

25. As an example of this activity, see Università popolare milanese, *Relazione per l'anno didattico, 1909–10* (Milan: Guttenberg, 1910).

26. For the elections of 1905, see *Il tempo*, 10 and 28 June 1905.

27. Marchetti, *La Confederazione generale del lavoro*, p. xviii.

28. *Avanti!*, 25 February 1906.

29. A list of those accepting is in Rigola, *Storia del movimento operaio*, p. 306.

30. See, for example, Turati to Kuliscioff, 15 March 1906.

31. Fausto Pagliari, "Cronache sociali: Camere del lavoro e federazioni," *Il tempo*, 4 March 1906; see also Cartiglia, *Rinaldo Rigola*, pp. 58–59. Pagliari had the "German" model in mind.

32. Rigola, *Storia del movimento operaio*, pp. 306–7. There was to be one delegate for each hundred members of an organization or fraction thereof. Votes were to be counted according to the number of people the delegates represented.

33. See Constantino Lazzari, "Un attentato alla resistenza dei lavoratori," and "Una prima vittoria," *Avanguardia socialista*, 10 March 1906.

34. Kuliscioff to Turati, 10 March 1906. See also the appeal for people to attend the meetings of the FSM in *Avanguardia socialista*, 10 February 1906, in the column, "Federazione socialista milanese."

35. On the elections, see *Il tempo*, 26, 27 April and 3 May 1906, and "Per le elezioni della commissione esecutiva della camera del lavoro," *Avanguardia socialista*, 24 March 1906. Anna Kuliscioff interpreted these elections as the repudiation of revolutionary syndicalism by the Milanese working class. See Kuliscioff to Turati, 3 May 1906.

36. L'avanguardia, "Contro la frazione sindacalista: Il colpo di stato di E. Ferri," *Avanguardia socialista*, 3 June 1905; Arfé, *Storia dell'Avanti!*, 1:65–67; and Marucco, *Labriola*, p. 153.

37. See the 3 and 10 February 1906 issues of *Avanguardia socialista*: Costantino Lazzari, "Parlamentarismo borghese e parlamentarismo socialista," and g.a., "Il neoministerialismo"; see also "Ferri all'estrema destra," 3 March 1906.

38. For example, see *Avanguardia socialista*, 10, 17, 24 and 31 March 1906.

39. "Analisi della crisi: Intervista con Walter Mocchi," *Avanguardia socialista*, 17 March 1906.

40. See *Avanguardia socialista*, 24 March 1906.

41. See Arfé, *Storia del socialismo*, p. 113.

42. See Kuliscioff to Turati, 12, 14, and 16 March 1906.

43. See Adolfo Pepe, "La costituzione della Confederazione generale del lavoro e il PSI (1906–1908)," *Storia contemporanea 1*, no. 4 (December 1970):692–95; and Marchetti, *La Confederazione generale del lavoro*, pp. 3–16, which gives the stenographic report of this congress. Pepe's research has been incorporated in his *Storia della Confederazione generale del lavoro dalla fondazione alla guerra di Libia, 1905–1911*.

44. Marchetti, *La Confederazione generale del lavoro*, pp. 6–8; and Rigola, *Storia del movimento operaio*, p. 309.

45. See Pepe, "La costituzione della Confederazione," pp. 695–99.

46. See c.t., "Tutto e nulla," *Il tempo*, 3 October 1906.

47. F. G. Paoloni, *Salviamo il partito*, pp. 9–12.
48. Partito socialista italiano, *Resoconto stenografico del IX congresso nazionale*, pp. 158–72.
49. La critica sociale, "Bisogna decidersi!" *Critica sociale*, 1 April 1907.
50. La critica sociale, "Il logogrifo integralista: Al di là del bene e del male," *Critica sociale*, 16 August 1906.
51. Kuliscioff to Turati, 13 August 1906.
52. Turati's speech is in PSI, *Resoconto stenografico del IX congresso*, pp. 196–224.
53. Labriola's speech is in ibid., pp. 101–30. See also Marucco, *Labriola*, pp. 187–201.
54. PSI, *Resoconto stenografico del IX congresso*, pp. 274–76.
55. Ibid., pp. 277–78.
56. Ibid., pp. 293–97.
57. See ibid., p. 28.
58. Marchetti, *La Confederazione generale del lavoro*, pp. 23–24, 27–78, 37.
59. See Pepe, "La costituzione della Confederazione," pp. 703–8; Marchetti, *La Confederazione generale del lavoro*, pp. 30–33, 35–36; and *Avanti!*, 13 and 15 January 1907.
60. See Cartiglia, *Rinaldo Rigola*, pp. 70–71. The effects on the reformists in the Party will be discussed in the following chapter.
61. La critica sociale, "Rinnovazione: Programma del'annata imminente," *Critica sociale*, 16 December 1906, "La nostra azione parlamentare," 1 January 1907, "L'inazione parlamentare socialista: L'indennità ai deputati," 16 January 1907; and F. Turati, "Bisogna decidersi! Il disegno di legge per l'indennità ai deputati," 1 April 1907. See also Marchetti, *La Confederazione generale del lavoro*, p. 37; and Pepe, "La costituzione della Confederazione," pp. 709–14.
62. Marchetti, *La Confederazione generale del lavoro*, pp. 38–40; and *Avanti!*, 21, 26 March and 22 April 1907.
63. See *Avanti!*, 14 August 1907; and Marchetti, *La Confederazione generale del lavoro*, pp. 42–48.
64. See Rigola's letter dated 11 August 1907 in Gianni Bosio, "Nascita e sviluppo della Confederazione generale del lavoro nel carteggio Turati-Rigola," *Rivista storica del socialismo* 1 (1958): 85.
65. Marchetti, *La Confederazione generale del lavoro*, pp. 48–49; and Pepe, "La costituzione della Confederazione," pp. 727–33.
66. For the activities of the CGL during this period, see Marchetti, *La Confederazione generale del lavoro*, pp. 52–55.
67. See Cartiglia, *Rinaldo Rigola*, pp. 76–77; and Rigola, *Storia del movimento operaio*, pp. 317–22.
68. Turati came out strongly against a railway strike in 1907, as did the CGL; see Filippo Turati, "Il nostro tradimento" and "Turati e lo sciopero," *Critica sociale*, 16 October–1 November 1907. Anna Kuliscioff was even more adamantly opposed to the strikes; see her letters of 15, 16, 17, 18, and 19 October 1907.
69. The program included maternity benefits, arbitration of labor disputes in public service industries, abolition of night shifts for certain kinds of workers, salaries for deputies, and measures designed to prevent proletarian "massacres." See Filippo Turati, "La riapertura," *Critica sociale*, 1 December 1907.
70. Filippo Turati, "Il più grande blocco," *Critica sociale*, 1 February 1908. Turati's suggested program involved fiscal and educational reform, social legislation, reduction of military and colonial expenditures, and parliamentary salaries.
71. Marchetti, *La Confederazione generale del lavoro*, pp. 61–62.

72. Cartiglia, *Rinaldo Rigola*, pp. 68–73.
73. La critica sociale, "La politica del sottomano," *Critica sociale*, 1 March 1908; and Marchetti, *La Confederazione generale del lavoro*, pp. 62–63.
74. Bosio, "Nascita e sviluppo della Confederazione," pp. 94–95.
75. Ibid., pp. 95–96.
76. Ibid., p. 97. Turati wrote:\"It would be impossible to organize a greater fiasco."
77. Pepe, "La costituzione della Confederazione," pp. 749–50.
78. The Directorate also announced that the results of the Rome meeting would have no binding effect on the Party. On these points, see Marchetti, *La Confederazione generale del lavoro*, pp. 63–64, and *Avanti!*, 26 March 1908.
79. La critica sociale, "Il proletariato contro se stesso," *Critica sociale*, 1 April 1908.
80. Pepe, "La costituzione della Confederazione," pp. 756–60.
81. Rigola defined the cGL as "reformist socialist." See Rinaldo Rigola, *Rinaldo Rigola e il movimento operaio nel Biellese: Autobiografia* (Bari: Laterza, 1930), pp. 196–98, *Ventun mesi di vita della Confederazione generale del lavoro* (Turin: S.E., 1908), pp. 47–48, and *Storia del movimento operaio*, pp. 343–44.
82. Rigola, *Ventun mesi*, pp. 27–29, 33–34. See also Carl E. Schorske, *German Social Democracy, 1905–1917* (Cambridge: Harvard University Press, 1955), pp. 39–40, 49–53; and Gay, *Dilemma of Democratic Socialism*, pp. 140, 243. Rigola often referred to the "German model."
83. See Mammarella, *Riformisti e rivoluzionari*, pp. 214–17.
84. In 1907, there were 2,278 strikes involving 452,910 strikers compared to 642 strikes and 101,327 strikers in 1905. See *Annuario statistico italiano* (1905–1907), 2:838–45; Cartiglia, *Rinaldo Rigola*, pp. 73–74.
85. La critica sociale, "Il problema più urgente," *Critica sociale*, 16 April 1907. See also Umberto Romagnoli, "La IX sessione del Consiglio superiore del lavoro," *Studi storici* 12, no. 2 (April–June 1971): 356–65. Turati emphasized the high cost of strikes to the workers, argued that they were obsolete, and believed that arbitration conformed to the ideas of socialism.
86. For details on the collective contracts and the proposed legislation (whose chief spokesman was Gino Murialdi, who was close to Turati), see Rigola, *Storia del movimento operaio*, pp. 323–27.
87. Ibid., pp. 366–68.
88. Cartiglia, *Rinaldo Rigola*, pp. 71–72. A stenographic report of the congress is in Marchetti, *La Confederazione generale del lavoro*, pp. 77–80.
89. Rigola, *Storia del movimento operaio*, p. 372.
90. See La critica sociale, "In vista del nuovo anno" and "Partendo per Firenze: Fra due congressi," *Critica sociale*, 16 September 1908. For the process leading up to the split, see the April and May issues of *Lotta di classe*.
91. Partito socialista italiano, *Resoconto stenografico del X congresso nazionale*, pp. 205–19; see also Rinaldo Rigola, *Il partito socialista e il movimento operaio*.
92. PSI, *Resoconto stenografico del X congresso*, pp. 297–309.
93. Ibid., pp. 322–33.
94. Ibid., pp. 334–36, also includes the opposing motions.
95. La critica sociale, "La vittoria delle cose," *Critica sociale*, 10 October 1908.
96. For details, see Cartiglia, *Rinaldo Rigola*, pp. 78–87.
97. Longobardi's speech is in PSI, *Resoconto stenografico del X congresso*, pp. 223–39. See also his *Direttive del partito in rapporto al movimento operaio*.

Chapter VIII

1. Graziadei, *La produzione capitalistica.*
2. Antonio Graziadei, "Sindicalismo, riformismo, rivoluzionarismo," *Critica sociale,* 1 July 1905.
3. Antonio Graziadei and La critica sociale, "Sindicalismo riformista?" *Critica sociale,* 16 July–1 August 1905.
4. Antonio Graziadei and La critica sociale, "Politica di partito e politica di classe," *Critica sociale,* 16 August 1905. Critics have also emphasized the relationship between "reformist" and "revolutionary" syndicalism. See Arfé, *Storia del socialismo,* pp. 126–29, and Santarelli, *La revisione del marxismo,* p. 105.
5. See *Critica sociale,* 16 November 1907.
6. Bonomi, *Le vie nuove,* pp. 26–69; Leonida Bissolati, "Il congresso socialista italiano," *Nuova antologia* 41, no. 835 (1 October 1906): 473; and Bonomi, *Le vie nuove,* pp. 72–73.
7. Bonomi, *Le vie nuove,* pp. 104–05.
8. Ibid., pp. 109–10.
9. See ibid., pp. 62–63, 232. See also Kuliscioff to Turati, 16 December 1905.
10. Arfé, *Storia del socialismo,* pp. 123–24, 129.
11. Ivanoe Bonomi, *Leonida Bissolati e il movimento socialista in Italia,* p. 73. Bonomi wrote that Turati's socialism "is and remains, in its essential points, within the purest orthodoxy."
12. Turati to Kuliscioff, 2 and 3 December 1904. According to Turati, Ferri was in a minority of two in the group.
13. Kuliscioff to Turati, 4, 6, and 12 December 1904 and 17 December 1905. "Do you think you would be able to retire almost into the shadows for a few years to study, to work, to prepare a plan of action for the real revival of the country?"
14. See Turati to Kuliscioff, 30 and 31 January 1906.
15. Turati, *Discorsi parlamentari,* 1:431–38. For Turati's demonstration that state and Church were silently cooperating, see "Scaramuccie," *Critica sociale,* 16 May 1907.
16. On the Church's role in education, see Francesco Ciccotti, *Azione e legislazione anticlericale,* pp. 5–9. On the large-scale banking and other economic activities of the Catholics during this period, see Candeloro, *Il movimento cattolico,* pp. 341–45. Catholic scholars praise Giolitti for his "silent reconciliation" with the Church by building a "tunnel" between the two parallels; see Spadolini, *Giolitti e i cattolici,* pp. 353–86. See also Jemolo, *Chiesa e stato,* pp. 161–67; and Candeloro, *Il movimento cattolico,* p. 320. Turati criticized the excesses of the campaign; see *Critica sociale,* 16 January and 1 February 1907. The mayor of Rome was Ernesto Nathan.
17. Ferri cited this factor in his speech to the Chamber supporting Sonnino on 31 January 1906.
18. Turati, *Discorsi parlamentari,* 1:441–43.
19. Sonnino's speech is in *Atti parlamentari,* 1 February 1906.
20. Ivanoe Bonomi, "Situazione nuova: Il significato e gli effetti del ministero Sonnino," *Critica sociale,* 16 February 1906; see also Bonomi, *La politica italiana,* p. 181; and Raffaele Colapietra, *Leonida Bissolati,* p. 107, who writes, "Turati manteneva una sua acciagliata e diffidente riservatezza che nulla sembrava poter giustificare se non il suo personale, geloso e fiducioso attacamento a Giolitti."
21. Turati to Kuliscioff, 2 February 1906 and 3 March 1906; see also the letter of 2 March.

22. Colapietra, *Bissolati*, p. 107.
23. La critica sociale, "Coll'arme al piede," *Critica sociale*, 16 February 1906.
24. "Riunione plenaria del Gruppo parlamentare e della Direzione del partito," *Avanti!*, 10 March 1906. Turati accused Ferri of pursuing a contradictory policy—supporting Sonnino while trying to maintain his "revolutionary" image; see Turati, "Coll'arme al piede."
25. Kuliscioff to Turati, 9 and 11 March 1906. Sonnino's program is in *Atti parlamentari XXII Leg., 1ª sess.*, 8 March 1906, pp. 6400–406.
26. Costantino Lazzari, "La polvere per i gonzi," *Avanguardia socialista*, 17 March 1906; Enrico Ferri, "Parole e fatti nell'attuale momento politico," *Avanti!*, 11 March 1906.
27. See Mocchi's interview with the *Messagiero*, reprinted in *Avanguardia socialista*, 17 March 1906. See also Costantino Lazzari, "Parlamentarismo borghese e parlamentarismo socialista," g.a., "Il neo-ministerialismo," and "Ferri all'estrema destra," *Avanguardia socialista*, 3 March 1906.
28. See "Il socialismo ministeriale dei deputati" and "La figura geniale di Enrico Ferri," *Avanguardia socialista*, 10 March 1906; g.a., "Espedienti ministeriali," R. Momigliano, "D'accordo con Bissolati," and "Fatiche ministerialiste," 17 March 1906. See also Kuliscioff to Turati, 12 and 14 March 1906; and "Alle sezioni," *Avanguardia socialista*, 17 March 1906.
29. "In difesa del Partito socialista," *Avanguardia socialista*, 17 March 1906, and "Il Convengno rivoluzionario di Milano," *Avanti!*, 14 March 1906. The meeting, called at the initiative of the Milanese revolutionaries, was held on 12 and 13 March.
30. L'avanguardia, "Partito e Gruppo," *Avanguardia socialista*, 31 March 1906.
31. *Bollettino della Direzione*, 30 April 1906, p. 30.
32. The declaration, written by E. C. Longobardi, is in ibid., pp. 32–35. See also "Per la mozione di Bologna," *Avanguardia socialista*, 24 March 1906.
33. "Dichiarazione del Gruppo parlamentare," *Critica sociale*, 16 March 1906.
34. Ausonio Semita, "Ministeriali!" *Avanguardia socialista*, 17 March 1906.
35. See Turati's comments on the deputies' statement in *Critica sociale*, 16 March 1906. Bissolati also approved; see Colapietra, *Bissolati*, p. 108.
36. Filippo Turati, "Agli elettori del V Collegio di Milano," *Critica sociale*, 16 May–1 June 1906; Turati to Kuliscioff, 9 May 1906.
37. Turati to Kuliscioff, 11 May 1906; Turati, "Agli elettori del V Collegio"; and *Il tempo*, 13 May 1906. Turati's action was not motivated by a change of heart about Sonnino, whom he continued to consider a poor politician; see Turati to Kuliscioff, 31 March and 6 April 1906.
38. The events are described by Colapietra, *Bissolati*, pp. 108–10.
39. Turati, "Agli elettori del V Collegio"; Turati to Kuliscioff, 11 May 1906; Kuliscioff to Turati, 10 May 1906, and two letters dated 12 May 1906. These letters express the same themes as Turati's open letter. After the resignations, which the Chamber at first refused to accept, the Socialists ran again for their empty seats in the by-elections, and most were reelected.
40. "Dissensi in famiglia," *Critica sociale*, 16 June 1906.
41. Kuliscioff to Turati, 5 July 1906. Giolitti's followers feared that Sonnino might be able to dissolve the Chamber and hold new elections; see Giolitti, *Quarant'anni*, 2:417–18.
42. Rerum scriptor [Gaetano Salvemini], "La questione meridionale e il federalismo," *Critica sociale*, 16 July, 1 and 16 August, 1 and 16 September 1900; reprinted in Salvemini, *Opere IV*, 2:157–91. Rerum scriptor, "Nord e sud nel partito socialista italiano," *Critica sociale*, 16 December 1902. Gaetano Salvemini,

"Riforme sociali e riforme politiche," *La battaglia* (Palermo), April–May 1904 (*Opere IV*, 2:299–313).

43. Rerum scriptor, "I socialisti meridionali," *La battaglia*, May 1904 (*Opere IV*, 2:313–19).

44. Gaetano Salvemini, *Il ministro della mala vita e altri scritti sull'Italia giolittiana*, in *Opere IV* (Milan: Feltrinelli, 1962), 1:137–41.

45. See Massimo L. Salvadori, *Gaetano Salvemini*, pp. 62–64.

46. La critica sociale, "Finanza feudale," *Critica sociale*, 1 December 1895.

47. For the exchange, see Salvemini's articles, "Polemica meridionale" and "Sempre polemiche meridionali," and Turati's comments in *Critica sociale*, 1, 16 January and 1 February 1903.

48. See Turati's comments in *Il tempo*, 1 May 1904, reprinted also in Salvemini, *Opere IV*, 2:321.

49. "Suffragio universale, questione meridionale e riformismo," in Salvemini, *Opere IV*, 2:337–52. Salvemini also argued that without universal suffrage the voting population of the country (which he estimated at 8.6 pereent) was too slim to support a program of reforms. See "Suffragio universale (specialmente in rapporto al problema meridionale)," in ibid., 2:402–3. This is Salvemini's report to the national congress of 1910.

50. Salvemini, "Suffragio universale," pp. 417–20. See also his "Suffragio universale e clerieialismo," in *Opere IV*, 2:227–32.

51. Rerum scriptor, "Sempre polemiche meridionali!" *Critica sociale*, 16 January and 1 February 1903, and "La questione meridionale e i partiti politici," 16 August 1903. See also Ivanoe Bonomi, "Polemiche doganali," and Salvemini's answer, "L'intrigo doganale e la questione del Mezzogiorno," in *Critica sociale*, 1 and 16 September and 1 October 1903.

52. Salvadori, *Salvemini*, pp. 66–68.

53. Tre stelle [Gaetano Salvemini], "Spettri e realtà," *Critica sociale*, 1 March 1907, and the commentary by Noi.

54. "La nuova crisi del partito socialista mentre si prepara il Congresso di Milano: Intervista con il prof. Salvemini," *Il giornale d'Italia*, 10 June 1910, reprinted in Salvemini, *Opere IV*, 2:354–58.

55. Gaetano Salvemini, "Cooperative di lavoro e movimento socialista," *Avanti!*, 24 and 28 June and 10 July 1910, reprinted in *Opere IV*, 2:359–84. See also Salvadori, *Salvemini*, p. 76.

56. See the comments following Salvemini's articles in *Avanti!*, 24 and 28 June and 10 July 1910. These have been reprinted in *Opere IV*, 2:384–89; see also the note on p. 359.

57. Filippo Turati, "A proposito di Nord e Sud," *Critica sociale*, 10 June 1900.

58. "Polemica meridionale" and "Sempre polemiche meridionali!" *Critica sociale*, 1, 16 January and 1 February 1903.

59. The summary of the GSM meeting, with an editorial by Treves, is in *Il tempo*, 23 November 1905. For Turati's commentary, see La critica sociale, "Per trovare una via d'uscita," *Critica sociale*, 16 November–1 December 1905. See also Salvadori, *Salvemini*, pp. 68–69.

60. Kuliscioff to Turati, 14 March 1908; Turati to Kuliscioff, 15, 19, 21 March 1908.

61. Kuliscioff to Turati, 17 and 26 May 1909.

62. Filippo Turati, "La leva elettorale," *Critica sociale*, 1 May 1908, and La critica sociale and E. Ciccotti, "La leva elettorale," 1 December 1909.

63. See La critica sociale, "In vista del congresso," *Critica sociale*, 1 August 1908, and "Il Punto," 16 September 1909.

64. See Anna Kuliscioff and Filippo Turati, "Suffragio universale?" *Critica sociale*,

16 March–1 April 1910; "Ancora del voto alle donne," 16 April 1910; and Anna Kuliscioff, "Per concludere sul voto alle donne," 1 May 1910. These articles were also printed as a pamphlet by *Critica sociale*. For further information on this issue, see Anna Kuliscioff, *Proletariato femminile e Partito socialista*; Anna Kuliscioff, *Per il suffragio universale*; and an interesting early presentation by Turati, "Il voto anche alle salariate dell'amore," which is in *Discorsi politici celebri* (Milan, 1957) but which can be found in several editions printed as an independent work.

65. Turati to Kuliscioff, 19 February and 12 March 1910.

66. Turati to Kuliscioff, 12 June 1910; Kuliscioff to Turati, 26 June 1910; Turati to Kuliscioff, 7 July 1910.

67. Brunello Vigezzi, *Giolitti e Turati*, 1 : 53–56. Vigezzi has published a selection of the Turati-Kuliscioff letters of this period. The material in the first volume originally appeared in Istituto Giangiacomo Feltrinelli, *Annali XIV, 1972* (Milan: Feltrinelli, 1972), pp. 184–356.

68. Salvemini's speech is in Partito socialista italiano, *Resoconto stenografico del XI congresso nazionale* (Milano, 1910), pp. 59–70. See his special report, *Suffragio universale*, reprinted in *Opere IV*, 2 : 391–435. See also Arfé, *Storia del socialismo*, p. 142.

69. See Turati's speech in psi, *Resoconto stenografico del XI congresso*, pp. 43–56. See also Turati to Kuliscioff, 6 and 10 June 1910.

70. psi, *Resoconto stenografico del XI congresso*, pp. 265–78, 361–62. See the letter from Anna Kuliscioff to Ivanoe Bonomi, dated 19 March 1909, in *Rivista storica del socialismo*, 1958, pp. 118–19.

71. psi, *Resoconto stenografico del XI congresso*, pp. 278–80.

72. Turati to Kuliscioff, 29 April, 30 April, and 1 May 1910. Turati's speech is in his *Discorsi parlamentari*, 2 : 885–88.

73. Kuliscioff to Turati, 2, 3, 9, 15 May 1910; and Turati to Kuliscioff, 2, 3, 10 May and also 30 May and 2 June 1910.

74. See Vigezzi, *Giolitti e Turati*, 1 : 29–44. The reformist Directorate's vote on this issue was 5 to 4; see Turati to Kuliscioff, 6 June 1910.

75. See Turati to Kuliscioff, 9, 14, 15, and 20 December 1910; and Kuliscioff to Turati, 17 and 20 December 1910 and 28 January 1911.

76. For this debate, see Salvemini's articles in *Avanti!*, 3, 11, 14 January 1911 (*Opere IV*, 2 : 459–69), and, in *Critica sociale*, Salvemini's "Il progetto Bonomi (ripristino dell'art. 100)," 1 February 1911, and especially "Il socialista che si contenta," 1 March 1911, and Turati's note to it. See also Bissolati's speech in psi, *Resoconto stenografico del XI congresso*, pp. 182–87.

77. G. Salvemini, "Che fare?" *Critica sociale*, 1 January 1911 (*Opere IV*, 1 : 215–24).

78. See Turati's comments to Salvemini's article in *Critica sociale*, 1 January 1911.

79. Comments of Noi, on Salvemini's article, "Nord e Sud nel Partito socialista italiano," *Critica sociale*, 16 December 1902.

80. See Salvemini's preface (written in 1949) to Bruno Caizzi, *Nuova antologia della questione meridionale* (Milan: Ed. di comunità, 1962), and Giustino Fortunato's articles in the anthology, pp. 193–204; see also pp. 153–63. It is, of course, beyond the scope of this essay to discuss all the ramifications of the southern problem. Salvemini's writings on the South have been collected into two volumes of his collected works *Opere IV*, vols. 1 and 2. Besides Caizzi's anthology, the collection by Rosario Villari, *Il Sud nella storia d'Italia*, 2 vols. (Bari: Laterza, 1966), is excellent, as is Massimo L. Salvadori, *Il mito del buongoverno* (Turin: Einaudi, 1961). For economic aspects of the question, see Clough, *Economic History of Italy*, pp. 163–69; Vera Lutz, *Italy: A Study in*

Economic Development (London, New York, Toronto: Oxford University Press, 1962), pp. 95–98; and *Storia d'Italia, vol. 4, Dall'unità a oggi* (Turin: Einaudi, 1975), pp. 45–72, 168–71, 188–90. For voting patterns in the South, see Istituto centrale di statistica e Ministero per la costituente, *Compendio delle statistiche elettorali italiane dal 1848 al 1934,* 2:110–20, 125–28.

81. The historiographical debate between the "good" and the "bad" Giolitti has been continuing apace since World War II, when Salvemini himself reopened it in his introductory essay to A. William Salomone, *Italy in the Giolittian Era.* See also Giovanni Ansaldo, *Il ministro della buona vita,* especially pp. 324–54. For Salvemini's last word on this issue, see his essay, "Fu l'Italia prefascista una democrazia," which originally appeared in *Il ponte* but is now in Salvemini's *Opere IV,* 2:540–67.

82. Turati to Kuliscioff, 20 December 1910; see also the letter of 17 December. For Giolitti's intervention, see his *Discorsi parlamentari,* 3:1364–65; see also Giolitti, *Memorie,* p. 187.

83. La critica sociale, "Il capitombolo," *Critica sociale,* 16 March 1911.

84. See Vigezzi, *Giolitti e Turati,* 1:13–15.

85. The "Inchiesta sulla partecipazione dei socialisti al governo" began on 28 November 1909 and ended with the 6 February 1910 issue of *Il viandante* (Milan), a journal edited by the former revolutionary syndicalist Tomaso Monicelli. See the 13 February 1910 issue for an analysis of the results by Colajanni. The Turatians took an aloof stand, their spokesman Treves answering only that the question was not "attuale"; see the 12 December 1909 issue.

86. Kuliscioff to Turati, 19 March 1911.

87. Turati to Kuliscioff, 20 March and 22 March (first letter) 1911.

88. Giolitti, *Quarant'anni,* 3:44–45. The Socialist deputy and labor expert Giovanni Montemartini had secretly visited the monarch in 1908—much to Turati's chagrin; see Turati to Kuliscioff, 11 February 1908.

89. Turati to Kuliscioff, 23 March 1911; see also 22 March 1911 (third letter).

90. Turati to Kuliscioff, 22 March 1911 (first letter); Vigezzi, *Giolitti e Turati,* 1:72–80. See also Bonomi, *Bissolati,* pp. 109–11; Giolitti, *Memorie,* pp. 191–93.

91. Turati to Kuliscioff, 26 March 1911; *Avanti!,* 18 October 1911.

92. See Turati to Kuliscioff, 27 March 1911. Bissolati's letter was published by Natale, *Giolitti,* p. 727.

93. Kuliscioff to Turati, 23 and 24 March 1911; and Vigezzi, *Turati e Giolitti,* 1:81–92.

94. Filippo Turati, "Dura salita," *Critica sociale,* 1 April 1911.

95. The Socialist deputies could not bring themselves to vote against Giolitti's program or his new cabinet, which included Radical representatives. Giolitti's program, with his presentation, is in his *Discorsi parlamentari,* 3:1366–69.

96. Antonio Graziadei, "Socialismo e Partito socialista," *Il viandante,* 20 June 1909; and Ivanoe Bonomi, "La crisi dei partiti storici in Italia: Il partito socialista," *Il viandante,* 17 October 1909. See also Santarelli, *La revisione del marxismo,* pp. 137–39.

97. PSI, *Resoconto stenografico del XI congresso,* pp. 188–89.

98. See Rigola's speech in ibid., pp. 220–31.

99. See Arfé, *Storia del socialismo,* p. 144; and Pedone, *Il Partito socialista,* 2:132; see also pp. 124, 145.

Chapter IX

1. See Turati to Kuliscioff, 20 May 1908 and 24 June 1908; Kuliscioff to Turati, 21, 22, 25 May 1908; Turati to Kuliscioff, 26 June 1908. For a clear exposition of

Bissolati's ideas on military expenses, see Leonida Bissolati, *La politica estera dell'Italia dal 1897 al 1920*, p. 104.

2. "Il convegno italo-austriaco a Trieste," *Il tempo*, 13 April 1905. The idea for the meeting came from Milanese Socialists and was also sanctioned by the Directorate. Subsequent to this meeting a very pessimistic article appeared on its chances for success; see L'italiano errante, "Dissolvere, non risolvere," *Il tempo*, 6 May 1905.

3. *Il tempo*, 23 May 1905 and 23 October 1906. Bissolati revealed the refusal of the Austrians to sabotage mobilization in case of war only on the latter date; reprinted in Bissolati, *La politica estera dell'Italia*, pp. 111–15.

4. See c.t., "Il convegno di Trieste e il riformismo," *Il tempo*, 25 May 1905; Bissolati, *La politica estera dell'Italia*, pp. 126–38, 144–48.

5. Bissolati, *La politica estera dell'Italia*, pp. 160–63.

6. Ibid., pp. 167–68.

7. La critica sociale, "Il riformismo alla prova," *Critica sociale*, 1 November 1908. Anna Kuliscioff had previously suggested such a campaign in her letters of 21, 22, 25 May 1908.

8. C. Braccialarghe and Leonida Bissolati, "A proposito di patria e di guerra," *Avanti!*, 7 April 1909.

9. Filippo Turati, "Le spese militari: Lettera aperta a Leonida Bissolati," *Critica sociale*, 16 April 1909. Leonida Bissolati, "Le spese militari e il Partito socialista: Risposta a Filippo Turati," *Avanti!*, 6 May 1909.

10. Turati to Kuliscioff, 5, 6, and 7 May 1909. Noi, "Due anni e mezzo prima!" *Critica sociale*, 1–16 December 1911.

11. See Turati to Kuliscioff, 3 May 1909, and Kuliscioff to Turati, 4, 11 May and 3 June 1909.

12. La critica sociale, "Il Partito socialista alla prova (seguito della polemica sulle spese militari)," *Critica sociale*, 16 May 1909.

13. See Filippo Turati, "Militaristi senza saperlo," *Critica sociale*, 1 May 1909, and "Momento di sosta," 16 June 1909.

14. See Richard A. Webster, *Industrial Imperialism in Italy, 1908–1915*, pp. 3–4, 44–46, 51. After examining the budget deficits and the percentages spent on arms during this period (which Turati also did in his articles), Webster writes: "Italy simply could not afford to pay for war programs and social progress at the same time." On the issue of foreign policy, he states: "Thus precariously perched on the outer edge of the industrial world, the Italians made up for their economic deficiencies with political audacity. A restless and adventurous spirit entered their foreign policy from 1911 on, and by 1914 they had become objects of suspicion and alarm in the European diplomatic world." The affinities with the later Fascist period are also thoroughly investigated by Webster. See also his article, "Autarchy, Expansion, and the Underlying Continuity of the Italian State," *Italian Quarterly* 8, no. 32 (Winter 1964): 3–18.

15. Bissolati's speech to the Chamber is in his *La politica estera dell'Italia*, pp. 175–93. See Turati to Kuliscioff, 5 May and 30 June 1909, and Kuliscioff to Turati, 11 May, and 9 June 1909.

16. Turati to Kuliscioff, 1 and 2 June 1911.

17. Filippo Turati, "Da Jena al Marocco e a Tripoli, passando per Roma," *Critica sociale*, 16 September 1911.

18. Marchetti, *La Confederazione generale del lavoro*, pp. 146–47. Pedone, *Il Partito socialista*, 2:159–60.

19. For a complete discussion of this meeting, see Noi, "La politica di Tecoppa: L'ordine del giorno di Bologna e il nostro suicidio politico," *Critica sociale*, 1

October 1911. On the general strike, see "Il proletariato italiano contro la guerra," *Avanti!*, 27 September 1911.

20. Giolitti, *Quarant'anni*, 3 : 61.

21. La critica sociale, "La guerra contro l'Italia," *Critica sociale*, 16 November 1911. Carocci, *Giolitti*, p. 139, writes: "La riforma elettorale e l'impresa libica furono concepite da Giolitti simultaneamente come le due facce di una unica, grande manovra politica la quale, interpretando e le tendenze di destra e le tendenze di sinistra, contribuisse a mantenerle nell'ambito del suo sistema." Webster sees Giolitti's actions as part of a bold plan, "according to which industrial Italy would constitute the vital center of a new political order, with conservative Catholic agrarian voters balancing the red urban proletariat and the Socialist day laborers of the Po valley farms"; see *Industrial Imperialism*, p. 26.

22. La critica sociale, "Anche soli!" *Critica sociale*, 1 October 1911, and Filippo Turati, "Nella Tagiola," 1 November 1911. Turati to Kuliscioff, and Kuliscioff to Turati, both letters dated 1 December 1911.

23. See *Avanti!*, 1 October 1911; Kuliscioff to Turati, 27 and 29 November 1911; and Turati to Kuliscioff, 3 March 1912. See also Turati to Kuliscioff, 30 November 1911, and Kuliscioff to Turati, 30 November 1911.

24. "L'altro pericolo," *Il secolo*, 15 September 1911, reprinted in Bissolati, *La politica estera dell'Italia*, pp. 229–32; for a fuller discussion of the Balkan problem by Bissolati, see pp. 245–48. See also di San Giuliano's "promemoria," in Giolitti; *Quarant'anni*, 3 : 52–56.

25. "Il nuovo compito nostro," *Il secolo*, 7 October 1911 (Bissolati, *La politica estera dell'Italia*, pp. 232–35).

26. See "Le ragioni del gruppo Bissolati," *Avanti!*, 13 October 1911; Ivanoe Bonomi and La critica sociale, "Il dissidio sul terreno concreto," *Critica sociale*, 16 October 1911.

27. Albertini, *Venti anni*, 1, pt. 2: 118–24, 55–62. See also Sidney Sonnino, *Scritti e discorsi extraparlamentari*, 2 vols. (Bari: Laterza, 1972), 2 : 1596–98. For a diplomatic history of the war, see William Askew, *Europe and Italy's Acquisition of Libya* (Durham, N.C.: Duke University Press, 1942).

28. Natale, *Giolitti*, pp. 726–31.

29. See Albertini, *Venti anni*, 1, pt. 2: 116–17, 123–24. In the *Corriere*, see especially, "L'Italia e la questione di Tripoli: Il momento di risolversi," 10 September 1911; "Turchia e Tripolitania," 12 September 1911; "Il valore della Tripolitania," 15 September 1911; and "La soluzione," 22 September 1911, all by Andrea Torre. Albertini himself did not consider Libya an economic asset. See also Giolitti, *Memorie*, pp. 218–19, for the importance of the period during which these articles were written.

30. "Alla vigilia dell'azione la concordia del paese" and "La protesta socialista," *Corriere della sera*, 24 and 25 September 1911.

31. Albertini, *Venti anni*, 1 : pt. 2 : 98.

32. See Enrico Corradini, *Discorsi politici, 1902–1923* (Florence: Vallecchi, 1923), and his *Il nazionalismo italiano* (Milan: Treves, 1914). Perhaps the best work in English on the Nationalists and the rise of a "new" Right is Salvatore Saladino's essay on Italy in Hans Rogger and Eugen Weber, eds., *The European Right: A Historical Profile* (Berkeley and Los Angeles: University of California Press, 1966), pp. 208–60. See also Pier Ludovico Occhini, *Enrico Corradini e la nuova coscienza nazionale* (Florence: Vallecchi, 1925), p. 202.

33. The Nationalist newspaper *Idea nazionale* was the main focus of the campaign, but the following works may also be consulted: Enrico Corradini, *L'ora di Tripoli* (Milan: Treves, 1911), especially pp. 93–95, 152–55, 159–75, 179–89,

227–36; P. Vinassa de Regny, *Libya italica* (Milan: Hoepli, 1913), especially pp. 94–95; see also pp. 99–115, 131–44, 185–93, and the collection on the issue made by Gaetano Salvemini, *Come siamo andati in Libia* (Florence: La voce, 1914). For a scholarly analysis, see Ronald S. Cunsolo, "Libya, Italian Nationalism, and the Revolt against Giolitti," *Journal of Modern History* 37, no. 2 (June 1965): 188; see also Occhini, *Corradini*, pp. 202–3. On the role of the bank in Libya and domestic politics, see Webster, *Industrial Imperialism*, pp. 152–58; Candeloro, *Il movimento cattolico*, pp. 343–45; and G. Volpe, *L'impresa di Tripoli* (Rome: Ed. Leonardo, 1946), pp. 32–36. The director of the bank was Ernesto Pacelli, uncle of the rising star of Vatican diplomacy and future Pius XII.

34. Morgari's views are quoted by Guido Podrecca, *Libia: Impressioni e polemiche* (Rome: Podrecca e Galantara, 1912), pp. 35–36; see pp. 5–12, 17, 29–30, 37–38, 40–58, 131–40 for the high points of Podrecca's own argument. Corradini reminded the Socialists that Antonio Labriola had sanctioned imperialism as a necessary stage in the development of the bourgeoisie, without which socialism would be impossible; see Corradini, *L'ora di Tripoli*, pp. 236–40.

35. Arturo Labriola, *La guerra di Tripoli e l'opinione socialista*, pp. 7–25, 38–54, 69–85, 103–9. See also Marucco, *Labriola*, pp. 203–7. For the revolutionary syndicalist repudiation of pacifism, see L'avanguardia, "La pace," *Avanguardia socialista*, 5 September 1905.

36. On this point, see Salvemini's preface to *Come siamo andati in Libia*; Cunsolo, "Libya, Nationalism, and Giolitti," pp. 186–207; Rogger and Weber, *The European Right*, p. 244; and Webster, *Industrial Imperialism*, p. 39.

37. Turati to Kuliscioff, 15 October 1911.

38. Bissolati's speech is in *Avanti!*, 18 October 1911. Bonomi and Cabrini were even more sympathetic to Giolitti.

39. *Avanti!*, 18 October 1911.

40. Kuliscioff to Turati, 17 October 1911. Turati's motion is referred to in the stenographic report, published in *Avanti!*, as the Treves-Bussi motion (Turati was among its signers). Turati, however, was the author of the motion—see Turati to Kuliscioff, 16 October 1911. The motion is reprinted in Pedone, *Il Partito socialista*, 2:175–77.

41. The stenographic report of this congress is in *Avanti!*, 18 and 19 October 1911. There is a summary in Pedone, *Il Partito socialista*, 2:157–83. See also *Critica sociale*, 1 November 1911.

42. *Guerin meschino*, 22 October 1911.

43. See M., "Alla vigilia del congresso socialista: I problemi del congresso," *Avanti!*, 14 October 1911. Lerda's motion is in Pedone, *Il Partito socialista*, 2:177–78. For Turati's article, see La critica sociale, "Quel che he detto il Congresso di Modena," *Critica sociale*, 1 November 1911.

44. Noi, "L'accordo dei contrari," *Critica sociale*, 16 November 1911.

45. La critica sociale, "La riunione del Gruppo," *Critica sociale*, 1 February 1912; see also Filippo Turati, "La riapertura," 16 February 1912.

46. Vigezzi, *Giolitti e Turati*, 2:287–93.

47. Ibid., pp. 294–308; Kuliscioff to Turati, 23 February 1912, and especially her letters of 25 and 28 February 1912.

48. Bissolati's speech is in Bonomi, *La politica italiana*, pp. 248–55. The annexation decrees were issued on 5 November 1911 by the government in order to prevent mediation of the Libyan dispute by the European powers. See Bonomi, *La politica italiana*, p. 229, and Kuliscioff's letter to Turati of 24 February 1912.

Turati's speech to the Chamber opposing conversion of the decrees is in his *Discorsi parlamentari*, 2:1068–81.

49. "La scissione del Gruppo socialista," *Critica sociale*, 1 March 1912.

50. Some Socialist deputies who had voted against the annexation decrees in the open vote had voted for them in the secret vote. By a process of elimination, some of these had to be reformists of the Left. See Turati to Kuliscioff, 26 February 1912.

51. Turati to Kuliscioff, 29 February 1912. Kuliscioff to Turati, 1 and 2 March 1912.

52. La critica sociale, "All'opposizione!" *Critica sociale*, 16 March 1912.

53. Il Comitato centrale della frazione rivoluzionaria intransigente del PSI, "Ai socialisti e ai lavoratori d'Italia," *La soffitta*, 1 May 1911. The title of the newspaper, "The Attic," refers to a remark by Giolitti that the Socialists had relegated Marx to the attic.

54. Untitled editorial by Giovanni Lerda, *La soffitta*, 1 May 1911. See also Alceste della Seta, "La soffitta," in the same issue.

55. Angelica Balabanoff, "Chi siamo e chi non siamo," *La soffitta*, 15 May 1911.

56. Angelica Balabanoff, "Una pregiudiziale," *La soffitta*, 15 June 1911.

57. See Pedone, *Il Partito socialista*, 2:132. See also G. Plechanoff, "Il caso Bissolati," *La soffitta*, 1 May 1911, and Rosa Luxemburg, "Rinascenza socialista," 15 May 1911.

58. "Atti ufficiale del Comitato C. della frazione," *La soffitta*, 15 June 1911, and "Il pensiero della frazione," 1 May 1911.

59. For a discussion of Mussolini, the Forlì schism, and the reaction of the Central Committee, see Renzo De Felice, *Mussolini il rivoluzionario* (Turin: Einaudi, 1965), pp. 96–103. The most important article in *La soffitta* is Franceso Ciccotti, "Per i ... fuorusciti forlivesi: A Benito Mussolini," in the 15 September 1911 issue. See also Adolfo Zerbini, "Verso la scissione?" *La soffitta*, 15 September 1911.

60. See Oda Lerda Olberg, "Movimento di resistenza e partito del lavoro," *La soffitta*, 15 June 1911.

61. See "Per il congresso della Confederazione Generale del Lavoro," *La soffitta*, 15 May 1911; Enrico Mastracchi, "Per il congresso della resistenza," 30 May 1911, and "Ancora il congresso di Padova," 1 July 1911. Pepe considers reformist power in the CGL to have peaked during this congress. See his *Storia della Confederazione generale del lavoro*, pp. 471–79.

62. "Atti ufficiali del Comitato C. della frazione," *La soffitta*, 15 June 1911.

63. "Atti ufficiali del Comitato centrale della frazione: Communicazioni del segretario," *La soffitta*, 1 July 1911. Lists of the *fiduciari* are printed in the 1 September and subsequent issues. See also "I nostri fiduciari," in the same issue; "Atti ufficiali del Comitato centrale della frazione," 31 July 1911, and "Atti ufficiali del Comitato centrale della frazione: Communicazioni del segretario, pel congresso," 15 August 1911. For the completed draft of the motion presented at Modena, see "Per il Congresso di Modena," 1 September 1911.

64. See "Ai compagni dell'Unione socialista romana," *La soffitta*, 1 September 1911, and "La battaglia all'U.S.R.," 15 September 1911.

65. Giovan[sic] Lerda, "Monito!" *La soffitta*, 1 October 1911, and "Atti ufficiali," 8 October 1911.

66. Arturo Vella, "Che fare?" *La soffitta*, 8 October 1911; see also Vella, "La vigilia," 15 October 1911.

67. See Costantino Lazzari, "Le lezioni della storia," and N. P., "L'insucesso dello sciopero generale," both in *La soffitta* of 8 October 1911.

68. "Attività della frazione," *La soffitta*, 12 November 1911.
69. "A tutti i compagni," *La soffitta*, 19 November 1911. The members of the new Central Committee were Lerda, della Seta, Balabanoff, Pittaluga, Patriarca, Zerbini, and Vella.
70. Giovanni Lerda, "Dichiarazione," *La soffitta*, 29 October 1911. For a wider discussion of the ideological issues, see Santarelli, *La revisione del marxismo*, pp. 149–52. See also De Felice, *Mussolini il rivoluzionario*, pp. 117–18.
71. Angelica Balabanoff, "Seguiamo l'esempio," *La soffitta*, 12 November 1911; see also Francesco Ciccotti, "Giovanni Lerda e . . . il programma," 19 November 1911. Vittorio Badaloni, "Per il nostro programma," *La soffitta*, 12 November 1911. Giovanni Lerda, *Il socialismo e la sua tattica*, pp. 9–16, 44–57.
72. "Quel che la detto il Congresso di Modena," in *Critica sociale*, 1 November 1911.
73. Oda Lerda Olberg, "Tutti d'accordo," *La soffitta*, 12 November and her "Scaramuccie . . . (Risposta all'Onorevole Filippo Turati)," 3 December 1911. Giovanni Lerda, "Per parlar chiaro," *La soffitta*, 15 January 1912.
74. Arturo Vella, "Per la restaurazione del partito," *La soffitta*, 15 January 1912. See also Angelica Balabanoff, "Cause ed effetti," *La soffitta*, 27 January 1912, and "Le riserve di Treves," in the same issue.
75. See Il Comitato centrale della frazione rivoluzionaria intransigente del PSI, "Contro l'avventura di Tripoli: Il nostro manifesto," O. L., "Eran pronti," A. V., "Quella direzione del partito!" *La soffitta*, 1 October 1911; Alceste della Seta, "Il navarca," Giovanni Lerda, "Vicolo cieco del . . . riformismo," 8 October 1911.
76. See a.v., "L'ultimissima 'enormità' della direzione del partito," *La soffitta*, 19 November 1911.
77. "Atti ufficiali," *La soffitta*, 3 December 1911 and 12 January 1912, and "La nostra dimostrazione contro la guerra in Campidoglio," 3 December 1911; see also "Atti ufficiali," 17 December 1911.
78. Maurizio Degl'Innocenti, "La guerra libica, la crisi del riformismo, e la vittoria degli intransigenti," *Studi storici* 13, no. 3 (July–September 1972):472–80.
79. On these issues, see Il Comitato centrale della frazione rivoluzionaria intransigente del PSI, "Ai socialisti d'Italia!," *La soffitta*, 15 February 1912. For Lerda's arguments and reasoning during the debate on his draft of the manifesto, see "Atti ufficiali del Comitato centrale della frazione," his "L'autonomia trionfante," and also "Le due deliberazioni," all in the same issue of *La soffitta*.
80. "Verso il congresso," *La soffitta*, 4 March 1912.
81. Kuliscioff to Turati, 1 March 1912. Turati to Kuliscioff, 2 March 1912.
82. La critica sociale, "Pro o contro il congresso," *Critica sociale*, 16 April 1912; and see La critica sociale, "A Reggio Emilia: Ritorno dopo un ventennio," *Critica sociale*, 1 July 1912.
83. See La critica sociale, "All'opposizione," *Critica sociale*, 16 March 1912, and Kuliscioff to Turati, 2 and 5 March 1912. The vote in the Gruppo was 19 to 15.
84. See Bonomi, *La politica italiana*, p. 229; "Deputati socialisti al Quirinale," "L'attentato," and "Ed ora . . . la reazione?" in *La soffitta*, 15 March 1912.
85. Kuliscioff to Turati, 5 May and 23 June 1912.
86. Kuliscioff to Turati, 1 March 1912. Turati to Kuliscioff, 2 March 1912.
87. Kuliscioff to Turati, 4 March 1912, and Kuliscioff to Turati, 5 May 1912.
88. La critica sociale, "Verso il congresso," and G. E. Modigliani, "Le direttive del Partito socialista secondo i riformisti di sinistra," *Critica sociale*, 16 June 1912. See also Vigezzi, *Giolitti e Turati*, 2:319–28.
89. Kuliscioff to Turati, 19, 20, 21 June 1912.
90. See Turati to Kuliscioff, 3 March 1912; and Vigezzi, *Giolitti e Turati*, 2:311–12.

Alessandro Schiavi, one of Turati's firmest supporters, sponsored two motions in the Milanese Socialist section critical of the Party Directorate and the Parliamentary Group. For activity of this kind, see Degl'Innocenti, "La guerra libica," pp. 496–97.

91. Kuliscioff to Turati, 30 and 31 January 1911. Arfé, *Storia dell'Avanti!*, 1:91–92.

92. See Kuliscioff to Turati, 21 May 1911, and Turati to Kuliscioff, 22 May 1911. See Arfé, *Storia dell'Avanti!*, 1:92. Turati was head of the board of directors of the new company.

93. For articles on this issue, see, in *La soffitta*, 1911, "Il trasloco dell'*Avanti!*," 1 May; Giovanni Lerda, "Ancora l'*Avanti!*," 15 June; Adolfo Zerbini, "Le disavventure dell'Avanti," 1 July; Costantino Lazzari, "Un grosso affare," 15 September; editorial, "La censura riformista," 8 October; C. Lazzari, "Il giornale del partito," 19 November; editorial, "Contro l'*Avanti!*" 3 December; and, in 1912, editorial, "Per l'*Avanti!*," 4 March; editorial, "La direzione del partito a Milano?" 1 May; Cic, "Chi sara?"; C. Lazzari, "I sofismi dei riformisti," 2 June; and "A proposito dell'*Avanti!*," 15 June. See also Arfé, *Storia dell'Avanti!*, 1:91, 96. Kuliscioff, in her letter to Turati of 21 May 1911, referred to the Directorate's decision to transfer *Avanti!* as a "colpo di stato."

94. See Arfé, *Storia dell'Avanti!*, 1:96–97. Kuliscioff to Turati, 19 and 23 June 1912.

95. See Arfé, *Storia dell'Avanti!*, 1:101–3. See also Kuliscioff to Turati, 1, 2, 3 December 1912.

96. Kuliscioff to Turati, 21 May 1911. Turati accused Kuliscioff of being too pessimistic; see his letter to her of 22 May 1911. See also Vigezzi, *Giolitti e Turati*, 2:371–76.

97. The committee's proclamation, "Contro la guerra," is in *La soffitta*, 15 March 1912.

98. Il Comitato centrale della frazione rivoluzionaria intransigente del PSI, "Per il primo maggio e contro la guerra," *La soffitta*, 1 May 1912, and Giovanni Lerda, "Organizzazione economica e socialismo," 15 March 1912.

99. Costantino Lazzari, "Da Briand a Lloyd George," *La soffitta*, 6 April, and "Una grossa manovra riformista," 1 May 1912.

100. See, in *La soffitta*, 1912, Giovanni Lerda, "Per parlar chiaro," and Arturo Vella, "Per la restaurazione del partito: parole schiette per i destri e per . . . i sinistri," 15 January; Angelica Balabanoff, "Cause ed effetti," and editorial, "Le riserve di Treves," 27 January; Tommaso Sorricchio, "I riformisti di sinistra ed il marxismo," 4 March; A. V., "Per un convegnino milanese (Nuove chiare parole ai sinistri)," 6 April; and v.b., "Non dimentichiamo," 19 May.

101. See Vezio, "Aspettando il congresso," *La soffitta*, 1 May 1912, "Annotando il nostro ordine del giorno," 19 May 1912; Oda Lerda Olberg, "Per la disciplina," 15 March 1912, "Ritornando a Reggio Emilia" and "La direzione del Partito," both 3 July 1912.

102. For details, see G. L., "Ai compagni," *La soffitta*, 4 March 1912; "Per il congresso nazionale di Reggio Emilia," 15 March 1912; G. L., "Vive raccomandazioni," 19 May 1912; "Congresso nazionale di Reggio Emilia: Le direttive politiche del Partito socialista" and "Annotando il nostro ordine del giorno," 19 May 1912; "Per le deleghe," 15 June 1912; and L'organizatore, "Raccogliamo le forze," 2 June 1912.

103. See G.d.M., "Vittoria di Pirro," *La soffitta*, 15 February 1912; "L'Unione socialista romana," 4 March 1912; "L'attività della frazione: A Roma, per l'assemblea dell'Unione socialista romana," 15 March 1912; "Le manovre ostruzionistiche dei riformisti per salvare Bissolati e Bonomi," 6 April 1912; "L'Unione socialista romana," 14 April 1912; "Verso la vittoria" and g.a., "La

vittoria di Milano," 2 June 1912. See also Costantino Lazzari, "Fra rappresentanti e rappresentati," in the 15 March 1912 issue.

104. Arturo Vella, "Occhio al timone," *La soffitta*, 15 June 1912, and a.v., "La trionfale preparazione della nostra frazione," 3 July 1912. In June, Kuliscioff wrote that everywhere "si vota l'intransigenza assoluta e la eliminazione dei destri." Kuliscioff to Turati, 19 June 1912. See also "Il precongresso della frazione," *La soffitta*, 3 July 1912.

105. See Kuliscioff to Turati, 19, 21, 23 June 1912.

106. See Partito socialista italiano, *Resoconto stenografico del XIII congresso nazionale*, pp. 13–18. See also Pedone, *Il Partito socialista*, 2:190–93.

107. Turati to Kuliscioff, 22 June 1912.

108. See PSI, *Resoconto stenografico del XIII congresso*, pp. 18–24, 59–60.

109. Mussolini's speech and motion are in ibid., pp. 69–72.

110. Ibid., pp. 187–99.

111. For the relevant speeches, see ibid., pp. 74–84, 94–106, 151–65. See also Arturo Vella, "Da Bonomi ai . . . milanesi," *La soffitta*, 2 June 1912.

112. PSI, *Resoconto stenografico del XIII congresso*, pp. 111–13, 234; and Pedone, *Il Partito socialista*, 2:203–4.

113. De Felice, *Mussolini il rivoluzionario*, p. 126. PSI, *Resoconto stenografico del XIII congresso*, pp. 240–70.

114. PSI, *Resoconto stenografico del XIII congresso*, pp. 270.

115. Francesco Ciccotti, "Dopo il congresso," *La soffitta*, 20 July 1912.

116. See De Felice, *Mussolini il rivoluzionario*, pp. 116–18.

117. See Pedone, *Il Partito socialista*, 2:208.

118. On the political intransigence in Milan, see Kuliscioff to Turati, 15 June 1908; and *Il tempo*, 26 March, 3 April, 14, 20 June, 6, 28 August and 9, 19 September 1910.

119. See Arfé, *Storia dell'Avanti!*, 1:102–7; and De Felice, *Mussolini il rivoluzionario*, pp. 131–35. For the intimate details of Treves's ouster, see Kuliscioff to Turati, 1, 2, 10, 11 December 1912, and Turati to Kuliscioff, 3 December 1912.

120. La critica sociale, "I risultati del congresso: Di chi la vittoria?" *Critica sociale*, 16 July 1912.

121. Bissolati and his friends established the Reformist Socialist party and tried to get the support of the labor movement, an attempt that failed, according to Bonomi, because of Turati's opposition. On these points, see Bonomi, *La politica italiana*, p. 231, and Carocci, *Giolitti*, pp. 79–81. See also Degl'Innocenti, "La gierra libica," pp. 499–516.

SELECTED BIBLIOGRAPHY

Alati, Domenico. *Dall'inerzia socialista all'attività clericale*. Milan: Tip. degli operai, 1910.
——. *Rapporti fra resistenza e cooperazione*. Milan, 1909.
Albertini, Luigi. *Venti anni di vita politica*. 2 vols. Bologna: Zanichelli, 1969.
Allevi, Giovanni. *L'utopia riformista*. Ascoli Piceno: Tip. economica, 1901.
Angiolini, Alfredo. *Relazione sulla stampa al VI congresso nazionale*. Modena: Tip. degli operai, 1900.
——. *Socialismo e socialisti in Italia*. Florence: Nerbini, 1900.
Ansaldo, Giovanni. *Il ministro della buona vita*. Milan: Longanesi, 1950.
Anzi, Felice. *Il movimento operaio socialista italiano (1882–1894)*. Rome: Avanti!, 1946.
——. *Origini e funzioni delle camere del lavoro*. Milan: Camera del lavoro, n.d.
Arfé, Gaetano. *Storia dell'Avanti!*. 2 vols. Milan: Avanti!, 1956.
——. *Storia del socialismo italiano*. Turin: Einaudi, 1965.
Avanguardia socialista: Periodico settimanale di propaganda e di polemica. Milan.
Avanti!: Giornale socialista. Rome, then Milan.
L'Avanti!. *Relazione al XI congresso nazionale del Partito socialista italiano*. Rome: Tip. dell'Avanti!, 1910.
——. *Rendiconto al X congresso nazionale del Partito socialista italiano*. Rome: Tip. dell'Avanti!, 1908.
——. *Resoconto della direzione del giornale al VII congresso nazionale del Partito socialista italiano*. Imola: Coop. tip. ed., 1902.
Bacci, Giovanni. *Socialismo e antimilitarismo: Relazione al X congresso nazionale*. Rome: Tip. popolare, 1908.
Baldini, Nullo and Verganini, Antonio. *Cooperazione e socialismo: Relazione al XI congresso nazionale*. Reggio Emilia: Coop. lavoratori, 1910.
Barbato, Nicola. *Anarchici e socialisti*. Bologna: Tip. economica, 1896.
——. *Il socialismo difeso al tribunale di guerra*. Turin: Grido del popolo, 1896.
——. *Lettera aperta a Filippo Turati*. Milan: Assoc. elettorale socialista, 1901.
Bartalini, Ezio. *Il Partito socialista italiano e l'agitazione antimilitarista*. Imola: Coop. tip. ed. Paolo Galeati, 1904.
Belardinelli, Mario. *Un esperimento liberal-conservatore: I governi di Di Rudinì (1896–1898)*. Rome: Elia, 1976.

Bernaroli, E. *Manuale per la costituzione e il funzionamento delle Leghe dei contadini.* Rome: Lib. socialista italiana, 1902.

Bertoldo, contadino di Riese, risponde al suo compaesano, Giuseppe Sarto. Milan: Soc. tip. ed. popolare, 1904.

Bertoldo, contadino, ragiona sulle prediche del vescovo Bonomelli, e spiega il socialismo. Cremona: Tip. sociale, 1897.

Berutti, F. *Le bande svizzere: Episodi dei moti di maggio 1898.* Arona: Tip. Algonon, 1904.

Biel, Dott. *Il socialismo per tutti.* 2d ed. Colle d'Elsa: Tip. Meoni, 1896.

———. *Ai contadini d'Italia.* Colle d'Elsa: Tip. Meoni, 1896.

Bissolati, Leonida. *La politica estera dell'Italia dal 1897 al 1920.* Milan: Fratelli Treves, 1923.

———. *Relazione sull'Avanti!.* Modena: Tip. degli operai, 1900.

———. *Socialismo e governi: Relazione al VIII congresso nazionale.* Imola: Coop. tip. ed. Paolo Galeati, 1904.

Bollettino della Direzione del Partito socialista italiano. Rome.

Bonavita, F. *Questioni al congresso: Ferri o Turati?* Castrecoro: Tip. moderna, 1902.

Bonomi, Ivanoe. *La politica italiana da Porta Pia a Vittorio Veneto.* Turin: Einaudi, 1966.

———. *La riforma tributaria: Relazione al VIII congresso nazionale.* Imola: Tip. coop. Galeati, 1904.

———. *L'azione dei socialisti nei comuni: Relazione al X congresso nazionale.* Rome: Tip. popolare, 1908.

———. *L'azione politica del Partito socialista e i suoi rapporti con l'azione parlamentare.* Imola: Coop. tip. ed., 1902.

———. *Leonida Bissolati e il movimento socialista in Italia.* Milan: Martinelli, 1929.

———. *Le vie nuove del socialismo.* Rome: Sestante, 1944.

———. *Sull'azione del partito nelle amministrazioni locali: Relazione al VI congresso nazionale.* Modena: Tip. degli operai, 1900.

Bosio, Gianni, ed. *Karl Marx–Friedrich Engels: Scritti italiani.* Milan: Avanti!, 1955.

Bussi, A. *Socialismo e anticlericalismo: Relazione al X congresso nazionale.* Alfonsine: Tip. Ricci, 1908.

Bussi, Armando and Treves, Claudio. *Appoggio ad indirizzi di governo: Relazione al XI congresso nazionale.* Rome: Tip. dell'Avanti!, 1910.

Cabrini, Angiolo. *Il Partito socialista italiano e la politica dell'emigrazione: Relazione al X congresso nazionale.* Rome: Tip. popolare, 1908.

———. *La legislazione sociale, 1859–1913.* Rome: Bontempelli, 1913.

———. *Legislazione sociale: Relazione al XI congresso nazionale.* Rome: Coop. tip. Avanti!, 1910.

———. *Penetrazione: Linee e frammenti di legislazione sociale.* Milan: L'ed. operaia, 1910.

———, and Canepa, Giuseppe. *Legislazione sociale: Relazione al VII congresso nazionale.* Imola: Coop. tip. ed., 1902.

———, and Chiesa, Pietro. *Proposte di assicurazioni sociali in Italia: Relazione pel VII congresso nazionale delle società di resistenza.* Turin: Tip. coop., 1908.

Candeloro, Giorgio. *Il movimento cattolico in Italia.* Rome: Rinascita, 1953.

Carlantonio, B. *Briciole di socialismo: Individualismo e collettivismo.* Turin: Grido del popolo, 1895.

———. *Briciole di socialismo: L'arma del voto.* Turin: Grido del popolo, 1895.

Carocci, Giampiero. *Giolitti e l'età giolittiana.* 4th ed. Turin: Einaudi, 1961.

Cartiglia, Carlo. *Rinaldo Rigola e il sindacalismo riformista in Italia.* Milan: Feltrinelli, 1976.

Cassina, F. *Alle urne!* . . . Lodi: Tip. operaia, 1900.

Catalano, Franco. *Filippo Turati*. Milan: Avanti!, 1957.

Chiesa, P., and Murialdi, Gino. *Il Partito socialista italiano e l'organizzazione economica del proletariato industriale*. Imola: Coop. tip. ed., 1902.

————, and Schiavi, Alessandro. *Lotta di classe e conflitti di categoria: Relazione al XI congresso nazionale*. Rome: Coop. tip. Avanti!, 1910.

Ciacchi, Emilio. *Le nostre Leghe*. Florence: Nerbini, n.d.

Ciccotti, Ettore. *Il socialismo e i partiti borghesi*. Novara: Tip. novarese, 1895.

————. *I vindici della vera libertà*. Milan: Tip. Morosini, 1895.

Ciccotti, Francesco. *Azione e legislazione anticlericale: Relazione al XI congresso nazionale*. Rome: Tip. Avanti!, 1910.

————. *Il "caso Ferri" e la partecipazione dei socialisti al governo*. Florence: Nerbini, 1910.

————. *La calata in Italia dei Congregazionisti francesi e l'atteggiamento del Partito socialista italiano: Conclusioni del relatore*. Imola: Coop. tip. ed. Paolo Galeati, 1904.

————. *Socialismo e cooperativismo agricolo nell'Italia meridionale*. Florence: Nerbini, 1900.

Cilibrizzi, Saverio. *Storia parlamentare politica e diplomatica d'Italia da Novara a Vittorio Veneto*. 8 vols. Milan: Dante Alighieri, 1923–52.

Clough, Shepard B. *The Economic History of Modern Italy*. New York: Columbia University Press, 1964.

Colajanni, Napoleone. *Gli avvenimenti in Sicilia e le loro cause*. Palermo: Sandron, 1895.

————. *L'Italia nel 1898: Tumulti e reazione*. Milan: Universale economica, 1951.

Colapietra, Raffaele. *Il novantotto: La crisi politica di fine secolo*. Milan: Avanti!, 1959.

————. *Leonida Bissolati*. Milan: Feltrinelli, 1958.

Colliva, Paolo. *Camillo Prampolini e i lavoratori reggiani*. Rome: Opere nuove, 1958.

Comizio agrario lodigiano. *Nuovo libretto colonico*. Lodi: Tip. success. Wilmont, 1905.

Comune di Reggio nell'Emilia. *Dodici anni di amministrazione socialista*. Reggio Emilia: Coop. lavoratori, 1920.

Congresso operaio italiano tenutosi in Milano nei giorni 2–3 agosto 1891: Riassunto delle discussioni e deliberazioni. Milan: Tip. degli operai, n.d.

Cortesi, Luigi. *La costituzione del Partito socialista italiano*. Milan: Avanti!, 1962.

————, ed. *Turati Giovane: Scapigliatura, positivismo, marxismo*. Milan: Avanti!, 1962.

Costanzi, C. *Abbasso l'astensione!*. Milan: Tip. Morosini, 1896.

————. *Il prossimo*. Milan: Agenzia giornalistica internazionale, 1896.

Critica sociale. Milan.

Croce, Benedetto. *Materialismo storico ed economia marxista*. Milan: Sandron, 1900.

Cunsolo, Ronald. "Libya, Italian Nationalism, and the Revolt against Giolitti." *Journal of Modern History*, June 1965.

De Amicis, Edmondo. *Lavoratori alle urne!*. Rome: L'*Asino*, 1900.

De Fazio, L. *I coatti politici in Italia*. Rome: Tip. ed. sociale, 1895.

De Felice, Giuseppe Giuffrida. *Commenti e note alla sentenza di condanna pronunciata dal tribunale militare di Palermo nel 30 maggio 1894 contro de Felice, Bosco, Barbato, Ferro, Montallo, Petrine, e Benzi*. Florence: Tip. Bondiccione, 1894.

Degli'Innocenti, Maurizio. "La guerra libica, la crisi del riformismo, e la vittoria degli intransigenti." *Studi storici*, July–September 1972.

del Bo, Giuseppe, ed. *La corrispondenza di Marx e Engels con italiani*. Milan: Feltrinelli, 1964.

Della Seta, Alceste. *Il Partito socialista e le questioni dell'antimilitarismo: Relazione al XI congresso nazionale*. Rome: Coop. tip. Avanti!, 1910.

Dinale, Ottavio. *Il movimento dei contadini e il Partito socialista*. Florence: Nerbini, 1902.

Engels, Friedrich. *L'evoluzione della rivoluzione: con prefazione di F. Turati*. Ancona: Sezione del PSI, 1895.

Ente per la storia del socialismo e del movimento operaio italiano (Opere di G. E. Modigliani). *Attività parlamentare dei socialisti italiani*. Rome: Ed. E.S.M.O.I., 1967.

Fantoni, U. *Agli esercenti*. Milan: Tip. Angelo Monti, 1896.

Fascio operaio: Voce dei Figli del lavoro. Milan.

Federazione italiana delle camere del lavoro. *Congresso delle camere del lavoro, Reggio Emilia, 19–20 ottobre 1901*. Milan: Tip. degli operai, 1901.

———. *Relazioni ed ordini del giorno approvati nel Congresso delle camere del lavoro tenutosi a Milano nei giorni 1–2 luglio 1900*. Milan: Tip. degli operai, 1900.

Federazione postale-telegrafica e telefonica. *La bancarotta dei telegrafi*. Milan, 1906.

Federazione socialista milanese. *Alle donne italiane*. Milan: Tip. degli operai, 1897.

———. *Pane e alfabeto*. Milan: Uffici della Federazione, 1896.

———. *Né idoli, né vittime*. Milan: Ed. Lombarda, 1901.

———. *Regolamento della Federazione socialista milanese*. Milan: Tip. degli operai, n.d.

Ferri, Enrico, and Prampolini, Camillo. *Polemiche socialiste*. Genoa: Tip. operai, 1903.

Filippo Turati: Discorsi commemorativi di Mondolfo, Gonzales, Nenni. Milan: Rizzoli, 1947.

Fonzi, Fausto. *Crispi e lo "Stato di Milano."* Milan: Giuffré, 1965.

Gerschenkron, Alexander. "Notes on the Rate of Industrial Growth in Italy, 1881–1913." *Journal of Economic History*, December 1955.

Giolitti, Giovanni. *Dalle carte di Giovanni Giolitti: Quarant'anni di politica italiana*. 3 vols. Milan: Feltrinelli, 1962.

———. *Discorsi extraparlamentari*. Turin: Einaudi, 1952.

———. *Discorsi parlamentari*. 4 vols. Rome: Camera dei deputati, 1953–56.

———. *Memorie della mia vita*. Milan: Garzanti, 1967.

Gnocchi-Viani, Osvaldo. *Le borse del lavoro*. Alessandria: Tip. sociale, 1889.

Graziadei, Antonio. *La produzione capitalistica*. Turin: Bocca, 1899.

———. *Memorie di trent'anni*. Rome: Rinascita, 1950.

———. *Socialismo e sindacalismo*. Rome: Mongini, 1909.

Horowitz, Daniel. *The Italian Labor Movement*. Cambridge: Harvard University Press, 1963.

Hostetter, Richard. *The Italian Socialist Movement*. Vol. 1, *Origins (1860–1882)*. New York: D. Van Nostrand, 1958.

Hunecke, Volker. "Comune e classe operaia a Milano (1859–1898)." *Studi Storici* 18, no. 3 (July–September 1976).

Il villano. Socialismo e contadini. Rome: Tip. Appolinare, n.d.

Istituto centrale di statistica. *Sommario di statistiche storiche dell'Italia, 1861–1955*. Rome: ISTAT, 1958.

Istituto centrale statistico e Ministero per la costituente. *Compendio delle statistiche elettorali italiane dal 1848 al 1934*. 2 vols. Rome: F. Failli, 1946.

Kuliscioff, Anna. *Lettere d'amore a Andrea Costa, 1880–1909*. Milan: Feltrinelli, 1976.

———. *Per il suffragio universale: Donne proletarie, a voi! . . .* Milan: Avanti!, 1913.
———. *Proletariato femminile e Partito socialista: Relazione al XI congresso nazionale.* Milan: Tip. degli operai, 1910.
Kuliscioff, Anna, *in memoria: A Lei, agli intimi, a me.* Milan: E. Lazzari, 1926.
———, and Turati, Filippo. "Lettere a Ivanoe Bonomi." *Rivista storica del socialismo,* January–March 1959.
Labriola, Antonio. *Lettere a Engels.* Rome: Rinascita, 1949.
Labriola, Arturo. *La guerra di Tripoli e l'opinione socialista.* Naples: Scintilla, 1912.
———. *La politica del proletariato: Relazione al VIII congresso nazionale.* Imola: Coop. tip. ed. Paolo Galeati, 1904.
———. *Le convenzioni ferroviarie e il Partito socialista: Relazione al VII congresso nazionale.* Imola: Coop. tip. ed., 1902.
———. *Ministero e socialismo. Risposta a Filippo Turati.* Florence: Nerbini, 1901.
———. *Riforme e rivoluzione sociale.* 2d ed. Lugano: Cagnoni, 1906.
———. *Spiegazioni a me stesso: Note personali e colturali.* Naples: Ed. centro studi sociali problemi dopoguerra, 1945.
———. *Storia di dieci anni.* Milan: Il viandante, 1910.
Lazzari, Costantino. *Il voto per tutti.* Milan: Costantino Lazzari, 1910.
———. *I principii e i metodi del Partito socialista italiano.* Milan: Costantino Lazzari, 1911.
———. *Rapporti fra Gruppo parlamentare e partito: Relazione al XI congresso nazionale.* Rome: Tip. Avanti!, 1910.
———. *Relazione sulla tattica e programma per le prossime elezioni politiche e conseguente azione parlamentare: Relazione al X congresso nazionale.* Rome: Tip. popolare, 1908.
Lazzeri, Gerolamo. *Filippo Turati.* Milan: Rinaldo Caddeo, 1920.
Lega socialista milanese. *Programma socialista discusso e approvato dalla Lega socialista milanese nelle adunanze del 28 febbraio, 11, 12 marzo, e 1 aprile 1891.* Milan: Tip. degli operai, 1891.
Lerda, Giovanni. *Appoggio ad indirizzi di governo: Relazione al XI congresso nazionale.* Rome: Tip. Avanti!, 1910.
———. *Il socialismo e la sua tattica.* Genoa: Lib. moderna, 1902.
———. *Perchè gli operai sono poveri.* Genoa: Partito socialista italiano, 1896.
———. *Sull'organizzazione politica del Partito socialista italiano: Relazione al VII congresso nazionale.* Imola: Tip. coop., 1902.
Levra, Umberto. *Il colpo di stato della borghesia: La crisi politica di fine secolo in Italia, 1896–1898.* Milan: Feltrinelli, 1975.
Longobardi, E. C. *Direttive del partito in rapporto al movimento operaio: Relazione al X congresso nazionale.* Rome: Tip. popolare, 1908.
Lotta di classe: Giornale dei lavoratori italiani. Milan.
Lotta di classe: Giornale dei sindacalisti italiani. Milan.
Lotta di classe: Numero unico delle associazioni operaie democratiche socialiste di Milano per le elezioni amministrative. Milan.
Lotta di classe: Organo dell'Unione socialista milanese. Milan.
Macchi, G. *Il socialismo giudicato da letterati, artisti, e scienziati italiani.* Milan: Aliprandi, 1903.
Mammarella, Giuseppe. *Riformisti e rivoluzionari nel Partito socialista italiano.* Padua: Marsiglio, 1969.
Manacorda, Gastone. *Il movimento operaio italiano attraverso i suoi congressi (1853–1892).* Rome: Riuniti, 1953.
———. *Storiografia e socialismo.* Padua: Liviania, 1967.
——— et al. *I fasci siciliani.* 2 vols. Bari: De Donato, 1975.

Manualetto dell'elettore socialista. Rome: Tip. dell'Asino, 1901.

Marchetti, Luciana, ed. *La Confederazione generale del lavoro negli atti, nei documenti, nei congressi, 1906–1926*. Milan: Avanti!, 1962.

Mariotti, Giovanni. *Filippo Turati*. Florence: La voce, 1946.

Marucco, Dora. *Arturo Labriola e il sindacalismo rivoluzionario in Italia*. Turin: Fondazione Luigi Einaudi, 1970.

Mastrolonardo, G. *La bancarotta dell'internazionalismo*. Trieste: Tip. Unione E. Meneghelli, 1909.

Mattia, E. *L'ABC del socialismo per le campagne*. Milan: Critica sociale, 1894.

———. *Padroni e contadini*. Milan: Critica sociale, 1894.

Merlino, Francesco Saverio. *Collettivismo, lotta di classe, e . . . ministero! (Controreplica a Filippo Turati)*. Florence: Nerbini, 1901.

Merloni, G. *Azione e legislazione clericale: Relazione al XI congresso nazionale*. Rome: Coop. tip. Avanti!, 1910.

Michels, Roberto. *Il proletariato e la borghesia nel movimento socialista italiano*. Turin: Bocca, 1908.

———. *Saggi economico-statistici sulle classi popolari*. Milan: Sandron, 1913.

———. *Storia del marxismo in Italia*. Rome: Luigi Mongini, 1910.

Modigliani, G. E. *Per le prossime elezioni generali politche: Relazione al X congresso nazionale*. Rome: Tip. popolare, 1908.

Mongini, Luigi. *Relazione del segretario amministrativo al X congresso nazionale*. Rome: Tip. popolare, 1908.

Montemartini, Giovanni. *Il Gruppo parlamentare socialista: Relazione al X congresso nazionale*. Rome: Tip. popolare, 1908.

Morgari, Oddino. *L'arte della propaganda socialista*. Milan: Lotta di classe, 1896.

Murialdi, Gino. *Il Partito socialista italiano e la legislazione sociale*. Imola: Coop. tip. ed. Paolo Galeati, 1904.

Natale, Gaetano. *Giolitti e gli italiani*. Milan: Garzanti, 1949.

Neufeld, Maurice. *Italy: School for Awakening Countries*. Ithaca: Cornell University Press, 1961.

Nofri, Quirino. *Azione del partito in rapporto al problema ferroviario: Relazione al VIII congresso nazionale*. Imola: Coop. tip. ed. Paolo Galeati, 1904.

Oggero, G. *Sorgete!*. Turin: Partito socialista dei lavoratori italiani, 1894.

Olivetti, A. O. *Questioni contemporanee*. Naples: Società ed. Partenopea, 1913.

Palamenghi-Crispi, Tommaso. *Franceso Crispi: Politica interna. Diario e documenti raccolti e ordinati da T. Palamenghi-Crispi*. Milan: Treves, 1924.

Paoloni, F. G. *Salviamo il partito! Manifesto-programma pel "blocco socialista integrale."* Rome: Luigi Mongini, 1906.

Partito dei lavoratori italiani. *Rapport au Congrès international de Zurich (1893) sur la constitution et l'action du Parti des travailleurs italiens*. Milan: Impr. des ouvriers, 1893.

Partito socialista dei lavoratori italiani. *Il congresso di Reggio Emilia, verbale stenografico*. Milan: Tip. operai, 1893.

Partito socialista italiano. *Bilancio e relazione finanziaria del partito e bilanci della "Lotta di classe" e della libreria al congresso nazionale del Partito socialista italiano, 18–20 settembre 1897*. Milan: Tip. operai, 1897.

———. *Congresso nazionale del Partito socialista italiano: Bilancio e relazione finanziaria del partito*. Milan: Tip. degli operai, 1900.

———. *Congresso nazionale del Partito socialista italiano: Il programma minimo socialista*. N.p., n.d.

———. *Congresso socialista: Verbali delle discussioni (Firenze, 1896)*. Milan: Lib. della Lotta di classe, 1897.

———. *Congresso socialista: Verbali delle discussioni (Firenze, 1896)*. Milan: Lib. Lotta di classe, 1897.

———. *Da Parma a Firenze: Relazione morale e statistica presentato dall'Ufficio esecutivo centrale al congresso nazionale del Partito socialista italiano*. Milan: Tip. degli operai, 1896.

———. *Genova—1892: Nascita del Partito socialista in Italia*. Milan: Avanti!, 1952.

———. *Il Partito socialista italiano e le classi agricole al congresso del partito*. Milan: Tip. operai, 1897.

———. *I socialisti al comune: Programma della sezione milanese del Partito socialista italiano per le elezioni amministrative del 1910*. Milan: Coop. tip. operai, 1910.

———. *Programma, statuto, e tattica del Partito socialista dei lavoratori italiani*. Milan: Tip. degli operai, 1896.

———. *Proposte e ordini del giorno di compagni, circoli, e federazioni presente al congresso nazionale*. Milan: Tip. degli operai, 1897.

———. *Rapport du Parti socialiste italien au Congrès ouvrier-socialiste international (Londres, 1896)*. Milan: Impr. des ouvriers, 1896.

———. *Rapport du Parti socialiste italien: Son activité depuis 1907 jusq'au mois de juin 1910*. Rome: Impr. coop. Avanti!, 1910.

———. *Rapporto sull'azione del Gruppo parlamentare al congresso nazionale*. Milan: Tip. operai, 1897.

———. *Relazione della direzione del partito*. Imola: Coop. tip. ed., 1902.

———. *Relazione morale dell'Ufficio esecutivo centrale, 1896–1897*. Milan: Tip. degli operai, 1897.

———. *Relazione per la riforma del programma minimo politico e amministrativo al congresso nazionale del Partito socialista italiano, 20 settembre 1897*. Milan: Tip. operai, 1897.

———. *Relazione sul contegno del Partito socialista di fronte alle classi agricole, presentata al IV congresso nazionale in Firenze*. Milan: Tip. degli operai, 1896.

———. *Rendiconto del consiglio d'amministrazione dell'Avanti al X congresso nazionale*. Rome: Tip. Avanti!, 1908.

———. *Rendiconto del VI congresso nazionale*. Rome: Lib. soc. italiana, 1901.

———. *Rendiconto del VII congresso nazionale*. Rome: Lib. soc. italiana, 1903.

———. *Rendiconto del VIII congresso nazionale*. Rome: Luigi Mongini, 1905.

———. *Resoconto stenografico del IX congresso nazionale*. Rome: Luigi Mongini, 1907.

———. *Resoconto stenografico del X congresso nazionale*. Rome: Luigi Mongini, 1908.

———. *Resoconto stenografico del XI congresso nazionale*. Rome: Poligrafica italiana, 1911.

———. *Resoconto stenografico del XIII congresso nazionale*. Città di Castello: Unione arti grafiche, 1913.

———. *Sessant'anni di socialismo a Milano*. Milan: Avanti!, 1952.

———. *Statuto del Partito socialista italiano*. Milan: Ufficio esecutivo centrale del partito, 1896.

Pedone, Franco. *Il Partito socialista italiano nei suoi congressi*. 4 vols. Milan: Avanti!, 1959–63.

Pelloux, Luigi. *Quelques souvenirs de ma vie*. Rome: Istituto per la storia del Risorgimento italiano, 1967.

Pepe, Adolfo. *Storia della Confederazione generale del lavoro dalla fondazione alla guerra di Libia, 1905–1911*. Bari: Laterza, 1972.

———. *Storia della Confederazione generale del lavoro dalla guerra di Libia all'intervento.* Bari: Laterza, 1971.

Perticone, Giacomo. *Linee di storia del socialismo,* 2d ed. Milan: Antonio Cordoni, 1944.

La posta: Organo della Federazione postale italiana. Milan.

Prampolini, Camillo. *L'insurrezione e il Partito socialista.* Milan: Magnagli, 1899.

Procacci, Giuliano. "Geografia e struttura del movimento contadino della valle padana nel suo periodo formativo (1901–1906)." *Studi storici* 5, no. 1 (January–March 1964).

Ragionieri, Ernesto. *Socialdemocrazia tedesca e socialisti italiani, 1875–1895.* Milan: Feltrinelli, 1961.

Ratti, Celestino. *Lotta di classe e conflitti di categoria: Relazione al XI congresso nazionale.* Rome: Tip. Avanti!, 1910.

Relazione per il congresso di Trieste dei socialisti italiani. Trieste: Pittoni, 1905.

Rigola, Rinaldo. *Il Partito socialista e il movimento operaio: Relazione al X congresso nazionale.* Rome: Tip. popolare, 1908.

———. *La Confederazione generale del lavoro nel triennio 1911–1913.* Milan: Tip. degli operai, 1914.

Roselli, Enrico. *Cento anni di legislazione sociale.* 2 vols. Milan: Bernabò, 1951.

Rosselli, Carlo. *Socialismo liberale.* Rome: Edizioni U, 1945.

———. *Vita e opera di Filippo Turati.* N.p.: Quaderni di giustizia e libertà, 1932.

Salomone, A. William. *Italy in the Giolittian Era.* Philadelphia: University of Pennsylvania Press, 1960.

Salvadori, Massimo L. *Gaetano Salvemini.* Turin: Einaudi, 1963.

Salvemini, Gaetano. *Perchè vogliamo il suffragio universale.* Mantua: A. Frizzi, 1911.

———. *Suffragio universale: Relazione al XI congresso nazionale.* Rome: Tip. Avanti!, 1910.

Santarelli, Enzo. *La revisione del marxismo in Italia.* Milan: Feltrinelli, 1964.

Scalzotto, A. *La tattica economica del Partito socialista.* Turin: Tip. Locatelli, 1897.

Schiavi, Alessandro. *Anna Kuliscioff.* Rome: Opere nuove, 1955.

———. *Come nasce, vive, e muore la povera gente.* Rome: Laziello, 1902.

———. *Esilio e morte di Filippo Turati.* Rome: Opere nuove, 1956.

———. *Filippo Turati.* Rome: Opere nuove, 1955.

———. *Filippo Turati attraverso le lettere di corrispondenti (1880–1925).* Bari: Laterza, 1947.

———. *Lavoratori e padroni nel 1902.* Turin: Roux e Viarengo, 1903.

———, ed. *Omaggio a Turati nel centenario della nascita, 1857–1957.* Rome: Opere nuove, 1957.

Sestan, Ernesto. *Opere di Gaetano Salvemini.* Milan: Feltrinelli, 1961–63.

Società umanitaria. *Le condizioni generali della classe operaia in Milano.* Milan: Ufficio del lavoro, 1907.

La soffitta: Organo della frazione rivoluzionaria intransigente. Rome.

Soldi, Romeo. *L'azione politica del proletariato e i suoi rapporti coll'azione parlamentare: Relazione al VII congresso nazionale.* Imola: Coop. tip. ed., 1902.

Spadolini, Giovanni. *Giolitti e i cattolici, 1901–14.* Florence: Felice le Monnier, 1971.

———. *L'opposizione cattolica da Porta Pia al '98.* Florence: Vallecchi, 1961.

Strik Lievers, Lorenzo. "Turati, la politica delle alleanze, e una celebre lettera di Engels." *Nuova rivista storica* 57 (January–April 1973).

Il tempo: Giornale politico quotidiano. Milan.

Thayer, John. *Italy and the Great War: Politics and Culture, 1870–1915.* Madison: University of Wisconsin Press, 1964.

Treves, Claudio. *Un socialista: Filippo Turati*. Milan: Critica sociale, n.d.

Turati, Filippo. *Al salvataggio delle istituzioni: Micrologia politica*. Milan: Tip. degli operai, 1895.

———. *Discorsi parlamentari*. 3 vols. Rome: Tip. della Camera dei deputati, 1950.

———. *Il canto dei lavoratori*. Milan: Fantuzzi, 1889.

———. *Il carteggio Turati-Ghisleri*. Milan: Movimento operaio, 1956.

———. *Il delitto e la questione sociale*. Milan: Quadrio, 1883.

———. *Il Partito socialista e l'attuale momento politico*. Milan: Critica sociale, 1901.

———. *I tribunali del lavoro*. Rome: Tip. Naz. Bertero, 1904.

———. *La prima conquista dell'organizzazione Federale postale telegrafica italiana*. Milan: Unione postale telegrafica, 1904.

———. *L'azione politica del Partito socialista italiano: Relazione al XI congresso nazionale*. Milan: Tip. degli operai, 1910.

———. *Le otto ore di lavoro*. Milan: Critica sociale, 1892.

———. *Le vie maestre del socialismo*. Naples: Morano, 1966.

———. *Lo stato delinquente*. Milan: La plebe, 1883.

———. *Strofe*. Milan: Quadrio, 1883.

———. *Trent'anni di Critica sociale*. Bologna: Zanichelli, 1921.

———. *Uomini della politica e della cultura*. Bari: Laterza, 1949.

———, and Kuliscioff, Anna. *Carteggio*. 7 vols. Turin: Einaudi, 1949–78.

———, and Venturi, S. *Le quote minime della delinquenza*. Milan: Tip. degli operai, n.d.

"Turati, Filippo." Police file in Archivio centrale dello stato (Rome), Casellario politico centrale, Ufficio riservato.

L'Unione postale-telegrafica telefonica. Milan.

Valiani, Leo. *Questioni di storia del socialismo*. Turin: Einaudi, 1958.

Vigezzi, Brunello. *Giolitti e Turati: Un incontro mancato*, 2 vols. Milan: Ricciardi, 1976.

Viviani, Sylva. *Antimilitarismo*. Florence: Tip. Polli, 1914.

Volpe, Gioacchino. "Partiti politici e contrasti sociali in Italia all'inizio del nuovo secolo." *Nuova antologia* 441, no. 1764 (December 1947).

Webster, Richard A. *Industrial Imperialism in Italy, 1908–1915*. Berkeley and Los Angeles: University of California Press, 1975.

Zerboglio, Alfredo. *La tattica: Relazione al VI congresso nazionale*. Modena: Tip. degli operai, 1900.

Zibordi, Giovanni. *Dialoghi campagnuoli*. Mantua: Arturo Frizzi, 1896.

———. *L'organizzazione del partito e azione relativa (Conclusioni)*. Imola: Coop. tip. ed. Paolo Galeati, 1904.

———. *Scritti vari di propaganda socialista*. Reggio Emilia: Tip. coop., 1907.

Zoppi, Sergio. *Romolo Murri e la prima democrazia cristiana*. Florence: Vallecchi, 1968.

Zorli, Alberto. *Sulla base teorica del riformismo (lettera aperta all'on. Filippo Turati)*. Rome, 1907.

INDEX

Library of Congress Cataloging in Publication Data
Di Scala, Spencer.
Dilemmas of Italian socialism.
Bibliography: p.
Includes index.
1. Partito socialista italiano—History. 2. Turati, Filippo, 1857–1932. I Title.
JN5657.S6D53   329.9'45   79–10274
ISBN 0-87023-285-1